Mike Geig

Sams **Teach Yourself**

Unity® 2018

Game
Development

in **24**
Hours

SAMS   800 East 96th Street, Indianapolis, Indiana 46240 USA

Sams Teach Yourself Unity® 2018 Game Development in 24 Hours

ISBN-13: 978-0-13-499813-8

ISBN-10: 0-13-499813-8

Library of Congress Control Number: 2018902432

01   18

Trademarks

All terms mentioned in this book that are known to be trademarks or service marks have been appropriately capitalized. Sams Publishing cannot attest to the accuracy of this information. Use of a term in this book should not be regarded as affecting the validity of any trademark or service mark.

Warning and Disclaimer

Every effort has been made to make this book as complete and as accurate as possible, but no warranty or fitness is implied. The information provided is on an "as is" basis. The author and the publisher shall have neither liability nor responsibility to any person or entity with respect to any loss or damages arising from the information contained in this book.

The Unity name, logo, brand, and other trademarks or images featured or referred to within this book are licensed from and are the property of Unity Technologies. Neither this book or the publisher is affiliated with, endorsed by, or sponsored by Unity Technologies.

All images herein of the Unity editor are provided courtesy of Unity Technologies.
© 2017–18 Unity Technologies

Microsoft and/or its respective suppliers make no representations about the suitability of the information contained in the documents and related graphics published as part of the services for any purpose all such documents and related graphics are provided "as is" without warranty of any kind. Microsoft and/or its respective suppliers hereby disclaim all warranties and conditions with regard to this information, including all warranties and conditions of merchantability, whether express, implied or statutory, fitness for a particular purpose, title and non-infringement. In no event shall Microsoft and/or its respective suppliers be liable for any special, indirect or consequential damages or any damages whatsoever resulting from loss of use, data or profits, whether in an action of contract, negligence or other tortious action, arising out of or in connection with the use or performance of information available from the services.

The documents and related graphics contained herein could include technical inaccuracies or typographical errors. Changes are periodically added to the information herein. Microsoft and/or its respective suppliers may make improvements and/or changes in the product(s) and/or the program(s) described herein at any time. Partial screen shots may be viewed in full within the software version specified.

Microsoft® Windows®, and Microsoft Office® are registered trademarks of the Microsoft Corporation in the U.S.A. and other countries. This book is not sponsored or endorsed by or affiliated with the Microsoft Corporation.

Special Sales

For information about buying this title in bulk quantities, or for special sales opportunities (which may include electronic versions; custom cover designs; and content particular to your business, training goals, marketing focus, or branding interests), please contact our corporate sales department at corpsales@pearsoned.com or (800) 382-3419.

For government sales inquiries, please contact governmentsales@pearsoned.com.

For questions about sales outside the U.S., please contact intlcs@pearson.com.

Editor-in-Chief
Mark Taub

Acquisition Editors
Laura Lewin
Malobika Chakraborty

Development Editor
Michael Thurston

Managing Editor
Sandra Schroeder

Project Editor
Mandie Frank

Copy Editor
Kitty Wilson

Indexer
Erika Millen

Proofreader
Gill Editorial
Services

Technical Editor
Michael Wu

Editorial Assistant
Courtney Martin

Designer
Chuti Prasertsith

Compositor
codemantra

Contents at a Glance

Table of Contents

Preface

The Unity game engine is an incredibly powerful and popular choice for professional and amateur game developers alike. This book has been written to get readers up to speed and working in Unity as fast as possible (in about 24 hours, to be exact) while covering fundamental principles of game development. Unlike other books that cover only specific topics or spend the entire time teaching a single game, this book covers a large array of topics while still managing to contain four games. Talk about a bargain! By the time you are done reading this book, you won't have just theoretical knowledge of the Unity game engine. You will have a portfolio of games to go with it.

About the Author

Mike Geig is the global head of evangelism content at Unity Technologies, where he helps democratize game development by developing and delivering high-impact learning resources. Mike has experience as an indie game developer, a university educator, and an author. A gamer at heart, Mike works to make the development of interactive entertainment fun and accessible for all skill sets. Hi, Mom!

Dedication

*Kara, I decided to wait until the third edition to dedicate this book
to you so that later, when you say, "You never dedicated a book to me,"
I can respond with, "Guess again!" Thank you for
continuing to be my foundation.*

Acknowledgments

A big thank-you goes out to everyone who helped me write this book.

First and foremost, thank you, Kara, for keeping me on track. I don't know what we'll be talking about when this book comes out, but whatever it is, you are probably right. Love ya, babe.

Link and Luke: We should take it easy on Mommy for a little while. I think she's about to crack.

Thanks to my parents. As I am now a parent myself, I recognize how hard it was for you not to strangle or stab me. Thanks for not strangling or stabbing me.

Thanks to Angelina Jolie. Due to your role in the spectacular movie *Hackers* (1995), I decided to learn how to use a computer. You underestimate the impact you had on 10-year-olds at the time. You're elite!

To the inventor of beef jerky: History may have forgotten your name but definitely not your product. I love that stuff. Thanks!

Thank you to Michael Wu for not only agreeing to be a technical editor on this book but also being the other Mike on our podcast "Mikes' Video Game Podcast." (I just had to get a plug in there.)

Thank you, Laura, for convincing me to write this book. Also, thank you for buying me lunch at GDC. I feel that lunch, the best of all three meals, specifically allowed me to finish this.

Finally, a thank-you is in order for Unity Technologies. If you'd never made the Unity game engine, this book would be very weird and confusing.

We Want to Hear from You!

As the reader of this book, *you* are our most important critic and commentator. We value your opinion and want to know what we're doing right, what we could do better, what areas you'd like to see us publish in, and any other words of wisdom you're willing to pass our way.

We welcome your comments. You can email or write to let us know what you did or didn't like about this book—as well as what we can do to make our books better.

Please note that we cannot help you with technical problems related to the topic of this book.

When you write, please be sure to include this book's title and author as well as your name and email address. We will carefully review your comments and share them with the author and editors who worked on the book.

Email: feedback@samspublishing.com

Mail: Sams Publishing

ATTN: Reader Feedback
         800 East 96th Street
         Indianapolis, IN 46240 USA

Reader Services

Register your copy of *Sams Teach Yourself Unity 2018 Game Development in 24 Hours* at informit.com for convenient access to downloads, updates, and corrections as they become available. To start the registration process, go to informit.com/register and log in or create an account*. Enter the product ISBN, 9780134998138, and click Submit. Once the process is complete, you will find any available bonus content under Registered Products.

*Be sure to check the box that you would like to hear from us in order to receive exclusive discounts on future editions of this product.

Who Should Read This Book

This book is for anyone looking to learn how to use the Unity game engine. Whether you are a student or a development expert, there is something to learn in these pages. It is not assumed that you have any prior game development knowledge or experience, so don't worry if this is your first foray into the art of making games. Take your time and have fun. You will be learning in no time.

How This Book Is Organized

Following the *Sam's Teach Yourself* approach, this book is organized into 24 chapters that should take approximately 1 hour each to work through. The chapters are as follows:

- ▶ Hour 1, "Introduction to Unity"—This hour gets you up and running with the various components of the Unity game engine.

- ▶ Hour 2, "Game Objects"—Hour 2 teaches you how to use the fundamental building blocks of the Unity game engine—game objects. You'll also learn about coordinate systems and transformations.

- ▶ Hour 3, "Models, Materials, and Textures"—In this hour, you'll learn to work with Unity's graphical asset pipeline as you apply shaders and textures to materials. You'll also learn how to apply those materials to a variety of 3D objects.

- ▶ Hour 4, "Terrain and Environments"—In Hour 4, you'll learn to sculpt game worlds using Unity's terrain system. Don't be afraid to get your hands dirty as you dig around and create unique and stunning landscapes.

- ▶ Hour 5, "Lights and Cameras"—Hour 5 covers lights and cameras in great detail.

- ▶ Hour 6, "Game 1: *Amazing Racer*": Time for your first game! In Hour 6, you'll create *Amazing Racer*, which requires you to apply all the knowledge you have gained so far.

- ▶ Hour 7, "Scripting, Part 1"—In Hour 7, you'll begin your foray into scripting with Unity. If you've never programmed before, don't worry. This hour takes it slow so you can learn the basics.

- ▶ Hour 8, "Scripting, Part 2"—This hour expands on what you learned in Hour 7, focusing on more advanced topics.

- ▶ Hour 9, "Collision"—Hour 9 walks you through the various collision interactions that are common in modern video games. You'll learn about physical as well as trigger collisions. You'll also learn to create physical materials to add some variety to your objects.

▶ Hour 10, "Game 2: *Chaos Ball*"—Time for another game! In this hour, you'll create *Chaos Ball*. This title certainly is apt, as the game involves various collisions, physical materials, and goals. Prepare to mix strategy with twitch reaction.

▶ Hour 11, "Prefabs"—Prefabs enable you to create repeatable game objects. In Hour 11, you'll learn to create and modify prefabs.

▶ Hour 12, "2D Game Tools"—In Hour 12, you'll learn about Unity's powerful tools for creating 2D games, including how to work with sprites and Box2D physics.

▶ Hour 13, "2D Tilemap"—In Hour 13, you'll learn how to construct complex 2D environments out of simple sprite tiles.

▶ Hour 14, "User Interfaces"—In this hour, you'll learn how to use Unity's powerful user interface system and how to create a menu for your game.

▶ Hour 15, "Game 3: *Captain Blaster*"—Game number 3! In this hour, you'll make *Captain Blaster*, a retro-style spaceship shooting game.

▶ Hour 16, "Particle Systems"—Time to learn about particle effects. In this chapter, you'll experiment with Unity's particle system to create cool effects and apply them to your projects.

▶ Hour 17, "Animations"—In Hour 17, you'll learn about animations and Unity's animation system. You'll experiment with 2D and 3D animation and some powerful animation tools.

▶ Hour 18, "Animators"—Hour 18 is all about Unity's Mecanim animation system. You'll learn how to use the powerful state machine and how to blend animations.

▶ Hour 19, "Timeline"—In this hour, you'll learn how to sequence many game object animations together by using the new Timeline system.

▶ Hour 20, "Game 4: *Gauntlet Runner*"—Lucky game number 4 is called *Gauntlet Runner*. This game explores a new way to scroll backgrounds and shows how to implement them for advanced gameplay functionality.

▶ Hour 21, "Audio"—Hour 21 has you adding important ambient audio effects. You'll learn about 2D and 3D audio and their different properties.

▶ Hour 22, "Mobile Development"—In this hour, you'll learn how to build games for mobile devices. You'll also learn to utilize a mobile device's built-in accelerometer and multi-touch display.

▶ Hour 23, "Polish and Deploy"—Time to learn how to add multiple scenes and persist data between scenes! You'll also learn about the deployment settings and playing your games.

▶ Hour 24, "Wrap-up"—Here, you'll look back on the journey you took to learn Unity. This hour provides useful information about what you have done and where to go next.

Thank you for reading my Preface! I hope you'll enjoy this book and learn much from it. Good luck on your journey with the Unity game engine!

Companion Files

Bonus files include full source code listings from every chapter, with author comments, all third-party art assets (textures, fonts, models), and all third-party sound assets. To gain access to the companion files navigate to

http://fixbyproximity.com/Downloads/UnityBook.html

Introduction to Unity

What You'll Learn in This Hour:

▶ How to install Unity

▶ How to create a new project or open an existing project

▶ How to use the Unity editor

▶ How to navigate inside the Unity Scene view

This hour focuses on getting you ready to rock and roll in the Unity environment. It starts by looking at the different Unity licenses and then installing the one you choose. This hour you'll also learn how to create new projects as well as open existing ones. You'll open the powerful Unity editor and examine its various components. Finally, you'll learn to navigate a scene by using mouse controls and keyboard commands. This lesson is meant to be hands-on, so download Unity while reading and follow along.

Installing Unity

Before you can begin using Unity, you first need to download and install it. Software installation is a pretty simple and straightforward process these days, and Unity is no exception. Before you can install anything, though, you need to look at the three available Unity license options: Unity Personal, Unity Plus, and Unity Pro. Unity Personal is free and has everything you need to complete all the examples and projects in this book. In fact, Unity Personal contains everything you need to make games commercially, up to an annual revenue of $100,000! If you're lucky enough to start earning more than this, or you want to access the advanced features of Unity Plus or Unity Pro (mainly aimed at teams), then you can always upgrade in the future.

NOTE

Unity Hub

At the time this book was published, a new method of accessing Unity installs and creating projects was under way. Unity Hub acts as a centralized launcher for your various projects. Unfortunately, it wasn't quite ready to be included in this book, but that doesn't mean this lesson is useless. You can still install Unity and create projects in the same manner as outlined in this hour if you'd like to. Even if you decide to use Unity Hub, the concepts behind the installations and projects are exactly the same. As the saying goes, "new packaging, same great taste!"

Downloading and Installing Unity

This lesson assumes that you are sticking with the Unity Personal license. If you instead choose the Plus or Pro version, the process is very similar, only deviating when it comes to choosing the license. When you are ready to begin downloading and installing Unity, follow these steps:

1. Download the Unity installer from the Unity download page at http://unity3d.com/ get-unity/download and proceed to follow the instructions to download the installer.

2. Run the installer and follow the prompts as you would with any other piece of software.

3. When prompted, be sure to leave the Unity 2018 and Standard Assets check boxes checked (see Figure 1.1). It is okay to install the example project and any other platforms you may want to build to if you have space; doing so won't affect your experience of the book.

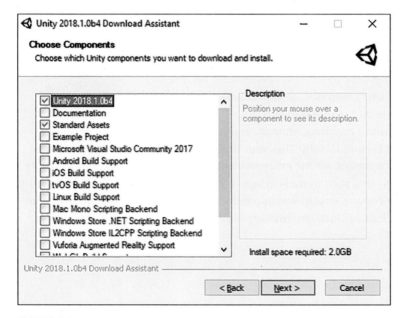

FIGURE 1.1
Choosing the components to install.

4. Choose an installation location for Unity. It is recommended to accept the default unless you know what you are doing. Unity takes some time to download, during which time you see a download screen (see Figure 1.2).

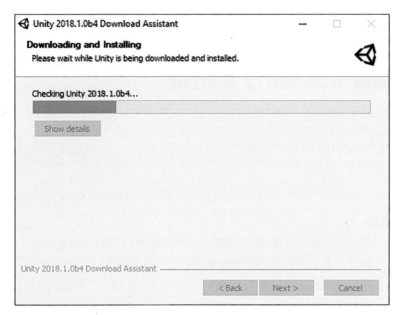

FIGURE 1.2
Be patient while Unity downloads.

5. If you already have a Unity account, you may be asked to log in with it. If you don't yet have a Unity account, follow the instructions to create one. Make sure you have access to your email to verify your address. That's it! Unity installation is now complete.

NOTE

Supported Operating Systems and Hardware

To use Unity, you must be using a Windows PC or a Macintosh computer. Although there is a version of the editor that runs on Linux machines, Linux is not a directly supported OS. Your computer must also meet the minimum requirements outlined here (taken from the Unity website at the time this book was published):

▶ Windows 7 SP1+, Windows 8, or Windows 10, 64-bit versions only; Mac OS X 10.9+. Note that Unity was not tested on server versions of Windows and OS X.

▶ Graphics card with DX9 (shader model 3.0) or DX11 with feature level 9.3 capabilities.

▶ A CPU that supports the SSE2 instruction set (most modern CPUs).

Note that these are *minimum* requirements.

NOTE

Internet Links

All Internet URLs in this book are current as of the time this book was published. Web locations do change sometimes, though. If the material you are looking for is no longer provided at the links listed, a good Internet search should turn up what you are looking for.

Getting to Know the Unity Editor

Now that you have Unity installed, you can begin exploring the Unity editor. The Unity editor is the visual component that enables you to build games in a "what you see is what you get" fashion. Because most interaction you have is actually with the editor, many people refer to it as simply Unity. This section examines all the different elements of the Unity editor and how they fit together to make games.

The Project Dialog

When opening Unity for the first time, you see the Project dialog (see Figure 1.3). You use this dialog to open recent projects, browse for projects that have already been created, or start new projects.

FIGURE 1.3
The Project dialog (Windows version shown; the Mac version is similar).

If you have created a project in Unity already, whenever you open the editor, you are taken directly to that project. To get back to the Project dialog, in Unity, select **File** > **New Project** to get to the Create New Project dialog or select **File** > **Open Project** to get to the Open Project dialog.

TIP

Opening the Project Dialog

You can choose whether you want Unity to open to the Project dialog or the last opened project by going to **Edit > Preferences (Unity > Preferences on a Mac)** and changing the value of the **Load Previous Project on Startup** check box.

TRY IT YOURSELF ▼

Creating Your First Project

You are ready to create a project. Pay special attention to where you save the project so that you can find it easily later if necessary. Figure 1.4 shows the dialog box you use to create the project. Follow these steps:

1. Open Unity and locate the New Project dialog. (If Unity opens to a project, click **File > New Project.**)

2. Select a location for your project. I recommend that you create a folder called Unity Projects to keep all your book projects together. If you are unsure where to put your project, you can leave the default location.

3. Name your project **Hour 1 TIY**. Unity creates a folder with the same name as the project, in the location specified in this dialog.

4. Leave 3D selected and ignore the Add Asset Package and Enable Unity Analytics options for now.

5. Click **Create Project.**

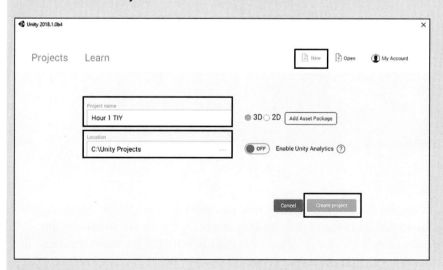

FIGURE 1.4
The settings for your first project.

NOTE

2D, 3D, Packages, Analytics?

You might be wondering what the other options on the New Project dialog are for. The 2D and 3D buttons allow you to select which type of game you are planning on making. Don't worry about picking the wrong one or being unsure. These just control editor settings and can be changed at any time. The Add Asset Package button allows you to add files that you commonly use in your projects into a new project automatically. Finally, the Enable Unity Analytics option is a very powerful tool that taps into Unity's Analytics service. Using it allows you to generate data about your game audience; while that is totally awesome for game developers, it isn't necessary for you at this time.

The Unity Interface

So far, you have installed Unity and looked at the Project dialog. Now it is time to dig in and start playing around. When you open a new Unity project for the first time, you see a collection of gray windows (called *views*), and everything is rather empty (see Figure 1.5). Never fear; you will quickly get this place hopping. The following section look at each of the unique views, one by one. First, though, let's talk about the layout as a whole.

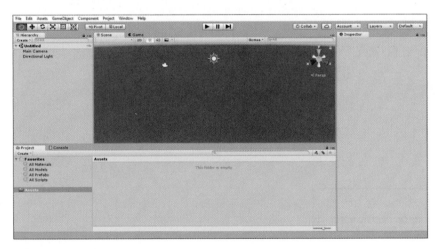

FIGURE 1.5
The Unity interface.

For starters, Unity allows you to determine exactly how you want to work. Any of the views can be moved, docked, duplicated, or changed. For instance, if you click the word **Hierarchy** (on the left) to select the Hierarchy view and drag it over to the Inspector (on the right), you can tab the two views together. You can also place your cursor on any line between views and resize the windows. In fact, why don't you take a moment to play around and move things so that they are to your liking? If you end up with a layout that you don't much care for, you can quickly and easily switch back to the built-in default view by going to **Window > Layouts > Default Layout**. While you are playing around, go ahead and try out a few of the other layouts. (I'm a fan of the Wide layout.) If you create a custom layout you like, you can save it by going to **Window > Layouts > Save Layout**. (I used a custom layout called Pearson for the writing of this book.) After you've saved a custom layout, if you accidentally change the layout, you can always get it back.

NOTE

Finding the Right Layout

No two people are alike, and likewise, no two ideal layouts are alike. A good layout will help you work on your projects and make things much easier for you. Be sure to take the time to fiddle around with the layouts to find the one that works best for you. You will be working a lot with Unity. It pays to set up your environment in a way that is comfortable for you.

Duplicating a view is a fairly straightforward process as well. You can simply right-click any view *tab* (such as Inspector in Figure 1.6), hover the mouse cursor over **Add Tab**, and a list of views pops up for you to choose from (see Figure 1.6). You may wonder why you would want to duplicate a view. Say that in your view-moving frenzy, you accidentally closed the view. Re-adding the tab will give it back to you. Also, consider the capability to create multiple Scene views. Each Scene view could align with a specific element or axis within your project. If you want to see this in action, check out the 4 Split built-in layout by going to **Window > Layouts > 4 Split**. (If you created a layout that you like, be sure to save it before you check out 4 Split.)

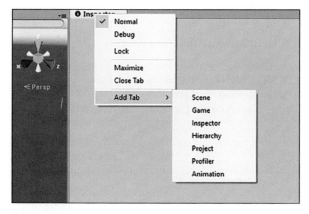

FIGURE 1.6
Adding a new tab.

Now, without further ado, let's look at the specific views themselves.

The Project View

Everything that has been created for a project (files, scripts, textures, models, and so on) can be found in the Project view (see Figure 1.7). This is the window that shows all the assets and organization of a project. When you create a new project, you see a single folder item called Assets. If you go to the folder on your hard drive where you save the project, you also find an Assets folder. This is because Unity mirrors the Project view with the folders on the hard drive. If you create a file or folder in Unity, the corresponding file or folder appears in the explorer (and vice versa). You can move items in the Project view simply by dragging and dropping. This enables you to place items inside folders or reorganize your project on-the-fly.

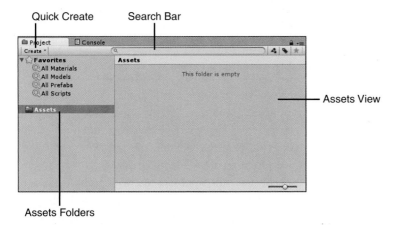

FIGURE 1.7
The Project view.

NOTE

Assets and Objects

An *asset* is any item that exists as a file in your Assets folder. All textures, meshes, sound files, scripts, and so on are considered assets. In contrast, a *game object* is an object that is part of a scene or a level. You can create assets from game objects, and you can create game objects from assets.

CAUTION

Moving Assets

Unity maintains links between the various assets associated with projects. As a result, moving or deleting items outside Unity could potentially cause problems. As a general rule, it is a good idea to do all your asset management inside Unity.

When you click a folder in the Project view, the contents of the folder are displayed under the Assets section on the right. As you can see in Figure 1.7, the Assets folder is currently empty; therefore, nothing appears on the right. If you would like to create assets, you can do so easily by clicking the **Create** drop-down menu. This menu enables you to add all manner of assets and folders to a project.

TIP

Project Organization

Organization is extremely important in project management. As your projects get bigger, the number of assets will grow, and eventually finding anything will be a chore. You can help prevent a lot of frustration by employing some simple organization rules:

- ► Every asset type (scenes, scripts, textures, and so on) should get its own folder.
- ► Every asset should be in a folder.
- ► If you use a folder inside another folder, make sure that the structure makes sense. Folders should become more specific and should not be vague or generalized.

Following these few simple rules will really make a difference.

The Favorites buttons enable you to quickly select all assets of a certain type. This makes it possible for you to get an "at a glance" view of your assets quickly. When you click one of the Favorites buttons (All Models, for instance) or perform a search with the built-in search bar, you can narrow down the results between Assets and Asset Store. If you click **Asset Store**, you can browse the assets that fit your search criteria from the Unity Asset Store (see Figure 1.8). You can further narrow your results by free and paid assets. This is a fantastic feature because it enables you to grab assets that you need for your project without ever leaving the Unity interface.

Favorite Buttons   Search for All Models   Search Asset Store

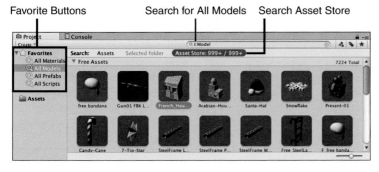

FIGURE 1.8
Searching the Unity Asset Store.

The Hierarchy View

In many ways, the Hierarchy view (see Figure 1.9) is a lot like the Project view. The difference is that the Hierarchy view shows all the items in the current scene instead of the entire project. When you first create a project with Unity, you get the default scene, which has just two items in it: Main Camera and Directional Light game objects. As you add items to your scene, they appear in the Hierarchy view. Just like with the Project view, you can use the Create menu to quickly add items to your scene, search using the built-in search bar, and click and drag items to organize and "nest" them.

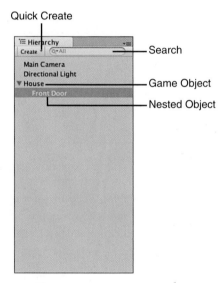

FIGURE 1.9
The Hierarchy view.

TIP

Nesting

Nesting is the term for establishing a relationship between two or more items. In the Hierarchy view, clicking and dragging an item onto another item nests the dragged item under the other one. This creates what is commonly known as a *parent/child relationship*. In this case, the object on top is the parent, and any objects below it are children. You can tell when an object is nested because it becomes indented. As you will see later, nesting objects in the Hierarchy view can affect how they behave.

TIP

Scenes

Scene is the term Unity uses to describe what you might already know as a level or map. As you develop a Unity project, each collection of objects and behaviors should be its own scene. Therefore, if you were building a game with a snow level and a jungle level, those would be separate scenes. You will see the words *scene* and *level* used interchangeably as you look for answers on the Internet.

TIP

Scene Organization

The first thing you should do when working with a new Unity project is create a Scenes folder under Assets in the Project view. This way, all your scenes (or levels) will be stored in the same place. Be sure to give your scenes descriptive names. Scene1 may sound like a great name now, but when you have 30 scenes, such unclear naming can get confusing.

The Inspector View

The Inspector view enables you to see all the properties of a currently selected item. Simply click any asset or object from the Project or Hierarchy view, and the Inspector view automatically propagates with information.

In Figure 1.10, you can see the Inspector view after the Main Camera object is selected from the Hierarchy view.

Let's break down some of this functionality:

▶ If you click the check box next to the object's name, it becomes disabled and does not appear in the project.

▶ Drop-down lists (such as the Layer and Tag lists; more on those later) are used to select from a set of predefined options.

▶ Text boxes, drop-downs, and sliders can have their values changed, and the changes are automatically and immediately reflected in the scene—even if the game is running!

▶ Each game object acts like a container for different components (such as Transform, Camera, and Audio Listener in Figure 1.10). You can disable these components by unchecking them or remove them by right-clicking and selecting **Remove Component**.

▶ Components can be added by clicking the **Add Component** button.

Name

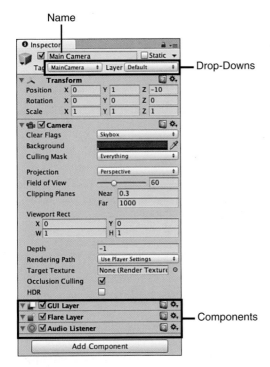

— Drop-Downs

— Components

FIGURE 1.10
The Inspector view.

CAUTION

Changing Properties While Running a Scene

The capability to change the properties of an object and see those changes reflected immediately in a running scene is very powerful. It enables you to tweak things like movement speed, jumping height, collision power, and so on, all on-the-fly, without stopping and starting the game. Be wary, though, as any changes you make to the properties of an object while a scene is running are reverted when the scene finishes. If you make a change and like the result, be sure to remember what it was so you can set it again when the scene is stopped.

The Scene View

The Scene view is the most important view you work with because it enables you to see your game visually as it is being built (see Figure 1.11). Using the mouse controls and a few hotkeys, you can move around inside your scene and place objects where you want them. This gives you an immense level of control.

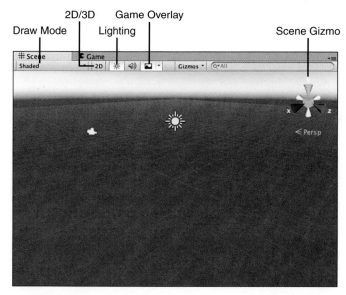

FIGURE 1.11
The Scene view.

In a little bit, you will learn about moving around within a scene, but for now, let's focus on the controls that are part of the Scene view:

▶ **Draw mode:** This controls how the scene is drawn. By default, it is set to Shaded, which means objects will be drawn with their textures in full color.

▶ **2D/3D view:** This control changes from a 3D view to a 2D view. Note that in 2D view, the scene gizmo (described later this hour) does not show.

▶ **Scene lighting:** This control determines whether objects in the Scene view are lit by default ambient lighting or only by lights that actually exist within the scene. The default is to include the built-in ambient lighting.

▶ **Audition mode:** This control sets whether an audio source in the Scene view functions.

▶ **Game overlay:** This control determines whether items like skyboxes, fog, and other effects appear in the Scene view.

▶ **Gizmo selector:** This control enables you to choose which *gizmos*—that is, indicators that help with visual debugging or aid in setup—appear in the Scene view. This control also determines whether the placement grid is visible.

▶ **Scene gizmo:** This control shows which direction you are currently facing and aligns the Scene view with an axis.

NOTE

The Scene Gizmo

The scene gizmo gives you a lot of power over the Scene view. As you can see, the control has X, Y, and Z indicators that align with the three axes. This makes it easy to tell exactly which way you are looking in the scene. You will learn more about axes and 3D space in Hour 2, "Game Objects." The scene gizmo also gives you active control over the scene alignment. If you click one of the gizmo's axes, the Scene view immediately snaps to that axis and gets set to a direction such as top or left. Clicking the box in the center of the gizmo toggles between Iso and Persp modes.

Iso, which stands for *isometric*, is the 3D view with no perspective applied. Persp, which stands for *perspective*, is the 3D view with perspective applied. Try it out for yourself and see how it affects the Scene view. You'll notice that the icon changes from parallel lines for isometric to diverging lines like crow's feet for perspective.

The Game View

The last view to go over is the Game view. Essentially, the Game view allows you to "play" the game inside the editor by giving you a full simulation of the current scene. All elements of a game function in the Game view just as they would if the project were fully built. Figure 1.12 shows what a Game view looks like. Note that although the Play, Pause, and Step buttons are not technically a part of the Game view, they control the Game view and therefore are included in the image.

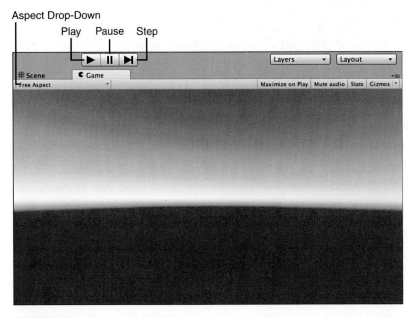

FIGURE 1.12
The Game view.

TIP

Missing Game View

If you find that the Game view is hidden behind the Scene view or that the Game view tab is missing entirely, don't worry. As soon as you click the **Play** button, a Game view tab appears in the editor and begins displaying the game.

The Game view comes with some controls that assist with testing games:

▶ **Play:** The Play button enables you to play the current scene. All controls, animations, sounds, and effects are present and working. Once a game is running, it should behave very closely to how it would behave if it were actually being run in a standalone player (such as on your PC or mobile device). To stop the game from running, click the Play button again.

▶ **Pause:** The Pause button pauses the execution of the currently running Game view. The game maintains its state and continues exactly where it was when paused. Clicking the Pause button again causes the game to continue running.

▶ **Step:** The Step button works while the Game view is paused and causes the game to execute a single frame of the game. This effectively allows you to "step" through the game slowly and debug any issues you might have. Clicking the Step button while the game is running causes the game to pause.

▶ **Aspect drop-down:** From this drop-down menu, you can choose the aspect ratio you want for the Game view window while running. The default is Free Aspect, but you can change this to match the aspect ratio of the target platform you are developing for.

▶ **Maximize on Play:** This button determines whether the Game view takes up the entirety of the editor when run. By default, this is off, and a running game is only the size of the Game view tab.

▶ **Mute Audio:** This button turns off the sounds when playing the game. This is handy when the person sitting next to you is getting tired of hearing your repeated play-testing!

▶ **Stats:** This button determines whether rendering statistics are displayed on the screen while the game is running. These statistics can be useful for measuring the efficiency of a scene. The stats are turned off by default.

▶ **Gizmos:** This is both a button and a drop-down menu. The button determines whether gizmos are displayed while the game is running. Game view gizmos are not displayed by default. The drop-down menu (the small arrow) on this button determines which gizmos appear if gizmos are turned on.

NOTE

Running, Paused, and Off

It can be difficult at first to determine what is meant by the terms *running*, *paused*, and *off*. When the game is not executing in the Game view, the game is said to be off. When a game is off, the game controls do not work, and the game cannot be played. When the Play button is pressed and the game begins executing, the game is said to be running. *Playing*, *executing*, and *running* all mean the same thing. If the game is running and the Pause button is pressed, the game stops running but still maintains its state. At this point, the game is paused. The difference between a paused game and an off game is that a paused game resumes execution at the point at which it was paused, whereas an off game begins executing at the beginning.

Honorable Mention: The Toolbar

Although not a view, the toolbar is an essential part of the Unity editor. Figure 1.13 shows the toolbar components:

▶ **Transform tools:** These buttons enable you to manipulate game objects and are covered in greater detail later in this book. Pay special attention to the button that resembles a hand. This is the Hand tool, and it is described later this hour.

▶ **Transform gizmo toggles:** These toggles allow you to manipulate how gizmos appear in the Scene view. Leave them alone for now.

▶ **Game view controls:** These buttons control the Game view.

▶ **Account and Services controls:** These buttons allow you to manage the Unity account you are using as well as the services you are using in your project.

▶ **Layers drop-down:** This menu determines which object layers appear in the Scene view. By default, everything appears in the Scene view. Leave this alone for now. Layers are covered in Hour 5, "Lights and Cameras."

▶ **Layout drop-down:** This menu allows you to quickly change the layout of the editor.

FIGURE 1.13
The toolbar.

Navigating the Unity Scene View

The Scene view gives you a lot of control over the construction of a game. The ability to place and modify items visually is very powerful. None of this is very useful, though, if you cannot move around inside the scene. This section covers a couple different ways to change your position and navigate the Scene view.

TIP

Zoom

Regardless of what method you are using for navigation, scrolling the mouse wheel always zooms the view within a scene. By default, the scene zooms in and out of the center of the Scene view. If you hold **Alt** while scrolling, however, you zoom in and out of wherever the mouse is currently pointing. Go ahead and give it a try!

The Hand Tool

The Hand tool (hotkey: **Q**) provides a simple way to move about the Scene view with the mouse (see Figure 1.14). This tool is especially useful if you are using a mouse with only a single button (because other methods require a two-button mouse). Table 1.1 briefly explains each of the Hand tool controls. (Don't worry about the other buttons next to the Hand tool yet. They are covered a little bit later.)

FIGURE 1.14
The Hand tool.

TABLE 1.1   The Hand Tool Controls

Action	Effect
Click-drag	Drags the camera around the scene
Hold **Alt** and **click-drag**	Orbits the camera around the current pivot point
Hold **Ctrl** (**Command** on Mac) and **right-click-drag**	Zooms the camera

You can find all the Unity hotkeys at http://docs.unity3d.com/Manual/UnityHotkeys.html.

CAUTION

Different Cameras

When working in Unity, you deal with two types of cameras. The first is the standard game object camera. You can see that you already have one in your scene (by default). The second type is more of an imaginary camera than a camera in the traditional sense. It is what determines what you can see in the Scene view. When this hour's instructions mention the camera, it is talking about the second type. You do not actually manipulate the game object camera.

Flythrough Mode

Flythrough mode enables you to move about the scene using a traditional first-person control scheme. This mode feels like home for anyone who plays first-person games (such as first-person shooters). If you don't play those games, this mode might take a little getting used to. Once you become familiar with it, though, it will be second nature.

Holding down the right mouse button while your mouse cursor is over the Scene view puts you into Flythrough mode. All the actions laid out in Table 1.2 require that the right mouse button be held down.

TABLE 1.2   Flythrough Mode Controls

Action	Effect
Move the mouse	Causes the camera to pivot, which gives the feeling of "looking around" within the scene.
Press the **WASD** keys	The WASD keys move you about the scene. Each key corresponds with a direction: forward, left, back, and right, respectively.
Press the **QE** keys	The QE keys move you up and down, respectively, within the scene.
Hold **Shift** while pressing the **WASD** or **QE** keys	Has the same effect as using the WASD or QE keys but much faster. Consider Shift to be your "sprint" button.

TIP

Snap Controls

You have many ways to attain precise control over scene navigation. Sometimes, you just want to quickly get around the scene, though. For times like these, it is good to use what I call *snap controls*. If you want to quickly navigate to, and zoom in on, a game object in a scene, you can do so by highlighting the object in the Hierarchy view and pressing **F** (short for *Frame Select*). The scene then "snaps" to that game object. You can also achieve the same effect by double-clicking any object in the Hierarchy view. Another snap control is one you have seen already: The scene gizmo allows you to quickly snap the camera to any axis. This way, you can see an object from any angle without having to manually move the scene camera around. Be sure to practice using the snap controls, and navigating through your scene quickly will become a snap!

TIP
_____

Additional Learning

When using the New Project or Open Project dialog, your eyes may have magically been draw to the Learn button present there (see Figure 1.15). Clicking that button displays Unity's new learning resources. These resources are a fantastic augmentation and are well worth your time if you'd like even more practice getting to know the basics of the Unity engine. (I am a little biased: I helped make them.)

FIGURE 1.15
The Learn section of the Project dialog.

_____

Summary

In this hour, you took your first look at the Unity game engine. You started off by downloading and installing Unity. From there, you learned how to open and create projects. Then you learned about all the different views that make up the Unity editor. You also learned how to navigate around the Scene view.

Q&A

Q. Are assets and game objects the same?

A. Not exactly. The big difference is that an asset has a corresponding file or group of files on the hard drive, whereas a game object does not. An asset may or may not contain a game object.

Q. There are a lot of different controls and options. Do I need to memorize them all right away?

A. Not at all. Most controls and options are already set to default states that cover most situations. As your knowledge of Unity grows, you will continue to learn more about the different controls available to you. This lesson is just meant to show you what's there and to give you a bit of familiarity.

Workshop

Take some time to work through the questions here to ensure that you have a firm grasp of the material.

Quiz

1. True or False: You must purchase Unity Pro to make commercial games.

2. Which view enables you to manipulate objects in a scene visually?

3. True or False: You should always move your asset files around within Unity and not use the operating system's file explorer.

4. True or False: When creating a new project, you should include every asset that you think is awesome.

5. What mode do you enter in the Scene view when you hold down the right mouse button?

Answers

1. False. You can make games with Unity Personal or Unity Plus.

2. Scene view

3. True. This helps Unity keep track of the assets.

4. False. This takes up space and slows down your project.

5. Flythrough mode

Exercise

Take a moment to practice the concepts presented in this hour. It is important to have a strong foundational understanding of the Unity editor because everything you will learn from here on out will utilize it in some way. To complete this exercise, do the following:

1. Create a new scene by going to **File > New Scene** or by pressing **Ctrl+N (Command+N** on a Mac).

2. Create a folder in the Project view by right-clicking **Assets** and selecting **Create > Folder**. Name the folder **Scenes**.

3. Save your scene by going to **File > Save Scene** or by pressing **Ctrl+S (Command+S** on a Mac). Be sure to save the scene in the Scenes folder you created and give it a descriptive name.

4. Add a cube to your scene. You can do this in one of three ways.

   ▶ Click the **GameObject** menu at the top of the editor and select **3D Object > Cube**.

   ▶ Click **Create > 3D Object > Cube** in the Hierarchy view.

   ▶ Right-click in the Hierarchy view and select **3D Object > Cube**.

5. Select the newly added cube in the Hierarchy view and experiment with its properties in the Inspector view.

6. Practice navigating around the Scene view by using Flythrough mode, the Hand tool, and snap controls. Use the cube as a point of reference to help navigate.

HOUR 2
Game Objects

What You'll Learn in This Hour:

▶ How to work with 2D and 3D coordinates
▶ How to work with game objects
▶ How to work with transforms

Game objects are the foundational components of a Unity game project. Every item that exists in a scene is, or is based on, a game object. In this hour, you'll learn about game objects in Unity. Before you can start working with objects in Unity, however, you must learn about the 2D and 3D coordinate systems. After you learn about those systems in this hour, you will begin working with the built-in Unity game objects, and you will wrap up the hour by learning about the various game object transformations. Information gained in this hour is foundational to everything else in this book. Be sure to take your time and learn it well.

Dimensions and Coordinate Systems

For all their glitz and glamour, video games are mathematical constructs. All the properties, movements, and interactions can be boiled down to numbers. Luckily for you, a lot of the groundwork has already been laid. Mathematicians have been toiling away for centuries to discover, invent, and simplify different processes, and all their work means you can more easily build games with modern software. You may think the objects in a game just exist in space randomly, but really every game space has dimensions, and every object is placed in a coordinate system (or grid).

Putting the D in 3D

As mentioned previously, every game uses some level of dimensions. The most common dimension systems, the ones you are most likely familiar with, are 2D and 3D (short for two-dimensional and three-dimensional). A 2D system is a flat system. In a 2D system, you deal only with vertical and horizontal elements (or, to put it another way: up, down, left, and right). Games like *Tetris*, *Pong*, and *Pac Man* are good examples of 2D games. A 3D system is like a

2D system, but it obviously has one more dimension. In a 3D system, you have not only horizontal and vertical (up, down, left, and right) but also depth (in and out). Figure 2.1 does a good job of illustrating the differences between a 2D square and a 3D square, otherwise known as a *cube*. Notice how the inclusion of the depth axis in the 3D cube makes it seem to "pop out."

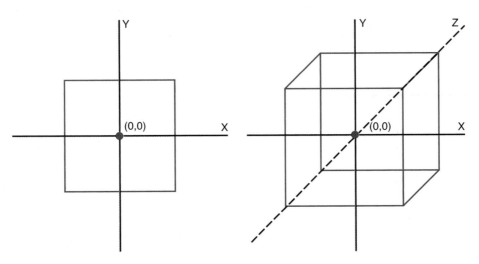

FIGURE 2.1
2D square versus 3D cube.

NOTE

Learning About 2D and 3D

Unity is a 3D engine. Therefore, all the projects made with it inherently use all three dimensions. The real secret is that there is no such thing as a true 2D game anymore. Modern hardware renders everything as 3D. 2D games still have the z axis but just don't use it. You might be wondering why this book bothers to cover 2D systems at all. The truth is that even in 3D projects, there are still a lot of 2D elements. Textures, screen elements, and mapping techniques all use a 2D system. Unity has a powerful set of tools to work with 2D games, and 2D systems aren't going away anytime soon.

Using Coordinate Systems

The mathematical equivalent of a dimension system is a coordinate system. A coordinate system uses a series of lines, called *axes* (the plural of axis), and locations, called *points*. These axes correspond directly with the dimensions they mimic. For instance, a 2D coordinate system has the x axis and y axis, which represent the horizontal and vertical directions, respectively. If an object is moving horizontally, we say it is moving "along the x axis." Likewise, the 3D coordinate system uses the x axis, the y axis, and the z axis for horizontal, vertical, and depth movement and positioning, respectively.

NOTE

Common Coordinate Syntax

When referring to an object's position, you generally list its coordinates. Saying that an object is 2 on the x axis and 4 on the y axis can be a little cumbersome. Luckily, a shorthand way of writing coordinates exists. In a 2D system, you write coordinates like (x, y), and in a 3D system, you write them like (x, y, z). Therefore, for an object that is 2 on the x axis and 4 on the y axis, you simply write (2, 4). If that object were also 10 on the z axis, you would write (2, 4, 10).

Every coordinate system has a point at which all the axes intersect. This point is called the *origin*, and the coordinates for the origin are always (0, 0) in a 2D system and (0, 0, 0) in a 3D system. This origin point is very important because it is the basis from which all other points are derived. The coordinates for any other point are simply the distance of that point from the origin along each axis. A point's coordinates get larger as it moves away from the origin. For example, as a point moves to the right, its x axis value gets larger. When it moves left, the x axis value gets smaller until it passes through the origin. At that time, the x value of the point begins getting larger again, but it also becomes negative. Consider Figure 2.2. This 2D coordinate system has three points defined. The point (2, 2) is 2 *units* away from the origin in both the x and the y directions. The point (–3, 3) is 3 units to the left of the origin and 3 units above the origin. The point (2, –2) is 2 units to the right of the origin and 2 units below the origin.

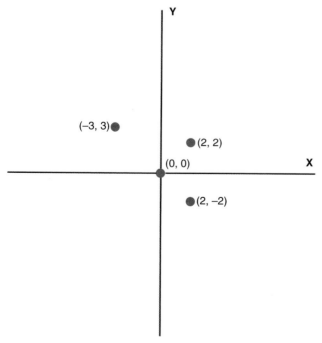

FIGURE 2.2
Points in relation to the origin.

World Versus Local Coordinates

You have now learned about the dimensions of a game world and about the coordinate systems that compose them. What you have been working with so far is considered the *world* coordinate system. At any given time, there is only a single x axis, a single y axis, and a single z axis in the world coordinate system. Likewise, there is only one origin that all objects share. What you might not know is that there is also something called the *local* coordinate system. This system is unique to each object, and it is completely separate from the local coordinate systems of other objects. This local system has its own axes and origin that other objects don't use. Figure 2.3 illustrates the world versus local coordinate systems by showing the four points that make up a square for each.

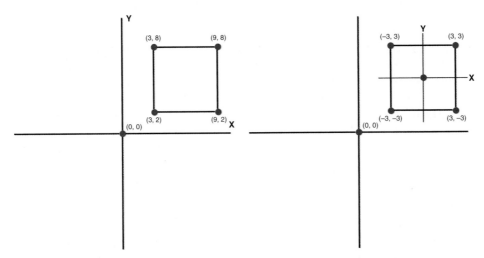

FIGURE 2.3
World coordinates (left) versus local coordinates (right).

You might be wondering what the local coordinate system is for if the world coordinate system is used for the positions of objects. Later in this hour, you will look at transforming game objects and at parenting game objects. Both of these require the local coordinate system.

Game Objects

All shapes, models, lights, cameras, particle systems, and so on in a Unity game have one thing in common: They are all game objects. The game object is the fundamental unit of any scene. Even though they are simple, game objects are very powerful. At their root, game objects are little more than transforms (discussed in greater detail later in the hour) and containers. The container part of a game object exists to hold the various components that make the object more dynamic and meaningful. What you add to your game objects is up to you. There are many components, and they add a huge amount of variety. Throughout the course of this book, you will be learning to use many of these components.

NOTE

Built-in Objects

Not every game object you use will start as an empty object. Unity has several built-in game objects available to use right out of the box. You can see the many items available by clicking the **GameObject** menu item at the top of the Unity editor. A large portion of learning to use Unity is learning to work with built-in and custom game objects.

TRY IT YOURSELF ▼

Creating Some Game Objects

Let's take some time now to work with game objects. Follow these steps to create a few basic objects and examine their different components:

1. Create a new project or create a new scene in an existing project.

2. Add an empty game object by clicking the **GameObject** menu item and selecting **Create Empty**. (Note that you could also create an empty game object by pressing **Ctrl+Shift+N** on a PC or **Command+Shift+N** on a Mac.)

3. Look in the Inspector view and notice that the game object you just created has no components other than a transform. (Every game object has a transform.) Click the **Add Component** button in the Inspector to see all the components you could add to the object. Don't select any components at this time.

4. Add a cube to your project by clicking the **GameObject** menu item, hovering the cursor over **3D Object**, and selecting **Cube** from the list.

5. Notice the various components the cube has that the empty game object doesn't. The mesh components make the cube visible, and the collider makes it able to interact with other objects on a physical level.

6. Add a point light to your project by clicking the **Create** drop-down in the Hierarchy view and selecting **Light > Point Light** from the list.

7. Notice that the point light only shares the transform component with the cube. It is focused entirely on emitting light. The light emitted by this point light adds to the directional light already in the scene.

Transforms

So far in this hour, you have learned and explored the different coordinate systems and experimented with some game objects. It is time to put the two together. When dealing with 3D objects, you often hear the term *transform*. Depending on the context, transform is either a noun or a verb. All objects in 3D space have a position, a rotation, and a scale. If you combine them, you get an object's transform (noun). Alternatively, *transform* can be a verb if it refers to changing an object's position, rotation, or scale. Unity combines the two meanings of the word with the *transform component*.

Recall that the transform component is the only component that every game object has to have. Even empty game objects have transforms. Using this component, you can both see the current transform of the object and change (or transform) the transform of the object. It might sound confusing now, but it is fairly simple. You will get the hang of it in no time. Because the transform is made up of the position, rotation, and scale, it stands to reason that there are three separate methods (called *transformations*) of changing the transform: translation, rotation, and scaling. These transformations can be achieved using either the Inspector or the transform tools. Figures 2.4 and 2.5 illustrate which Inspector components and tools correlate with the various transforms.

FIGURE 2.4
Transform options in the Inspector.

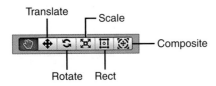

FIGURE 2.5
The transform tools.

TIP

Check Yourself Before You Rect Yourself

The term Rect (short for rectangle) can often be seen in conjunction with 2D game objects. For instance, while 2D objects like sprites have the same type of transform as 3D objects, you can use the simpler Rect tool to control their position, rotation, and scale all at once. (Refer to Figure 2.5 for the location of the Rect tool.) Furthermore, user interface (UI) objects in Unity have a different type of transform called a Rect transform. Hour 14, "User Interfaces," covers this in more detail; for now, just understand that they are the 2D equivalent of the normal transform that is used exclusively for UI.

Translation

The process of changing the coordinate position of an object in a 3D system is called *translation*, and it is the simplest transform you can apply to an object. When you translate an object, it is shifted along an axis. Figure 2.6 demonstrates a square being translated along the x axis.

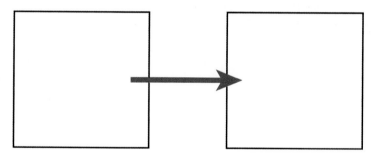

FIGURE 2.6
Sample translation.

When you select the Translate tool (hotkey: **W**), whatever object you have selected changes slightly in the Scene view. More specifically, you see three arrows appear, pointing away from the center of the object along the three axes. These are translation gizmos, and they help you move your objects around in the scene. Clicking on and holding any of these axis arrows causes them to turn yellow. Then, if you move your mouse, the object moves along that axis. Figure 2.7 shows what the translation gizmos look like. Note that the gizmos appear only in the Scene view.

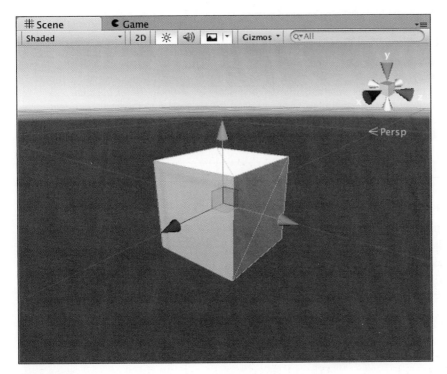

FIGURE 2.7
Translation gizmos.

TIP

The Transform Component and Transform Tools

Unity provides two ways to manage the transforms of your objects. Knowing when to use each is important. When you change an object's transform in the Scene view with a transform tool, the transform data also changes in the Inspector view. It is often easier to make large changes to an object's transform using the Inspector view because you can just change the values to what they need to be. The transform tools, however, are more useful for quick, small changes. Learning to use both together will greatly improve your workflow.

Rotation

Rotating an object does not move it in space. Instead, it changes the object's relationship to that space. More simply stated, rotation enables you to redefine which directions the x, y, and z axes point for a particular object. When an object rotates around an axis, it is said to be rotating *about* that axis. Figure 2.8 shows a square being rotated about the z axis.

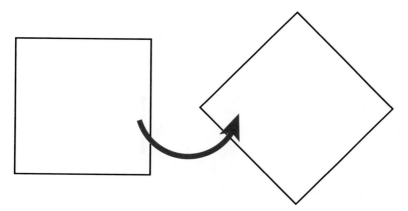

FIGURE 2.8
Rotation about the z axis.

TIP

Determining the Axis of Rotation

If you are unsure which axis you need to rotate an object about to get a desired effect, you can use a simple mental method. One axis at a time, pretend that the object is stuck in place by a pin that is parallel with that axis. The object can only spin around the pin stuck in it. Now, determine which pin allows the object to spin the way you want. That is the axis you need to rotate the object about.

Just as with the Translate tool, selecting the Rotate tool (hotkey: **E**) causes rotation gizmos to appear around your object. These gizmos are circles representing the object's rotation path about the axes. Clicking and dragging on any of these circles turns it yellow and allows you to rotate the object about that axis. Figure 2.9 shows what the rotation gizmos look like.

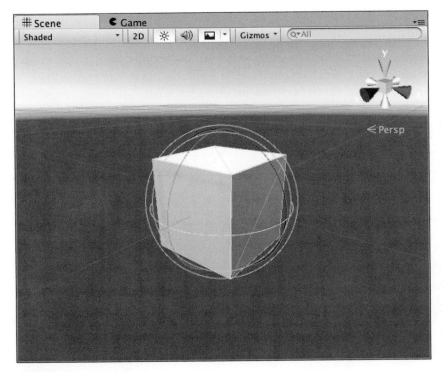

FIGURE 2.9
The Rotate tool gizmos.

Scaling

Scaling causes an object to grow or shrink within a 3D space. This transform is really straightforward and simple to use. Scaling an object on any axis causes its size to change on that axis. Figure 2.10 demonstrates a square being scaled down on the x and y axes. Figure 2.11 shows what the scaling gizmos look like when you select the Scaling tool (hotkey: **r**).

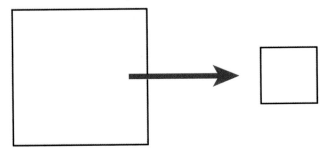

FIGURE 2.10
Scaling on the x and y axes.

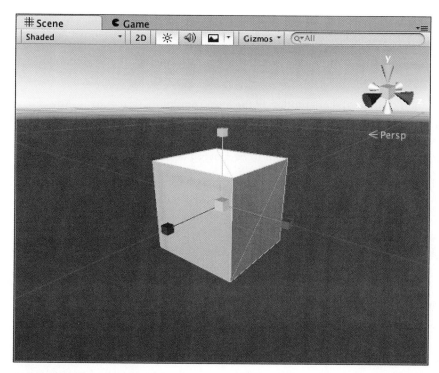

FIGURE 2.11
The scaling gizmos.

Hazards of Transformations

As mentioned earlier in this hour, transformations use the local coordinate system. Therefore, the changes that are made can potentially impact future transformations. For example, in Figure 2.12, notice how the same two transformations, when applied in reverse order, have very different effects.

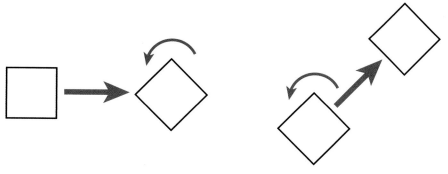

FIGURE 2.12
Effects of transformation order.

As you can see, not paying attention to transformation order can have unexpected consequences. Luckily, the transformations have consistent effects that can be planned on:

▶ **Translation:** Translation is a fairly inert transformation. This means that any changes applied after it generally are not affected.

▶ **Rotation:** Rotation changes the orientation of the local coordinate system axes. Any translations applied after a rotation cause the object to move along the new axes. If you were to rotate an object 180 degrees about the z axis, for example, and then move in the positive y direction, the object would appear to be moving down instead of up.

▶ **Scaling:** Scaling effectively changes the size of the local coordinate *grid*. Basically, when you scale an object to be larger, you are really scaling the local coordinate system to be larger. This causes the object to seem to grow. This change is multiplicative. For example, if an object is scaled to 1 (its natural, default size) and then translated 5 units along the x axis, the object appears to move 5 units to the right. If the same object were to be scaled to 2, however, then translating 5 units on the x axis would result in the object appearing to move 10 units to the right. This is because the local coordinate system is now double the size, and 5 times 2 equals 10. Inversely, if the object were scaled to .5 and then moved, it would appear to move only 2.5 units (.5 × 5 = 2.5).

Once you understand these rules, determining how an object will change with a set of transformations is easy. These effects depend on whether you have Local or Global selected, and they take some getting used to, so it is a good idea to experiment.

TIP

All Tools at Once

The last scene tool on the toolbar is a new Composite tool (hotkey: **y**). This tool allows you to translate, rotate, and scale a 3D object all at once.

Gizmo Positions

The gizmo placement options can be very confusing for a new user who doesn't know what they do. Effectively, these options control the position and alignment of the transform gizmos in the scene view. Check out Figure 2.13 to see how the alignment of the translate gizmos changes depending on whether you have the option set to Local or Global coordinate space.

In addition, see Figure 2.14 to learn how the placement of the gizmos changes when you have multiple objects selected. With the Pivot option selected, the gizmos function centers on the first object selected. With the Center option selected, the gizmos are placed and function in the center of all of the selected objects.

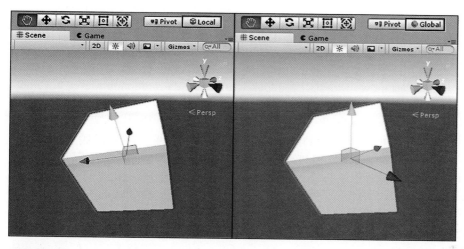

FIGURE 2.13
The alignment of the gizmos for Local versus Global.

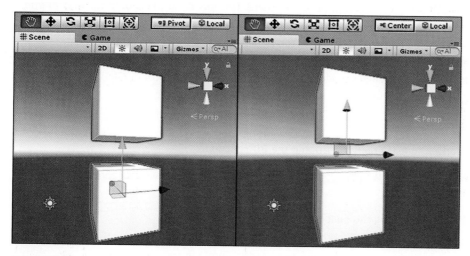

FIGURE 2.14
The position of the gizmos for Pivot versus Center.

Generally speaking, you should keep your gizmos set to Pivot and Local to avoid confusion and to make your day-to-day work in Unity easier.

Transforms and Nested Objects

In Hour 1, "Introduction to Unity," you learned how to nest game objects in the Hierarchy view (by dragging one object onto another one). Recall that when you have an object nested inside another one, the top-level object is the parent, and the other object is the child. Transformations applied to the parent object work as normal. The object can be moved, scaled, and rotated. What's special is how the child object behaves. Once nested, a child object's transform is relative to that of the parent object—not relative to the world. Therefore, a child object's position is not based on its distance from the origin but the distance from the parent object. If the parent object is rotated, the child object moves with it. If you looked at the child's rotation, however, it would not register that it had rotated at all. The same goes for scaling. If you scale the parent object, the child also changes in size. The scale of the child object remains unchanged. You might be confused by this. Remember that when a transformation is applied, it is not applied to the object but to the object's coordinate system. An object isn't rotated; its coordinate system is rotated. The effect is that the object *seems* to turn. When a child object's coordinate system is based on the local coordinate system of the parent, any changes to the parent system directly change the child (without the child knowing about it).

Summary

In this hour, you have learned all about game objects in Unity. You started off by learning all about the differences between 2D and 3D. From there, you looked at the coordinate system and how it breaks down the "world" concepts mathematically. You then began working with game objects, including some of the built-in ones. You ended by learning about transforms and the three transformations. You got to try out the transforms, learn about some of the hazards, and see how transforms affect nested objects.

Q&A

Q. Is it important to learn both the 2D and the 3D concepts?

A. Yes. Even games that are entirely 3D still use some of the 2D concepts on a technical level.

Q. Should I learn to use all the built-in game objects right away?

A. Not necessarily. There are many game objects, and it can be overwhelming to attempt to learn them all right away. Take your time and learn about the objects as they are covered here.

Q. What is the best way to get familiar with transforms?

A. Practice. Keep working with them; eventually, they will become quite natural.

Workshop

Take some time to work through the questions here to ensure that you have a firm grasp of the material.

Quiz

1. What does the *D* in 2D and 3D stand for?

2. How many transformations are there?

3. True or False: Unity has no built-in objects, and you must create your own.

4. Say you have an object at (0, 0, 0). What is its new position if you move it 1 unit on the x axis and then rotate it 90 degrees about the z axis? What if, instead, you rotated it before moving it?

Answers

1. Dimension

2. Three

3. False. Unity provides many built-in objects.

4. Moving and then rotating results in a position of (1, 0, 0). Rotating and then moving results in a position of (0, 1, 0). If this is confusing to you, be sure to revisit the section "Hazards of Transformations" in this hour.

Exercise

Take a moment to experiment with the way transformations work in a parent/child object scenario. You will get a better feel for exactly how the coordinate systems change the way things are oriented.

1. Create a new scene or a project.

2. Add a cube to the scene and place it at (0, 2, −5). Remember the shorthand notation for coordinates: The cube you add should have an x value of 0, a y value of 2, and a z value of −5. You can set these values easily in the transform component in the Inspector view.

3. Add a sphere to your scene. Pay attention to the sphere's x, y, and z values.

4. Nest the sphere under the cube by dragging the sphere onto the cube in the Hierarchy view. Notice how the position values changed. The sphere is now located relative to the cube.

5. Place the sphere at (0, 1, 0). Notice how it doesn't go to right above the origin and instead sits right above the cube.

6. Experiment with the various transformations. Be sure to try them on the cube as well as the sphere and see how differently they behave for a parent than for a child object.

Models, Materials, and Textures

What You'll Learn in This Hour:

▶ The fundamentals of models
▶ How to import custom and premade models
▶ How to work with materials and shaders

In this hour, you'll learn all about models and how they are used in Unity. You'll start by looking at the fundamental principles of meshes and 3D objects. From there, you'll learn how to import your own models or use ones acquired from the Asset Store. You'll finish this hour by examining Unity's material and shader functionality.

The Basics of Models

Video games wouldn't be very *video* without the graphical components. In 2D games, the graphics consist of flat images called *sprites*. In 2D games, all you need to do is change the x and y positions of sprites and flip several of them in sequence, and the viewer's eye is fooled into believing that it sees true motion and animation. In 3D games, however, things aren't so simple. In worlds with a third axis, objects need to have volume to fool the eye. Games use a large number of objects; therefore, they need to process things quickly. Meshes make that possible. A mesh, at its most simple, is a series of interconnected triangles. These triangles build off each other in strips to form basic to very complex objects. These strips provide the 3D definitions of a model and can be processed very quickly. Don't worry, though: Unity handles all this for you so that you don't have to manage it yourself. Later in this hour, you'll see just how triangles can make up various shapes in the Unity Scene view.

NOTE

Why Triangles?

You might be wondering why 3D objects are made up entirely of triangles. The answer is simple: Computers process graphics as a series of points, otherwise known as *vertices*. The fewer vertices an object has, the faster it can be drawn. Triangles have two properties that make them desirable.

The first is that whenever you have a single triangle, you need only one more vertex to make another. So to make one triangle, you need three vertices, to make two triangles you need only four, and to make three triangles you need only five. This makes triangles very efficient. The second property that makes triangles desirable is that by making strips of triangles, you can model any 3D object. No other shape affords you that level of flexibility and performance.

NOTE

Terminology: Model or Mesh?

The terms *model* and *mesh* are similar, and you can often use them interchangeably. There is a difference, however. A mesh contains all the points and lines that define the 3D shape of an object. When you refer to the shape or form of a model, you are really referring to a mesh. A mesh can also be called a *model's geography*, or its *geo*. A model, therefore, is an object that contains a mesh.

A model has a mesh to define its dimensions, but it can also contain animations, textures, materials, shaders, and other meshes. A good general rule is this: If the item in question contains anything other than vertex information, it is a model; otherwise, it is a mesh.

NOTE

What About 2D?

This hour covers a lot of information about rendering 3D objects. While that is useful, what if you only want to make 2D games? Should you still bother with this lesson (or any others that don't cover 2D)? Of course! As mentioned in Hour 2, "Game Objects," there aren't really 2D games anymore. Sprites are just textures applied to flat 3D objects. Lighting can be applied to 2D objects. Even the cameras used for 2D and 3D games are identical. All the concepts learned here can be applied directly to your 2D games because 2D games are really 3D games. As you practice more with Unity, you will quickly come to see that the line between 2D and 3D is very blurred indeed!

Built-in 3D Objects

Unity comes with a few basic built-in meshes (or primitives) for you to work with. They tend to be simple shapes that serve simple utilities or can be combined to make more complex objects. Figure 3.1 shows the available built-in meshes. (You worked with the cube and sphere in the previous hours.)

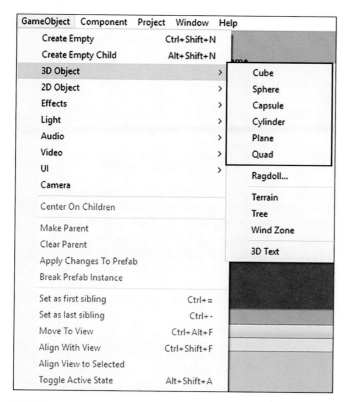

FIGURE 3.1
The built-in meshes in Unity.

TIP

Modeling with Simple Meshes

Do you need a complex object in your game but can't find the right type of model to use? By nesting objects in Unity, you can easily make simple models using the built-in meshes. Just place the meshes near each other so that they form the rough look you want. Then nest all the objects under one central object. This way, when you move the parent, all the children move, too. This might not be the prettiest way to make models for a game, but it will do in a pinch and is useful for prototyping!

Importing Models

Having built-in models is nice, but most of the time your games will require art assets that are a little more complex. Thankfully, Unity makes it rather easy to bring your own 3D models into your projects. Just placing a file containing a 3D model in your Assets folder is enough to bring it into the project. From there, you can drag it into the scene or hierarchy to build a game object around it. Natively, Unity supports .fbx, .dae, .3ds, .dxf, and .obj files. This enables you to work with just about any 3D modeling tool.

▼ TRY IT YOURSELF

Importing Your Own 3D Model

Follow these steps to bring a custom 3D modes into a Unity project:

1. Create a new Unity project or scene.

2. In the Project view, create a new folder named **Models** under the Assets folder by right-clicking the Assets folder and selecting **Create > Folder**.

3. Locate the Torus.fbx file provided for you in the Hour 3 folder of the book files.

4. With the operating system's file browser and the Unity editor open and side-by-side, click and drag the Torus.fbx file from the file browser into the Models folder that you created in step 2. In Unity, click the **Models** folder to see the new Torus file. If you do this correctly, your Project view should resemble Figure 3.2. (*Note:* If you are using an earlier version of Unity or have changed your editor settings, you may also have a Materials folder automatically created. If this is the case, it is not a problem. Materials are discussed in greater detail later in this hour.)

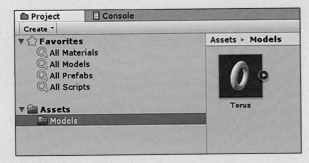

FIGURE 3.2
The Project view after the Torus model is added.

5. Drag the Torus asset from the Models folder onto the Scene view. Notice how a Torus game object is added to the scene containing a mesh filter and mesh renderer. These allow the Torus to be drawn to the screen.

6. Currently the torus in the scene is very small, so select the Torus asset in the project view and look at the Inspector view. Change the value of the scale factor from 1 to 100 and click the **Apply** button at the bottom right of the Inspector.

CAUTION

Default Scaling of Meshes

Most of the Inspector view options for meshes are advanced and are not covered right now. The property you are interested in is the scale factor. 3D software deals in generic units, and each software can use a different scale for units. By default, Unity treats one generic unit as one meter;

another software, such as Blender, might treat one unit as a centimeter. Normally when you import a model, based on the file type, Unity can guess the scale at which to import. Sometimes, however (as in this case), this doesn't work, and you can fine-tune it with the scale factor. By changing the value of the scale factor from 1 to 100, you are telling Unity to import the model 100 times larger, which converts the centimeters of the model into the meters of Unity.

Models and the Asset Store

You don't have to be an expert modeler to make games with Unity. The Asset Store provides a simple and effective way to find premade models and import them into your projects. Generally speaking, models in the Asset Store are either free or paid and come alone or in a collection of similar models. Some of the models come with their own textures, and some of them are simply the mesh data.

Downloading Models from the Asset Store

Let's look at how to find and download models from Unity's Asset Store. Follow these steps to acquire a model named Robot Kyle and import it into your scene:

1. Create a new scene (by selecting **File > New Scene**). In the Project view, type **Robot Kyle t: Model** in the search bar (see Figure 3.3).

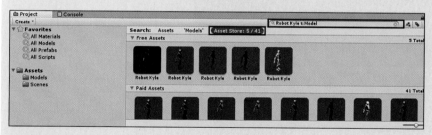

FIGURE 3.3
Locating a model asset.

2. In the search filter section, click the **Asset Store** button (refer to Figure 3.3). If these words aren't visible, you may need to resize your editor window or Project view window. You also need to be connected to the Internet.

3. Locate Robot Kyle, published by Unity Technologies. You can see the publisher by clicking on an asset and checking the Inspector view (see Figure 3.4).

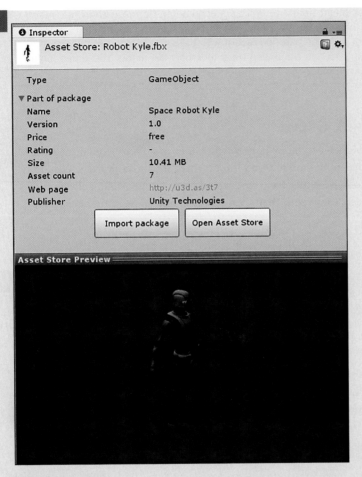

FIGURE 3.4
The asset Inspector view.

4. In the Inspector view, click **Import Package**. At this point, you may be prompted to provide your Unity account credentials. In case you have trouble with this, I have also provided the file in this hour's book files as a Unity package; simply double-click it to import it.

5. When the Importing Package dialog opens, leave everything checked and click **Import**.

6. Locate the robot model under Assets\Robot Kyle\Model and drag it into the Scene view. Note that the model will be fairly small in the Scene view; you might need to move closer to see it.

Textures, Shaders, and Materials

Applying graphical assets to 3D models can be daunting for beginners who are not familiar with the process. Unity uses a simple and specific workflow that gives you a lot of power in determining exactly how you want things to look. Graphical assets are broken down into textures, shaders, and materials. Each of these is covered individually in its own section, and Figure 3.5 shows how they fit together. Notice that textures are not applied directly to models. Instead, textures and shaders are applied to materials. Those materials are in turn applied to the models. This way, the look of a model can be swapped or modified quickly and cleanly without a lot of work.

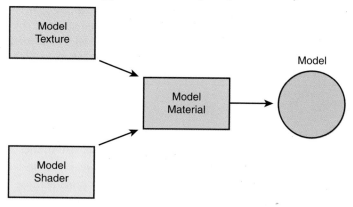

FIGURE 3.5
The model asset workflow.

Textures

Textures are flat images that get applied to 3D objects. They are responsible for models being colorful and interesting instead of blank and boring. It can be strange to think that a 2D image can be applied to a 3D model, but it is a fairly straightforward process once you are familiar with it. Think about a soup can for a moment. If you were to take the label off the can, you would see that it is a flat piece of paper. That label is like a texture. After a label is printed, it is wrapped around a 3D can to provide a more pleasing look.

Just as with all other assets, adding textures to a Unity project is easy. Start by creating a folder for your textures; a good name would be Textures. Then drag any textures you want in your project into the Textures folder you just created. That's it!

NOTE

That's an Unwrap!

Imagining how textures wrap around cans is fine, but what about more complex objects? When creating an intricate model, it is common to generate something called an *unwrap*. The unwrap is somewhat akin to a map that shows exactly how a flat texture will wrap back around a model. If you look in the Textures folder under the Robot Kyle folder from earlier this hour, you see the Robot_Color texture. It looks strange, but that is the unwrapped texture for the model. The generation of unwraps, models, and textures is an art form and is not covered in this text. A preliminary knowledge of how it works should suffice at this level.

CAUTION

Weird Textures

Later in this hour, you will apply some textures to models. You might notice that the textures warp a bit or get flipped in the wrong direction. Just know that this is not a mistake or an error. This occurs when you take a basic rectangular 2D texture and apply it to a model. The model has no idea which way is correct, so it applies the texture however it can. If you want to avoid this issue, use textures specifically designed for (that is, unwrapped for) the model you are using.

Shaders

Whereas the texture of a model determines what is drawn on its surface, the shader determines *how* it is drawn. Here's another way to look at this: A material is the interface between you and a shader. The material tells you what the shader needs to render an object, and you provide those items to make it look the way you want. This might seem nonsensical right now, but later, when you create materials, you will begin to understand how they work. Much of the information about shaders is covered later this hour because you cannot use a shader without a material. In fact, much of the information to be learned about materials is actually about materials' shaders.

TIP

Thought Exercise

If you are having trouble understanding how a shader works, consider this scenario: Imagine you have a piece of wood. The physicality of the wood is its mesh; the color, texture, and visible element are its texture. Now take that piece of wood and pour water on it. The wood still has the same mesh. It is still made of the same substance (wood). It looks different, though. It is slightly darker and shiny. In this example, you have two "shaders": dry wood and wet wood. The wet wood "shader" had something added that made it look a little different without actually changing it.

Materials

As mentioned earlier, materials are not much more than containers for shaders and textures that can be applied to models. Most of the customization of materials depends on which shader is chosen for it, although all shaders have some common functionality.

To create a new material, start by making a Materials folder. Then right-click the folder and select **Create > Material**. Give your material some descriptive name, and you are done. Figure 3.6 shows two materials with different shader settings. Notice how they both use the same Standard shader. Each has a base albedo color of white (more about albedo later), but they have different Smoothness settings. The Flat material has a low Smoothness, so the lighting looks very flat because the light bounces in a lot of directions. The Shiny material has a higher Smoothness, which creates a more focused light bounce. For both materials, there is also a preview of the material, so you can see what it will look like once it is on a model.

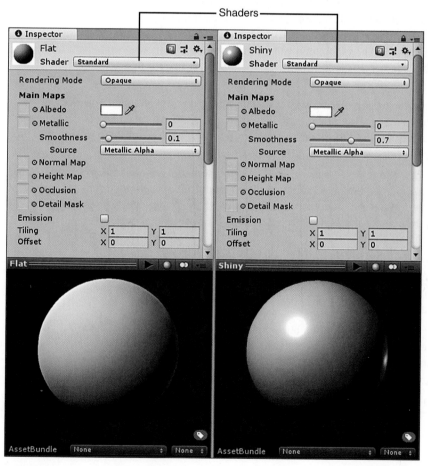

FIGURE 3.6
Two materials with different shader settings.

Shaders Revisited

Now that you have been introduced to textures, models, and shaders, it is time to look at how it all comes together. Unity has a very powerful Standard shader, which this book focuses on. Table 3.1 describes the common shader properties. In addition to the settings listing in Table 3.1, there are many other settings of the Standard shader; however, this book focuses on mastering the ones listed in the table.

TABLE 3.1 Common Shader Properties

Property	Description
Albedo	The Albedo property defines the base color of the object. With Unity's powerful physically based rendering (PBR) system, this color interacts with light as a real object would. For example, a yellow albedo will look yellow in white light but green under blue light. This is where you would apply a texture that contains the color information about your model.
Metallic	This setting does exactly what it sounds like it does: It changes how metallic the material looks. This setting can also take in a texture as a "map" of how metallic different parts of the model appear. For realistic results, set this property to either 0 or 1.
Smoothness	Smoothness is a key element in PBR as it represents various micro imperfections, details, marks, and age that control how smooth (or rough) a surface is. The result is that it makes a model look more or less shiny. This property uses the same texture map as the Metallic property. For realistic results, avoid extreme values like 0 and 1.
Normal Map	The Normal Map property contains the normal map that will be applied to the model. A normal map can be used to apply relief, or bumps, to a model. This is useful when calculating lighting to give the model more detail than it would otherwise have.
Tiling	The Tiling property defines how often a texture can repeat on a model. It can repeat in both the x and y axes. (Remember that textures are flat, which is why there is no z tiling axis.)
Offset	The Offset property defines where in the x and y axes of a texture to begin applying.

This might seem like a lot of information to take in, but once you become more familiar with the few basics of textures, shaders, and materials, you'll find that the Smoothness value of your understanding goes to 1 (classic comedy).

Unity also has several other shaders that this book doesn't cover. The Standard shader is very flexible and should work for most of your basic needs.

Applying Textures, Shaders, and Materials to Models

Follow these steps to put all your knowledge of textures, shaders, and materials together to create a decent-looking brick wall:

1. Start a new project or scene. Note that creating a new project causes the editor to close and reopen.

2. Create a **Textures** folder and a **Materials** folder.

3. Locate the Brick_Texture.png file in the book files and drag it into the Textures folder created in step 2.

4. Add a cube to the scene. Position it at (0, 1, -5). Give it a scale of (5, 2, 1). Figure 3.7 shows the cube's properties.

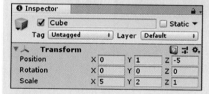

FIGURE 3.7
The properties of the cube.

5. Create a new material (by right-clicking the Materials folder and selecting **Create > Material**) and name it **BrickWall**.

6. Leave the shader as Standard, and under Main Maps click the circle selector (the little circle icon) to the left of the word Albedo. Select **Brick_Texture** from the pop-up window.

7. Click and drag the brick wall material from the Project view onto the cube in the Scene view.

8. Notice that the texture is stretched across the wall a little too much. With the material selected, change the value of the x tiling to be **3**. Make sure you do this in the Main Maps section, not the Secondary Maps section. Now the wall looks much better. You now have a textured brick wall in your scene. Figure 3.8 shows the final product.

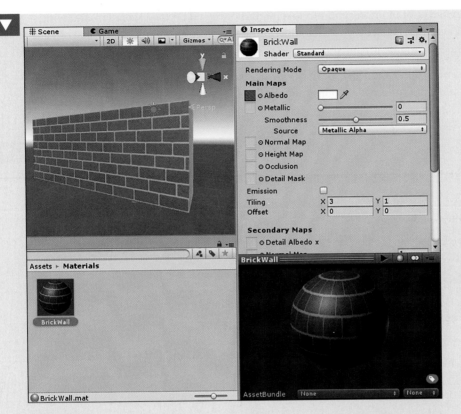

FIGURE 3.8
The final product of this Try It Yourself.

Summary

In this hour, you have learned all about models in Unity. You started by learning about how models are built with collections of vertices called meshes. Then you discovered how to use the built-in models, import your own models, and download models from the Asset Store. You then learned about the model art workflow in Unity. You experimented with textures, shaders, and materials. You finished by creating a textured brick wall.

Q&A

Q. Will I still be able to make games if I'm not an artist?

A. Absolutely. Using free online resources and the Unity Asset Store, you can find various art assets to put in your games.

Q. **Do I need to know how to use all the built-in shaders?**

A. Not necessarily. Many shaders are very situational. Start with the Standard shader covered in this lesson and learn more if a game project requires it.

Q. **If there are paid art assets in the Unity Asset Store, does that mean I can sell my own art assets?**

A. Yes, it does. In fact, the Asset Store is not limited to only art assets. If you can create high-quality assets, you can certainly sell them in the store.

Workshop

Take some time to work through the questions here to ensure that you have a firm grasp of the material.

Quiz

1. True or False: Because of their simple nature, squares make up meshes in models.

2. What file formats does Unity support for 3D models?

3. True or False: Only paid models can be downloaded from the Unity Asset Store.

4. Explain the relationship between textures, shaders, and materials.

Answers

1. False. Meshes are made up of triangles.

2. .fbx, .dae, .3ds, .dxf, and .obj files

3. False. There are many free models.

4. Materials contain textures and shaders. Shaders dictate the properties that can be set by a material and how the material gets rendered.

Exercise

In this exercise, you'll experiment with the effects shaders have on the way models look. You will use the same mesh and texture for each model; only the shaders will be different. The project created in this exercise is named Hour 3_Exercise and is available in the Hour 3 book files.

1. Create a new scene or project.

2. Add a **Materials** folder and a **Textures** folder to your project. Locate the files Brick_Normal.png and Brick_Texture.png in the Hour 3 book files and drag them into the Textures folder.

3. In the Project view, select Brick_Texture. In the Inspector view, change the aniso level to **3** to increase the texture quality for curves. Click **Apply**.

4. In the Project view, select Brick_Normal. In the Inspector view, change the texture type to **Normal Map**. Click **Apply**.

5. Select Directional Light in the Hierarchy view and give it the position (0, 10, -10) and the rotation (30, -180, 0).

6. Add four spheres to your project. Scale them each to (2, 2, 2). Spread them out by giving them the positions (1, 2, -5), (-1, 0, -5), (1, 0, -5), and (-1, 2, -5).

7. Create four new materials in the Materials folder. Name them **DiffuseBrick**, **SpecularBrick**, **BumpedBrick**, and **BumpedSpecularBrick**. Figure 3.9 shows all the properties of the four materials. Go ahead and set them as shown.

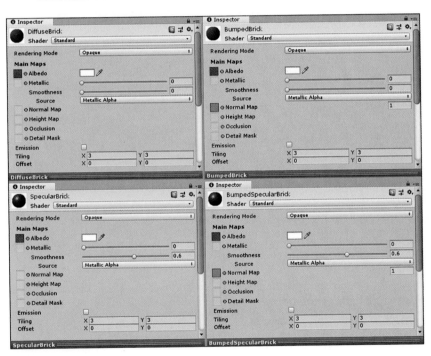

FIGURE 3.9
Material properties.

8. Click and drag each of the materials onto one of the four spheres. Notice how the light and the curvature of the spheres interact with the different shaders. Remember that you can move about the Scene view to see the spheres from different angles.

HOUR 4
Terrain and Environments

What You'll Learn in This Hour:

▶ The fundamentals of terrain
▶ How to sculpt terrain
▶ How to decorate your terrain with textures
▶ How to add trees and grass to your terrain
▶ How to move around in your terrain with a character controller

In this hour, you'll learn about terrain generation. You'll learn what terrain is, how to create it, and how to sculpt it. You will also get hands-on experience with texture painting and fine-tuning. In addition, you'll learn to make large, expansive, and realistic-looking terrain pieces for your games and how to use a controller to move around and explore.

Terrain Generation

All 3D game levels exist in some form of a world. These worlds can be highly abstract or realistic. Often, games with expansive "outdoor" levels are said to have a terrain. The term *terrain* refers to any section of land that simulates a world's external landscape. Tall mountains, far plains, and dank swamps are all examples of possible game terrain.

In Unity, terrain is a flat mesh that can be sculpted into many different shapes. It may help to think of terrain as the sand in a sandbox. You can dig into the sand or raise up sections of it. The only thing basic terrain cannot do is overlap. This means you cannot make things like caves or overhangs. Such items have to be modeled separately. Also, just as with any other object in Unity, terrain has position, rotation, and scale (although they aren't usually changed during gameplay).

Adding Terrain to a Project

Creating a flat terrain in a scene is an easy task with some basic parameters. To add terrain to a scene, just click **GameObject > 3D Object > Terrain**. An asset named New Terrain appears in the project view, and an object called Terrain is added to your scene. If you navigate around in the Scene view, you may also notice that the terrain piece is very large. In fact, the piece is much larger than you could possibly need right now. Therefore, you need to modify some of the properties of this terrain.

To make this terrain more manageable, you need to change the terrain resolution. By modifying the resolution, you can change the length, width, and maximum height of your piece of terrain.

The reason the term *resolution* is used will become more apparent later in this lesson, when you learn about heightmaps. To change the resolution of the terrain piece, follow these steps:

1. Select your terrain in the Hierarchy view. In the Inspector view, locate and click the **Terrain Settings** button (see Figure 4.1).

2. In the Resolution section, note that currently, Terrain Width and Terrain Length are set to 500. Change them both to **50**, which is a more manageable size.

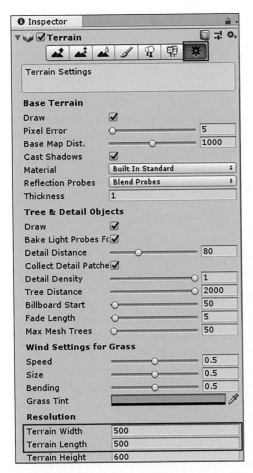

FIGURE 4.1
The Resolution settings.

The other options in the Resolution settings modify the way textures are drawn and the performance of your terrain. Leave these alone for now. After you change the width and length, you will see that the terrain is much smaller and more manageable. Now it is time to start sculpting.

NOTE

Terrain Size

Currently, you are working with terrain that is 50 units long and wide. This is purely for manageability while you're learning to use the various tools. In a real game, the terrain would probably be a bigger size to fit your needs. It is also worth noting that if you already have a heightmap (covered in the next section), you will want the terrain ratio (the ratio of length and width) to match the ratio of the heightmap.

Heightmap Sculpting

Traditionally, 256 shades of gray are available in 8-bit images. These shades range from 0 (black) to 255 (white). Knowing this, you can use a black-and-white image, often called a *grayscale* image, as something called a *heightmap*. A *heightmap* is a grayscale image that contains elevation information similar to a topographical map. The darker shades can be thought of as low points and the lighter shades as high points. Figure 4.2 shows an example of a heightmap. It might not look like much, but a simple image like this can produce some dynamic scenery.

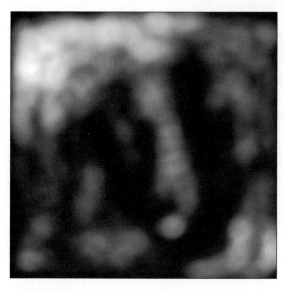

FIGURE 4.2
A simple heightmap.

Applying a heightmap to your currently flat terrain is simple. You simply start with a flat terrain and import the heightmap onto it, as shown in the following Try It Yourself.

▼ TRY IT YOURSELF

Applying a Heightmap to Terrain

Follow these steps to import and apply a heightmap:

1. Create a new Unity project or scene. Locate the terrain.raw file in the Hour 4 files and place it somewhere you can easily find it.

2. Create a new terrain using the steps outlined earlier in this hour. Be sure to set its width and height to **50**.

3. With your terrain selected in the Hierarchy view, click the **Terrain Settings** button in the Inspector view. (Refer to Figure 4.1 if needed.) In the Heightmap section, click **Import Raw**.

4. In the Import Raw Heightmap dialog, locate the terrain.raw file from step 1 and click **Open**.

5. In the Import Heightmap dialog, set the options as they appear in Figure 4.3. (*Note:* The Byte Order property isn't related to the operating system your computer in running. Instead, it relates to the operating system the heightmap was created in.)

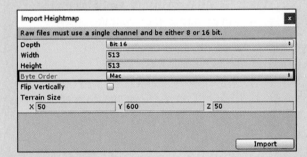

FIGURE 4.3
Import Heightmap dialog.

6. Click **Import**. Right about now, your terrain is looking strange. The problem is that when you set the length and width of your terrain to be more manageable, you left the height at 600. This is obviously much too high for your current needs.

7. Change the terrain resolution by going back to the Resolution section under Terrain Settings in the Inspector view. This time, change the height value to **60**. The result should be something much more pleasant, as shown in Figure 4.4.

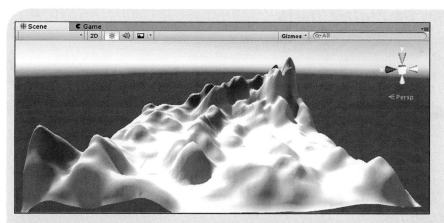

FIGURE 4.4
Terrain after you import a heightmap.

TIP

Calculating Height

So far, the heightmap might seem random, but it is actually quite easy to figure out. Everything is based on a percentage of 255 and the maximum height of the terrain. The max height of the terrain defaults to 600 but is easily changeable. If you apply the formula (Gray Shade)/255 × (Max Height), you can easily calculate any point on the terrain.

For instance, black has a value of 0, so any spot that is black is 0 units high (0/255 × 600 = 0). White has a value of 255; therefore, it produces spots that are 600 units high (255/255 × 600 = 600). If you have a medium gray with a value of 125, any spots of that color produce terrain that is about 294 units high (125/255 × 600 = 294).

NOTE

Heightmap Formats

In Unity, heightmaps must be grayscale images in the .raw format. There are many ways to generate these types of images; you can use a simple image editor or even Unity itself. If you create a heightmap using an image editor, try to make the map the same length and width ratio as your terrain. Otherwise, some distortion will be apparent. If you sculpt some terrain using Unity's sculpting tools and want to generate a heightmap for it, you can do so by going to the Heightmap section under Terrain Settings in the Inspector view and clicking **Export Raw**.

Generally for large terrains, or where performance is important, you should export your heightmap and convert your terrain to a mesh in another program. With a 3D mesh, you can then also add caves, overhangs, and so on before importing the mesh for use in Unity. Note, though, that if you import a mesh to use as a terrain, you won't be able to use Unity's terrain texturing and painting tools with it. (However, you can find third-party assets in the Asset Store that can provide this functionality.)

Unity Terrain Sculpting Tools

Unity gives you multiple tools for hand sculpting your terrain. You can see these tools in the Inspector view under the component Terrain. These tools all work basically the same way: You use a brush with a given size and opacity to "paint" terrain. In effect, what you are doing behind the scenes is painting a heightmap that is translated into changes for the 3D terrain. The painting effects are cumulative, which means the more you paint an area, the stronger the effect on that area. Figure 4.5 shows these tools, which you can use to generate nearly any landscape you can imagine.

FIGURE 4.5
The terrain sculpting tools.

The first tool you will learn to use is the Raise/Lower tool. This tool, just as it sounds, enables you to raise or lower the terrain wherever you paint. To sculpt with this tool, follow these steps:

1. Select a brush. (The brush determines the size and shape of the sculpting effect.)

2. Choose a brush size and opacity. (The opacity determines how strong the sculpting effect is.)

3. Click and drag over the terrain in the Scene view to raise the terrain. Holding **Shift** when you click and drag instead lowers the terrain.

Figure 4.6 illustrates some good starting options for sculpting given the terrain size 50 × 50 with a height of 60.

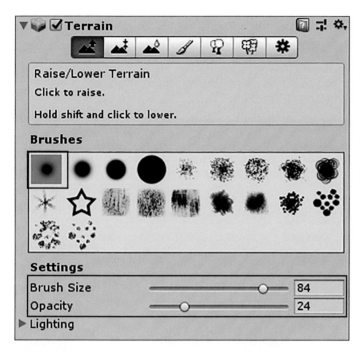

FIGURE 4.6
Good starting properties for sculpting.

The next tool is the Paint Height tool. This tool works almost exactly the same way as the Raise/Lower tool except that it paints your terrain to a specified height. If the specified height is higher than the current terrain, painting raises the terrain. If the specified height is lower than the current terrain, however, the terrain is lowered. This is useful for creating mesas and other flat structures in your landscape. Go ahead and try it out!

TIP

Flattening Terrain

If, at any time, you want to reset your terrain back to being flat, you can do so by going to the Paint Height tool and clicking **Flatten**. One benefit of doing this is that you can flatten the terrain to a height other than its default 0. If your maximum height is 60 and you flatten your heightmap to 30, you have the ability to raise the terrain by 30 units, but you can also lower it by 30 units. This makes it easy to sculpt valleys into your otherwise flat terrain.

The final tool you will use is the Smooth Height tool. This tool doesn't alter the terrain in highly noticeable ways. Instead, it removes a lot of the jagged lines that appear when sculpting terrain. Think of this tool as a polisher. You will use it only to make minor tweaks after your major sculpting is done.

▼ TRY IT YOURSELF

Sculpting Terrain

Now that you have learned about the sculpting tools, it's time to practice using them. In this exercise, you attempt to sculpt a specific piece of terrain:

1. Create a new project or scene and add a terrain. Set the resolution of the terrain to 50 × 50 and give it a height of 60.

2. Flatten the terrain to a height of 20 by clicking the **Paint Height** tool, changing the height to **20,** and clicking **Flatten**. (*Note:* If the terrain appears to disappear, it just moved up 20 units.)

3. Using the sculpting tools, attempt to create a landscape similar to that shown in Figure 4.7. (*Note:* The lighting in the image has been changed to make it easier to see.)

4. Continue to experiment with the tools and try to add unique features to your terrain.

FIGURE 4.7
A sample terrain.

TIP

Practice, Practice, Practice

Developing strong, compelling levels is an art form in itself. Much thought has to be given to the placement of hills, valleys, mountains, and lakes in games. Not only do the elements need to be visually satisfying, they also need to be placed in such a way as to make a level playable. Level-building skills don't develop overnight. Be sure to practice and refine your level-building skills to make exciting and memorable levels.

Terrain Textures

You now know how to make the physical dimensions of a 3D world. Even though there may be a lot of features to your landscape, it is still bland, shiny (due to the default material), and difficult to navigate. It is time to add some character to your level. In this section, you'll learn how to texture your terrain to give it an engaging look. Like sculpting terrain, texturing terrain works a lot like painting. You select a brush and a texture and paint it onto your world.

Importing Terrain Assets

Before you can begin painting the world with textures, you need some textures to work with. Unity has some terrain assets available to you, but you need to import them in order to use them. To load these assets, select **Assets > Import Package > Environment**. The Import Unity Package dialog appears (see Figure 4.8). You use this dialog to specify which assets you want to import. Deselecting unneeded items is a good idea if you want to keep your project size down. For now, though, just leave all options checked and click **Import**. You should now have a new folder under Assets in the Project view called Standard Assets. This folder contains all the terrain assets you will be using in the rest of this hour.

NOTE

Missing Packages

If you are missing the Environment asset package when you go to **Assets > Import Package**, that means that you did not select the Standard Assets option when installing Unity. If you would like these assets (and many more that will be used throughout this book), you can run the installer again and select to install the standard assets.

Texturing Terrain

In order to begin painting terrain, you need to load a texture. Figure 4.9 illustrates the Paint Texture tool in the Inspector, which you access after selecting the terrain in your Hierarchy. Pay attention to the three numeric properties: brush size, opacity, and target strength. You should be familiar with the first two properties, but the last one is new. The target strength is the maximum opacity that is achievable through constant painting. Its value is a percentage, with 1 being 100%. Use this as a control to avoid painting your textures too strongly.

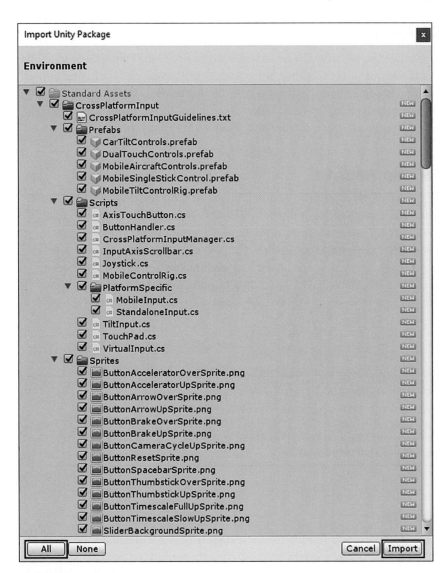

FIGURE 4.8
The Import Unity Package dialog.

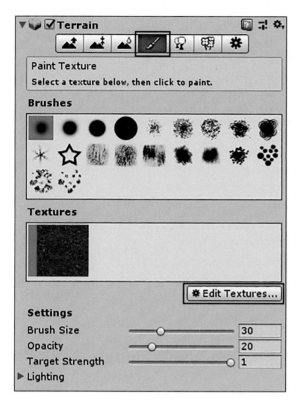

FIGURE 4.9
Paint Texture tool and properties.

To load a texture, follow these steps:

1. Select **Edit Textures** > **Add Texture** in the Inspector (not from the Unity menus).

2. In the Edit Terrain Texture dialog, click **Select** in the texture box (see Figure 4.10) and select the **GrassHillAlbedo** texture.

3. Click **Add**. There is no need to add a normal map, but you can if you have a texture with some bumpiness to it.

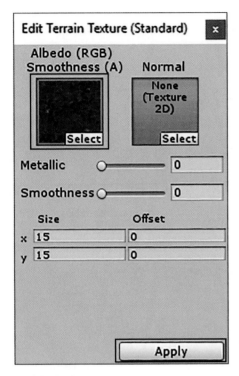

FIGURE 4.10
The Edit Terrain Texture dialog.

At this point, your entire terrain should be covered in patchy grass. This looks better than the white terrain you had before, but it is still far from realistic. Next, you will actually begin painting and making your terrain look better.

▼ TRY IT YOURSELF

Painting Textures onto Terrain

Follow these steps to apply a new texture to your terrain to give it a more realistic two-tone effect:

1. Using the steps listed earlier in this hour, add a new texture. This time, load the **GrassRockyAlbedo** texture. Once you have loaded it, be sure to select it by clicking it. (*Note:* A blue bar appears next to it if it is selected.)

2. Set the brush size to **30**, the opacity to **20**, and the target strength to **0.6**.

3. Sparingly paint (by clicking and dragging) on the steep parts and crevices of your terrain. This gives the impression that grass isn't growing on the sides of steep grades and in between hills (see Figure 4.11).

4. Continue experimenting with texture painting. Try loading the texture **CliffAlbedoSpecular** and applying it to steeper parts or the texture **SandAlbedo** and making a path.

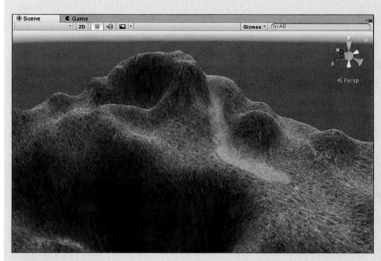

FIGURE 4.11
Example of a two-toned textured cliff with a sand path.

You can load as many textures as you want in this fashion and achieve some realistic effects. Be sure to practice texturing to determine the best-looking patterns.

NOTE

Creating Terrain Textures

Game worlds are often unique and require custom textures to fit within the context of the games they are created for. You can follow some general guidelines when making your own textures for terrain. The first is to always try to make the pattern repeatable. This means the textures can be tiled seamlessly. The larger the texture, the less obvious a repeating pattern is. The second guideline is to make the texture square. Finally, try to make the texture dimension a power of 2 (32, 64, 128, 512, and so on). The last two guidelines affect the compression of the texture and the texture's efficiency. With a little practice, you will be making brilliant terrain textures in no time.

TIP

Subtlety Is the Best Policy

When texturing, remember to keep your effects subtle. In nature, one element tends to fade to another without many harsh transitions. Your texturing efforts should reflect that. If you can zoom out away from a piece of terrain and tell the exact point where one texture starts, your effect is not subtle enough. It is often better to work in many small and subtle applications of a texture rather than with one broad application.

CAUTION

TerrainData Errors…What?

Depending on your project settings and the version of Unity you are using, you may get errors when you run your scene. One error says something like "TerrainData is missing splat texture…make sure it is marked for read/write in the importer." This error tells you that you are having runtime texture access issues. Luckily, the fix is very simple. All you need to do is click on the offending texture in the Project view, which causes the Inspector to show its Import settings. Then, in the Inspector view, expand **Advanced** and check the box next to **Read/Write Enabled**. Problem solved!

Generating Trees and Grass

A world with only flat textures would be boring. Almost every natural landscape has some form of plant life. In this section, you'll learn how to add and customize trees and grass to give your terrain an organic look and feel.

Painting Trees

Adding trees to your terrain works very much like sculpting and texturing; the whole process is very similar to painting. The basic premise is to load a tree model, set the properties for the trees, and then paint the area where you want the trees to appear. Based on the options you choose, Unity will spread out the trees and vary them to give a more natural and organic look.

You use the Paint Trees tool to spread out trees over the terrain. Once the terrain has been selected in the scene, select the **Paint Trees** tool in the Inspector view for the Terrain (Script) component. Figure 4.12 shows the Paint Trees tool and its standard properties.

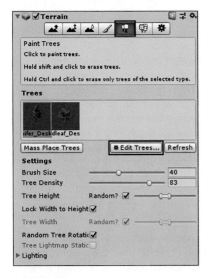

FIGURE 4.12
The Paint Trees tool.

Table 4.1 describes the Paint Trees tool's properties.

TABLE 4.1   The Paint Trees Tool's Properties

Property	Description
Brush Size	The size of the area to which trees are added when painting.
Tree Density	How densely the trees can be packed.
Tree Height/Width, Rotation, and so on	How all the trees differ from each other. Using these properties allows you to give the impression of many different trees instead of the same tree repeated.

TRY IT YOURSELF ▼

Placing Trees on a Terrain

Let's walk through the steps involved in placing trees onto terrain by using the Paint Trees tool. This exercise assumes that you have created a new scene and have already added a terrain. The terrain should be set to a length and width of 100. It will look better if the terrain has some sculpting and texturing done already. Follow these steps:

1. Click **Edit Trees > Add Tree** to pull up the Add Tree dialog (see Figure 4.13).

2. Clicking the **circle** icon to the right of the Tree Prefab text box on the Add Tree dialog pulls up the Tree Selector dialog.

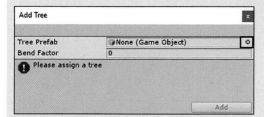

FIGURE 4.13
The Add Tree dialog.

3. Select **Conifer_Desktop** and click **Add**.

4. Set your brush size to **2** and your tree density to **10**. Leave the tree height/width set to **Random** but reduce the overall size.

5. Paint trees on the terrain by clicking and dragging over the areas where you want trees. Hold the **Shift** key while click-dragging to remove trees. If you can't paint, go to **Terrain Settings > Tree & Detail Objects** and ensure that the **Draw** check box is selected.

6. Continue to experiment with different brush sizes, densities, and trees.

Painting Grass

Now that you have learned how to paint trees, you'll learn how to apply grass and other small plant life to your world. Grass and other small plants are called *details* in Unity. Therefore, the tool used to paint grass is the Paint Details tool. Unlike trees, which are 3D models, details are billboards (see the note "Billboards"). Just as you have done over and over in this hour, you apply details to a terrain by using a brush and a painting motion. Figure 4.14 illustrates the Paint Details tool and some of its properties.

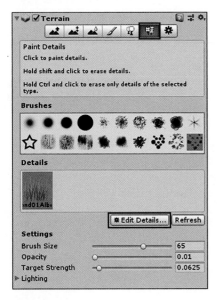

FIGURE 4.14
The Paint Details tool.

NOTE

Billboards

Billboards are a special type of visual component in a 3D world that give the effect of a 3D model without actually being a 3D model. Models exist in all three dimensions. Therefore, when moving around one, you can see the different sides. Billboards, however, are flat images that always face the camera. When you attempt to go around a billboard, the billboard turns to face your new position. Common uses for billboards are grass details, particles, and onscreen effects.

Applying grass to your terrain is a fairly straightforward process. You first need to add a grass texture:

1. Click **Edit Details** in the Inspector view and select **Add Grass Texture**.

2. In the Edit Grass Texture dialog, click the **circle** icon next to the Texture text box (see Figure 4.15). Select the **GrassFrond01AlbedoAlpha** texture. You can search for "grass" to help find it.

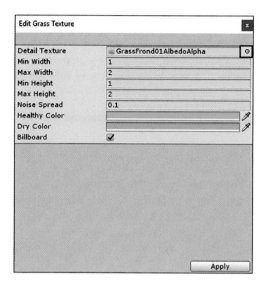

FIGURE 4.15
The Edit Grass Texture dialog.

3. Set your texture properties to whatever values you want. Pay special attention to the color properties because they establish the range of natural colors for your grass.

4. When you're finished changing settings, click **Apply**.

When you have your grass loaded, you just need to choose a brush and brush properties, and you are ready to begin painting grass.

TIP

Realistic Grass

You may notice that when you begin painting grass, it does not look realistic. You need to focus on a few things when adding grass to your terrain. The first is to pay attention to the colors you set for the grass texture. Try to keep them darker and earth toned. The next thing you need to do is choose a nongeometric brush shape to help break up hard edges. (Refer to Figure 4.14 for a good brush to use.) Finally, keep the opacity and target strength properties very low. Good settings to start with are .01 for opacity and .0625 for target strength. If you need more grass, you can just keep painting over the same area. You can also go back to Edit Details and change the grass texture properties.

CAUTION

Vegetation and Performance

The more trees and grass you have in a scene, the more processing is required to render it. If you are concerned about performance, keep the amount of vegetation low. Some of the properties you'll look at later in this hour can help you manage this, but as an easy rule, try to add trees and grass only to areas where they are really needed.

TIP

Disappearing Grass

As with trees, grass is affected by its distance from the viewer. Whereas trees revert to a lower quality when the viewer is far away, grass is just not rendered. The result is a ring around the viewer beyond which no grass is visible. Again, you can modify this distance by using properties discussed later in this hour.

Terrain Settings

The last of the terrain tools in the Inspector view is the Terrain Settings tool. This tool's settings control how the terrain, texture, trees, and details look and function overall. Figure 4.16 shows the Terrain Settings tool.

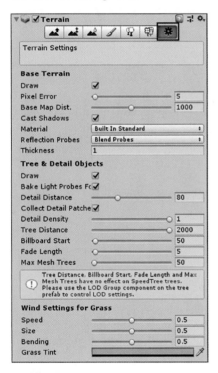

FIGURE 4.16
The Terrain Settings tool.

The first group of settings is for the overall terrain. Table 4.2 describes some of these settings.

TABLE 4.2   Base Terrain Settings

Setting	Description
Draw	Determines whether the terrain should be drawn.
Pixel Error	Specifies the number of allowable errors when displaying terrain geometry. The higher the value, the lower the detail of the terrain.
Base Map Dist.	Specifies the maximum distance from which high-resolution textures are displayed. When the viewer is farther than the distance set, textures degrade to a lower resolution.
Cast Shadows	Determines whether terrain geometry casts shadows.
Material	This slot is for assigning a custom material capable of rendering terrain. The material must contain a shader that can render terrain.
Reflection Probes	Specifies how reflection probes are used on terrain. This is effective only when using built-in standard material or a custom material that supports rendering with reflection. It is an advanced setting that is not covered in this text.
Thickness	Specifies how much the terrain collision volume should extend along the negative y axis. Objects are considered colliding with the terrain from the surface to a depth equal to the thickness. This helps prevent high-speed moving objects from penetrating into the terrain without the use of expensive continuous collision detection.

In addition, some settings directly affect the way trees and details (like grass) behave in a terrain. Table 4.3 describes these settings.

TABLE 4.3   Tree and Detail Object Settings

Setting	Description
Draw	Determines whether trees and details are rendered in the scene.
Bake Light Probes For	Makes real-time lighting more realistic and efficient. This is an advanced performance setting.
Detail Distance	Specifies the distance from the camera at which details are no longer drawn to the screen.
Collect Detail Patches	Preloads the terrain details to prevent hiccups when moving around terrain, at the cost of memory usage.
Detail Density	Specifies the number of detail/grass objects in a given unit of area. The value can be set lower to reduce rendering overhead.
Tree Distance	Specifies the distance from the camera at which trees are no longer drawn to the screen.

Setting	Description
Billboard Start	Specifies the distance from the camera at which 3D tree models begin to transition into lower-quality billboards.
Fade Length	Specifies the distance over which trees transition between billboards to higher-quality 3D models. The higher the setting, the smoother the transition.
Max Mesh Trees	Specifies the total number of trees able to be drawn simultaneously as 3D meshes and not billboards.

The next settings are for wind. Because you haven't had a chance to actually run around inside your world yet (although you will later in this hour), you might be wondering how wind works. Basically, Unity simulates a light wind over your terrain, and this light wind causes the grass to bend and sway and livens up the world. Table 4.4 describes the wind settings. (The Resolution settings are discussed earlier in this hour in the section "Adding Terrain to a Project").

TABLE 4.4   Wind Settings

Setting	Description
Speed	Specifies the speed, and therefore the strength, of the wind effect.
Size	Specifies the size of the area of grass affected by the wind at one time.
Bending	Specifies the amount of sway the grass has due to wind.
Grass Tint	Controls the overall coloration of all grass in a level. (This is not really a wind setting, but it is related.)

Character Controllers

At this point, you have finished your terrain. You have sculpted it, textured it, and covered it in trees and grass. It is now time to get into your level and see what it's like to play it. Unity provides two basic character controllers that allow you to easily get right into your scene without a lot of work on your end. Basically, you drop a controller into a scene and then move around with the control scheme common to most first-person games.

Adding a Character Controller

To add a character controller to your scene, you first need to import the asset by selecting **Assets > Import Package > Characters**. In the Import Package dialog, leave everything checked and click **Import**. A new folder named Characters is added to your Project view, under the Standard Assets folder. Because you don't have a 3D model to use as the player, in this case you are going to use the first-person controller. Locate the **FPSController** asset in the Character Controllers folder (see Figure 4.17) and drag it onto your terrain in the Scene view.

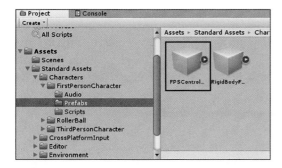

FIGURE 4.17
The FPSController character controller.

Now that the character controller has been added to your scene, you can move around in the terrain you created. When you play your scene, notice that you can now see from where the controller was placed. You can use the WASD keys to move around, the mouse to look around, and the spacebar to jump. Play around with the controls if they feel a bit unusual to you, and enjoy experiencing your world!

TIP

"2 Audio Listeners" Message

When you added the character controller to the scene, you might have noticed a message at the bottom of the editor that said, "There are 2 audio listeners in the scene." This is because the Main Camera (the camera that exists by default) has an audio listener component, and so does the character controller that you added. Because the cameras represent the player's perspective, only one of them can listen for audio. You can change this by removing the audio listener component from the Main Camera. You can even delete the Main Camera game object altogether if you wish, as FPSController has its own camera.

TIP

Falling Through the World

If you find the camera falling through the world whenever you run your scene, chances are that your character controller is stuck partially in the ground. Try raising your character controller up slightly above the ground. When the scene starts, the camera should fall just a little bit until it hits the ground and stops.

Summary

In this hour, you have learned all about terrains in Unity. You started by learning what terrains are and how to add them to a scene. From there, you looked at sculpting the terrain with both a heightmap and Unity's built-in sculpting tools. You learned how to make your terrains look more appealing by applying textures in a realistic fashion. Finally, you learned to add trees and grass to your terrain and explore it with a character controller.

Q&A

Q. Does my game have to have terrain?

A. Not at all. Many games take place entirely inside modeled rooms, in abstract spaces, or with meshes for exterior terrain.

Q. My terrain doesn't look very good. Is that normal?

A. It takes a while to gain proficiency with the sculpting tools. With some practice, your levels will begin looking much better. True quality comes from patience working on a level.

Workshop

Take some time to work through the questions here to ensure that you have a firm grasp of the material.

Quiz

1. True or False: You can make caves out of the Unity terrain.

2. What is a grayscale image containing terrain elevation information called?

3. True or False: Sculpting terrain in Unity is a lot like painting.

4. How do you access Unity's available terrain textures?

Answers

1. False. Unity's terrain cannot overlap.

2. A heightmap

3. True

4. You import the terrain assets by going to **Assets > Import Package > Environment**.

Exercise

Practice terrain sculpting and texturing. Sculpt a terrain that contains the following elements:

▶ Beach

▶ Mountain range

▶ Flat plains

You may need a slightly larger terrain to fit in everything you'd like to have. Once you have sculpted these elements, apply textures to your terrain in the following manner. You can find all textures listed here in the Terrain Assets package:

▶ The beach should use the texture SandAlbedo and should fade into GrassRockyAlbedo.

▶ Plains and all flat areas should be textured with GrassHillAlbedo.

▶ The texture GrassHillAlbedo should smoothly transition into GlassRockyAlbedo as the terrain gets steeper.

▶ The texture GlassRockyAlbedo should transition into Cliff at its steepest and highest points.

Finally, finish the terrain by adding trees and grass. Be as creative as you want with this exercise. Build a world that makes you proud.

Lights and Cameras

What You'll Learn in This Hour:

► How to work with lights in Unity

► The core elements of cameras

► How to work with multiple cameras in a scene

► How to work with layers

In this hour, you'll learn to use lights and cameras in Unity. You'll start by looking at the main features of lights. You'll then explore the different types of lights and their unique uses. When you are finished with lights, you'll begin working with cameras. You'll learn how to add new cameras, place them, and generate interesting effects with them. You'll finish this lesson by learning about layers in Unity.

Lights

In any form of visual media, lights go a long way in defining how a scene is perceived. Bright, slightly yellow light can make a scene look sunny and warm. Take the same scene and give it a low-intensity blue light, and it will look eerie and disconcerting. The color of the lights will also mix with the color of the skybox to give even more realistic-looking results.

Most scenes that strive for realism or dramatic effect employ at least one light (and often many). In previous hours, you briefly worked with lights to highlight other elements. In this section, you work with lights more directly.

NOTE

Repeat Properties

The different lights share many of the same properties. If a light has a property that has already been covered under a different light type, it isn't covered again. Just remember that if two different light types have properties with the same names, those properties do the same thing.

What Is a Light?

In Unity, lights are not objects themselves. Instead, a light is a component. This means that when you add a light to a scene, you are really just adding a game object with the Light component, which can be any of the types of light you can use.

Baking Versus Real Time

Before you get started actually working with lights, you need to understand two main ways of using light: baked and real time. The thing to keep in mind is that all light in games is more or less computational. Light has to be figured out by the machine in three steps:

1. The color, direction, and range of simulated light rays are calculated from a light source.

2. When the light rays hit a surface, they illuminate and change the color of the surface.

3. The angle of impact with the surface is calculated, and the light bounces. Steps 1 and 2 are repeated again and again (depending on the light settings). With each bounce, the properties of the light rays are changed by the surfaces they hit (just like in real life).

This process is repeated for every light in every frame and creates global illumination (where objects receive light and color based on the objects around them). This process is helped a little by the feature Precomputed Realtime GI, which is turned on by default and requires no effort from you. With this feature, a part of the light calculation process described above is calculated before the scene starts so only part of the calculations need to be done at runtime. You may have already seen this in operation. If you have ever opened a Unity scene for the first time and noticed that the scene elements are dark for a moment, you have seen the precalculation process.

Baking, on the other hand, refers to the process of completely precalculating light and shadow for textures and objects during creation. You can do this with Unity or with a graphical editor. For instance, if you were to make a wall texture with a dark spot on it that resembled a human shadow and then put a human model next to the wall it was on, it would seem like the model was casting a shadow on the wall. The truth is, though, that the shadow was "baked" into the texture. Baking can make your games run much more quickly because the engine doesn't have to calculate light and shadow every single frame; however, baking isn't very necessary for your current needs because the games discussed in this book are not complex enough to require it.

Point Lights

The first light type you will be working with is the point light. Think of a point light as a light bulb. All light is emitted from one central location out in every direction. The point light is the most common type of light for illuminating interior areas.

To add a point light to a scene, select **GameObject > Light > Point Light**. Once in the scene, the Point Light game object can be manipulated just like any other. Table 5.1 describes the point light properties.

TABLE 5.1   Point Light Properties

Property	Description
Type	Specifies the type of light that the component gives off. Because this is a point light, the type should be Point. Changing the Type property changes the type of light.
Range	Dictates how far the light shines. Illumination fades evenly from the source of light to the range dictated.
Color	Specifies the color the light shines. Color is additive, which means if you shine a red light on a blue object, it will end up purple.
Mode	Determines if the light is a real-time light, a baked light, or a mixture of the two.
Intensity	Dictates how brightly a light shines. Note that the light still shines only as far as the Range property dictates.
Indirect Multiplier	Determines how bright the light is after it bounces off objects. (Unity supports Global Illumination, meaning it calculates the results of bouncing light.)
Shadow Type	Specifies how shadows are calculated for this source in a scene. Soft shadows are more realistic but are also more performance intensive.
Cookie	Accepts a cubemap (like a skybox) that dictates a pattern for the light to shine through. Cookies are covered in more detail later in this hour.
Draw Halo	Determines whether a glowing halo appears around the light. Halos are covered in more detail later in this hour.
Flare	Accepts a light flare asset and simulates the effect of a bright light shining into a camera lens.
Render Mode	Determines the importance of this light. The three settings are Auto, Important, and Not Important. An important light is rendered in higher quality, whereas a less-important light is rendered more quickly. Use the Auto setting for now.
Culling Mask	Determines what layers are affected by the light. By default, everything is affected by the light. Layers are covered in detail later in this hour.

▼ TRY IT YOURSELF

Adding a Point Light to a Scene

Follow these steps to build a scene with some dynamic point lighting:

1. Create a new project or scene and delete the directional light that is there by default.

2. Add a plane to the scene (by selecting **GameObject > 3D Object > Plane**). Ensure that the plane is positioned at (0, .5, 0) and rotated to (270, 0, 0). The plane should be visible to the camera, but only from one side in the Scene view.

3. Add two cubes to the scene. Position them at (-1.5, 1, -5) and (1.5, 1, -5).

4. Add a point light to the scene (by selecting **GameObject > Light > Point Light**). Position the point light at (0, 1, -7). Notice how the light illuminates the inner sides of the cubes and the background plane (see Figure 5.1).

5. Set the light's shadow type to **Hard Shadows** and try moving it around. Continue exploring the light properties. Be sure to experiment with the light color, range, and intensity.

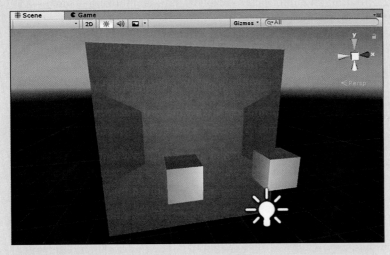

FIGURE 5.1
The results of this Try It Yourself.

Spotlights

Spotlights work a lot like the headlights of a car or flashlights. The light of a spotlight begins at a central spot and radiates out in a cone. In other words, spotlights illuminate whatever is in front of them while leaving everything else in the dark. Whereas a point light sends light in every direction, you can aim a spotlight.

To add a spotlight to a scene, select **GameObject > Create Other > Spotlight**. Alternatively, if you already have a light in your scene, you can change its type to **Spot**, and it becomes a spotlight.

Spotlights have only one property not already covered: Spot Angle. The Spot Angle property determines the radius of the cone of light emitted by the spotlight.

TRY IT YOURSELF ▼

Adding a Spotlight to a Scene

You now have a chance to work with spotlights in Unity. For brevity, this exercise uses the project created in the previous Try It Yourself for point lights. If you have not completed that exercise, do so and then continue with the following steps:

1. Duplicate the Point Light scene from the previous project (by selecting **Edit > Duplicate**) and name the new scene **Spotlight**.

2. Right-click **Point light** in the Hierarchy view and select **Rename**. Rename the object **Spotlight**. In the Inspector, change the Type property to **Spot**. Position the light object at (0, 1, -13).

3. Experiment with the properties of the spotlight. Notice how the range, intensity, and spot angle shape and change the effect of the light.

Directional Lights

The last type of light you'll work with in this hour is the directional light. A directional light is similar to a spotlight in that it can be aimed. Unlike a spotlight, though, a directional light illuminates an entire scene. You can think of a directional light as similar to the sun. In fact, you used a directional light as a sun in Hour 4, "Terrain and Environments." The light from a directional light radiates evenly in parallel lines across a scene.

A new scene comes with a directional light by default. To add a new directional light to a scene, select **GameObject > Light > Directional Light**. Alternatively, if you already have a light in a scene, you can change its type to Directional, and it becomes a directional light.

Directional lights have one additional property that hasn't been covered yet: Cookie Size. Cookies are covered later in this hour, but basically this property controls how big a cookie is and thus how many times it is repeated across a scene.

▼ TRY IT YOURSELF

Adding a Directional Light to a Scene

You will now add a directional light to a Unity scene. Once again, this exercise builds on the project created in the previous Try It Yourself. If you have not completed that exercise, do so, and then follow these steps:

1. Duplicate the Spotlight scene from the previous project (by selecting **Edit > Duplicate**) and name the new scene **Directional Light.**

2. Right-click **Spotlight** in the Hierarchy view and select **Rename**. Rename the object **Directional Light**. In the Inspector, change the Type property to **Directional.**

3. Change the light's rotation to (75, 0, 0). Notice how the sky changes when you rotate the light. This is due to the scene using a procedural skybox. Skyboxes are covered in more detail in Hour 6, "Game 1: *Amazing Racer.*"

4. Notice how the light looks on the objects in the scene. Now change the light's position to (50, 50, 50). Notice that the light does not change. Because the directional light is in parallel lines, the position of the light does not matter. Only the rotation of a directional light matters.

5. Experiment with the properties of the directional light. There is no range (because range is infinite), but notice how the color and intensity affect the scene.

NOTE

Area Lights and Emissive Materials

There are two more light types that are not covered in this text: area lights and emissive materials.

An area light is a feature that exists for a process called *lightmap baking*. These topics are more advanced than what you need for basic game projects so are not covered in this book. If you want to learn more about this, see Unity's wealth of online documentation.

An emissive material is a material applied to an object that actually transmits light. This type of light could be very useful for a TV screen, indicator lights, and so on.

Creating Lights Out of Objects

Because lights in Unity are components, any object in a scene can be a light. To add a light to an object, first select the object. Then, in the Inspector view, click the **Add Component** button. A new list should pop up. Select **Rendering** and then **Light**. Now your object has a light component. An alternative way to add a light to an object is to select the object and select **Component > Rendering > Light**.

Note a couple things about adding lights to objects. First, an object will not block the light. This means that putting a light inside a cube will not stop the light from radiating. Second, adding a light to an object does not make it glow. The object itself will not look like it is giving off light, but it is.

Halos

Halos are glowing circles that appear around lights in foggy or cloudy conditions (see Figure 5.2). They occur because light is bouncing off small particles all around the light source. In Unity, you can easily add halos to lights. Each light has a Draw Halo check box. If it is checked, a halo is drawn for the light. If you can't see the halo, you may be too close to the light, so try backing up a bit.

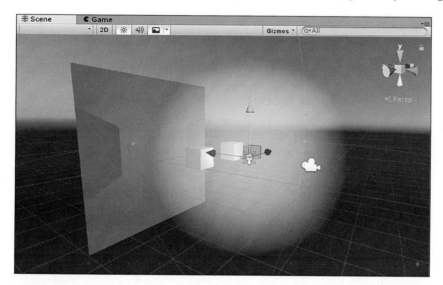

FIGURE 5.2
A halo around a light.

The size of a halo is determined by the light's range. The bigger the range, the bigger the halo. Unity also provides a few properties that apply to all halos in a scene. You can access these properties by selecting **Window > Lighting > Settings**. Expand **Other Settings**, and the settings then appear in the Inspector view (see Figure 5.3).

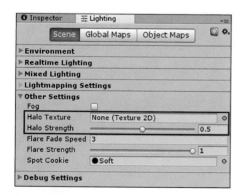

FIGURE 5.3
The scene lighting settings.

The Halo Strength property determines how big the halo will be, based on the light's range. For instance, if a light has a range of 10 and a strength of 1, the halo will extend out all 10 units. If the strength is .5, the halo extends out only 5 units (10 × .5 = 5). The Halo Texture property allows you to specify a different shape for a halo by providing a new texture. If you do not want to use a custom texture for a halo, you can leave it blank, and the default circular one is used.

Cookies

If you have ever shone a light on a wall and then put your hand in between the light and the wall, you've probably noticed that your hand blocks some of the light, leaving a hand-shaped shadow on the wall. You can simulate this effect in Unity by using cookies. Cookies are special textures that you can add to lights to dictate how the light radiates. Cookies differ a little for point, spot, and directional lights. Spotlights and directional lights both use black-and-white flat textures for cookies. Spotlights don't repeat the cookies, but directional lights do. Point lights also use black-and-white textures, but this type of light must be placed in a cubemap. A cubemap is six textures placed together to form a box (like a skybox).

Adding a cookie to a light is a fairly straightforward process. You simply apply a texture to the Cookie property of the light. The trick to getting a cookie to work is setting up the texture correctly ahead of time. To set up the texture correctly, select it in Unity and then change its properties in the Inspector window. Figure 5.4 shows the property settings for turning a texture into a cookie.

FIGURE 5.4
The texture properties of cookies for point, spot, and directional lights.

Adding a Cookie to a Spotlight

This exercise requires the biohazard.png image, available in the book assets for Hour 5. Follow these steps to add a cookie to a spotlight so that you can see the process from start to finish:

1. Create a new project or scene. Delete the directional light from the scene.

2. Add a plane to the scene and position it at (0, 1, 0) with a rotation of (270, 0, 0).

3. Add a spotlight to the Main Camera by selecting **Main Camera** and then clicking **Component > Rendering > Light** and changing the type to **Spot**. Set the range to **18**, the spot angle to **40**, and the intensity to **3**.

4. Drag the biohazard.png texture from the book assets into your Project view. Select the texture, and in the Inspector view, change the texture type to **Cookie**, set the light type to **Spotlight**, and set the alpha source to **From Grayscale**. This makes the cookie block light where it's black.

5. With the Main Camera selected, click and drag the biohazard texture into the Cookie property of the light component. You should see the biohazard symbol projected onto the plane (see Figure 5.5).

6. Experiment with different ranges and intensities of the light. Rotate the plane and see how the symbol warps and distorts.

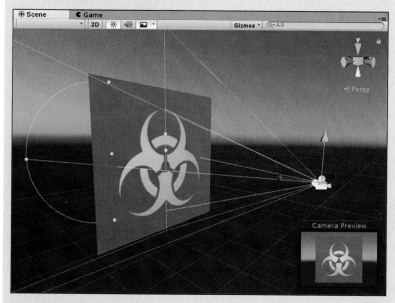

FIGURE 5.5
Spotlight with a cookie.

Cameras

The camera is the player's view into the world. It provides perspective and controls how things appear to the player. Every game in Unity has at least one camera. In fact, a camera is always added for you whenever you create a new scene. The camera always appears in the hierarchy as Main Camera. In this section, you'll learn all about cameras and how to use them for interesting effects.

Anatomy of a Camera

All cameras share the same set of properties that dictate how they behave. Table 5.2 describes all the camera properties.

TABLE 5.2   Camera Properties

Property	Description
Clear Flags	Determines what the camera displays in the areas where there are no game objects. The default is Skybox. If there is no skybox, the camera defaults to a solid color. Depth Only should be used only when there are multiple cameras. Don't Clear causes streaking and should be used only if you're writing a custom shader.
Background	Specifies the background color if there is no skybox present.
Culling Mask	Determines what layers are picked up by the camera. By default, the camera sees everything. You can uncheck certain layers (more on layers later in this hour), and they won't be visible to the camera.
Projection	Determines how the camera sees the world. The two options are Perspective and Orthographic. Perspective cameras perceive the world in 3D, with closer objects being larger and farther objects being smaller. This is the setting to use if you want depth in your game. The Orthographic setting ignores depth and treats everything as flat.
Field of View	Specifies how wide an area the camera can see.
Clipping Planes	Specifies the range where objects are visible to the camera. Objects that are closer than the near plane or farther from the far plane will not be seen.
View Port Rect	Establishes what part of the actual screen the camera is projected on. (View Port Rect is short for View Port Rectangle.) By default, x and y are both set to 0, which causes the camera to start in the lower left of the screen. The width and height are both set to 1, which causes the camera to cover 100% of the screen vertically and horizontally. This is discussed in more detail later in this hour.
Depth	Specifies the priority for multiple cameras. Lower numbers are drawn first, which means higher numbers may be drawn on top and may effectively hide them.
Rendering Path	Determines how the camera renders. It should be left set to Use Player Settings.

Property	Description
Target Texture	Enables you to specify a texture for the camera to draw to instead of the screen.
Occlusion Culling	Disables rendering of objects when they are not currently seen by the camera because they are obscured (occluded) by other objects.
Allow HDR	Determines whether Unity's internal light calculations are limited to the basic color range. (HDR stands for Hyper-Dynamic Range.) This property allows for advanced visual effects.
Allow MSAA	Enables a basic, but efficient, type of antialiasing called MultiSample antialiasing. Antialiasing is a method of removing pixelated edges when rendering graphics.
Allow Dynamic Resolution	Allows for dynamic resolution adjustment for console games.

Cameras have many properties, but you can set most and then forget about them. Cameras also have a few extra components. The flare layer allows a camera to see the lens flares of lights, and the audio listener allows the camera to pick up sound. If you add more cameras to a scene, you need to remove their audio listeners. There can be only one audio listener per scene.

Multiple Cameras

Many effects in modern games would not be possible without multiple cameras. Thankfully, you can have as many cameras as you want in a Unity scene. To add a new camera to a scene, select **GameObject > Camera**. Alternatively, you can add the camera component to a game object that is already in your scene. To do that, select the object and click **Add Component** in the Inspector. Select **Rendering > Camera** to add the camera component. Remember that adding a camera component to an existing object does not automatically give you the flare layer or audio listener components.

▼ TRY IT YOURSELF

Working with Multiple Cameras

The best way to understand how multiple cameras interact is to get some practice working with them. This exercise focuses on basic camera manipulation:

1. Create a new project or scene and add two cubes. Place the cubes at (-2, 1, -5) and (2, 1, -5).

2. Move the Main Camera to (-3, 1, -8) and change its rotation to (0, 45, 0).

3. Add a new camera to the scene (by selecting **GameObject > Camera**) and position it at (3, 1, -8). Change its rotation to (0, 315, 0). Be sure to disable the audio listener for the camera by unchecking the box next to the component.

4. Run the scene. Notice that the second camera is the only one displayed. This is because the second camera has a higher depth than the Main Camera. The Main Camera is drawn to the screen first, and then the second camera is drawn on top of it. Change the main camera depth to **1** and then run the scene again. Notice that the Main Camera is now the only one visible.

Split-Screen and Picture-in-Picture

As you saw earlier in this hour, having multiple cameras in a scene doesn't do much good if one of them simply draws over the other one. In this section, you'll learn to use the Normalized View Port Rect property to achieve split-screen and picture-in-picture effects.

The normalized view port basically treats the screen as a simple rectangle. The lower-left corner of the rectangle is (0, 0), and the upper-right corner is (1, 1). This does not mean that the screen has to be a perfect square. Instead, think of the coordinates as percentages of the size. So, a coordinate of 1 means 100%, and a coordinate of .5 means 50%. When you know this, placing cameras on the screen becomes easy. By default, cameras project from (0, 0) with a width and height of 1 (or 100%). This causes them to take up the entire screen. If you were to change those numbers, however, you would get a different effect.

▼ TRY IT YOURSELF

Creating a Split-Screen Camera System

This exercise walks through creating a split-screen camera system. This type of system is common in two-player games where the players have to share the same screen. This exercise builds on the previous Try It Yourself for multiple cameras earlier in this hour. Follow these steps:

1. Open the project that you created in the preceding Try It Yourself.

2. Ensure that the Main Camera has a depth of -1. Ensure that the X and Y properties of the camera's View Port Rect property are both **0**. Set the W and H properties to **1** and **.5**, respectively (that is, 100% of the width and 50% of the height).

3. Ensure that the second camera also has a depth of -1. Set the X and Y properties of the view port to (0, .5). This causes the camera to begin drawing halfway down the screen. Set the W and H properties to **1** and **.5**, respectively.

4. Run the scene and notice that both cameras are now projecting on the screen at the same time (see Figure 5.6). You can split the screen like this as many times as you want.

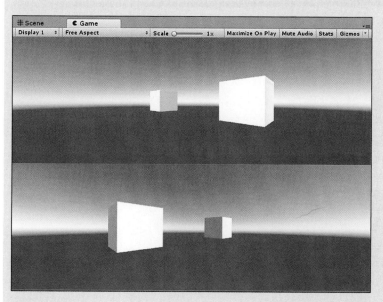

FIGURE 5.6
The split-screen effect.

Creating a Picture-in-Picture Effect

Picture-in-picture is commonly used to create effects like minimaps. With this effect, one camera draws over another one in a specific area. This exercise builds on the previous Try It Yourself for multiple cameras earlier in this hour:

1. Open the project that you created in the Try It Yourself "Working with Multiple Cameras."

2. Ensure that the Main Camera has a depth of -1. Ensure that the X and Y properties of the camera's Normalized View Port Rect property are both **0** and the W and H properties are both **1**.

3. Ensure that the depth of the second camera is 0. Set the X and Y property of the view
   port to (.75, .75) and set both the W and the H values to **.2**.

   4. Run the scene. Notice that the second camera appears in the upper-right corner of
   the screen (see Figure 5.7). Experiment with the different view port settings to get the
   camera to appear in the different corners.

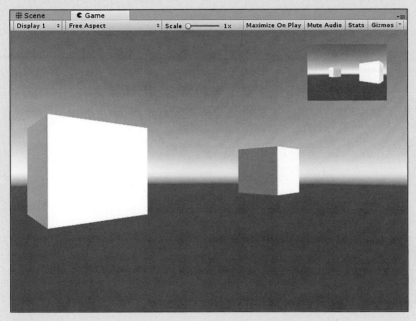

FIGURE 5.7
The picture-in-picture effect.

Layers

It can often be difficult to organize the many objects in a project and in a scene. Sometimes
you want items to be viewable by only certain cameras or illuminated by only certain lights.
Sometimes you want collisions to occur only between certain types of objects. Unity allows
you to organize by using layers. Layers are groupings of similar objects that can be treated a
certain way. By default, there are 8 built-in layers and 24 layers for the user to define.

Layer Overload!

Adding layers can be a great way to achieve complex behaviors without doing a lot of work. A word of warning, though: Do not create layers for items unless you need to. Too often, people arbitrarily create layers when adding objects to a scene with the thinking that they might need them later. This approach can lead to an organizational nightmare as you try to remember what each layer is for and what it does. In short, add layers when you need them. Don't try to use layers just because you can.

Working with Layers

Every game objects starts in the Default layer. That is, the object has no specific layer to belong to, so it is lumped in with everything else. You can easily add an object to a layer in the Inspector view. With the object selected, click the **Layer** drop-down in the Inspector and choose a new layer for the object to be a part of (see Figure 5.8). By default, there are five layers to choose from: Default, TransparentFX, Ignore Raycast, Water, and UI. You can safely ignore most of these for now because they are not very useful to you at this point.

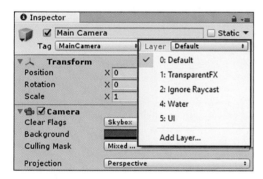

FIGURE 5.8
The Layer drop-down menu.

Although the current built-in layers aren't exactly useful to you, you can easily add new layers. You add layers in the Tags & Layers Manager, which you can open in three different ways:

▶ With an object selected, click the **Layer** drop-down and select **Add Layer** (refer to Figure 5.8).

▶ In the menu at the top of the editor, click **Edit > Project Settings > Tags and Layers**.

▶ Click the **Layers** selector in the scene toolbar and choose **Edit Layers** (see Figure 5.9).

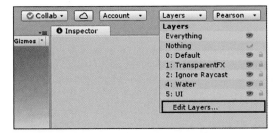

FIGURE 5.9
The Layers selector in the scene toolbar.

In the Tags & Layers Manager, click to the right of one of the user layers to give it a name. Figure 5.10 illustrates this process, showing two new layers being added. (They were added for this figure, and you won't have them unless you add them yourself.)

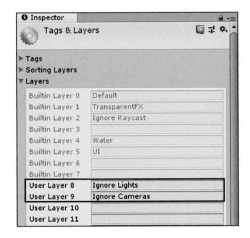

FIGURE 5.10
Adding new layers to the Tags & Layers Manager.

Using Layers

There are many uses for layers. The usefulness of layers is limited only by what you can think to do with them. This section covers four common uses.

One common use of layers is to hide them from the Scene view. By clicking the Layers selector in the Scene view toolbar (refer to Figure 5.9), you can choose which layers appear in the Scene view and which don't. By default, the scene is set up to show everything.

TIP

Invisible Scene Items

One common mistake is accidentally changing what layers are visible in the Scene view. If you are not familiar with the ability to make layers invisible, this can be quite confusing. Just note that if at any time items are not appearing in the Scene view when they should, you should check the Layers selector to ensure that it is set to show everything.

A second way to use layers is to exclude objects from being illuminated by light. This is useful if you are making a custom user interface, making a shadowing system, or using a complex lighting system. To prevent a layer from being illuminated by a light, select the light and then, in the Inspector view, click the **Culling Mask** property and deselect any layers that you want ignored (see Figure 5.11).

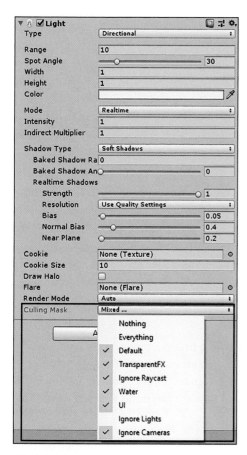

FIGURE 5.11
The Culling Mask property.

The third thing you can use layers for is to tell Unity which physics objects interact with each other. You can choose this in **Edit** > **Project Settings** > **Physics** and look for the Layer Collision Matrix (see Figure 5.12).

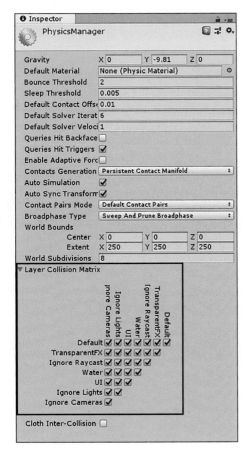

FIGURE 5.12
The Layer Collision Matrix.

The last thing to know about layers is that you can use them to determine what a camera can and cannot see. This is useful if you want to build a custom visual effect using multiple cameras for a single viewer. Just as previously described, to ignore layers, simply click the **Culling Mask** drop-down on the camera component and deselect anything you don't want to appear.

Ignoring Lights and Cameras

Follow these steps to briefly work with layers for both lights and cameras:

1. Create a new project or scene. Add two cubes to the scene and position them at (2, 1, -5) and (2, 1, -5).

2. Enter the Tags & Layers Manager using any of the three methods listed earlier and add two new layers: **Ignore Lights** and **Ignore Cameras** (refer to Figure 5.10).

3. Select one of the cubes and add it to the Ignore Lights layer. Select the other cube and add it to the Ignore Cameras layer.

4. Select the Directional Light in the scene, and in its Culling Mask property, deselect the **Ignore Lights** layer. Notice that now only one of the cubes is illuminated. The other one has been ignored because of its layer.

5. Select the Main Camera and remove the **Ignore Cameras** layer from its Culling Mask property. Run the scene and notice that only one nonilluminated cube appears. The other one has been ignored by the camera.

Summary

In this hour, you've learned about lights and cameras. You have worked with the different types of lights. You have also learned to add cookies and halos to the lights in a scene. This hour you have also learned all about the basics of cameras and about adding multiple cameras to create split-screen and picture-in-picture effects. You wrapped up the hour by learning about layers in Unity.

Q&A

Q. I noticed this lesson skipped lightmapping. Is it important to learn?

A. Lightmapping is a useful technique for optimizing the lighting of a scene. It's slightly more advanced, and you don't need to know how to use it to make your scenes look great.

Q. How do I know if I want a perspective camera or an orthographic camera?

A. As mentioned in this hour, a general rule of thumb is that you want perspective cameras for 3D games or effects and orthographic cameras for 2D games and effects.

Workshop

Take some time to work through the questions here to ensure that you have a firm grasp of the material.

Quiz

1. If you want to illuminate an entire scene with one light, which type should you use?

2. How many cameras can be added to a scene?

3. How many user-defined layers can you have?

4. What property determines which layers are ignored by lights and cameras?

Answers

1. A directional light is the only light that is applied evenly to an entire scene.

2. You can have as many as you want.

3. 24

4. Culling Mask property

Exercise

In this exercise, you have a chance to work with multiple cameras and lights. You have a bit of leeway in the construction of this exercise, so feel free to be creative:

1. Create a new scene or project. Delete the directional light. Add a sphere to the scene and place it at (0, 0, 0).

2. Add four point lights to your scene. Place them at (-4, 0, 0), (4, 0, 0), (0, 0, -4), and (0, 0, 4). Give each of them its own color. Set the ranges and intensities to create the visual effect on the sphere that you want.

3. Delete the Main Camera from your scene (by right-clicking **Main Camera** and selecting **Delete**). Add four cameras to the scene. Disable the audio listener on three of them. Position them at (2, 0, 0), (-2, 0, 0), (0, 0, 2), and (0, 0, -2). Rotate each of them about the y axis until it is facing the sphere.

4. Change the view port settings on the four cameras so that you achieve a split-screen effect with all four cameras. You should have a camera displaying in each corner of the screen taking up one-quarter of the screen's size (see Figure 5.13). This step is left for you to complete. If you get stuck, look for the completed version of this exercise in the Hour 5 book assets.

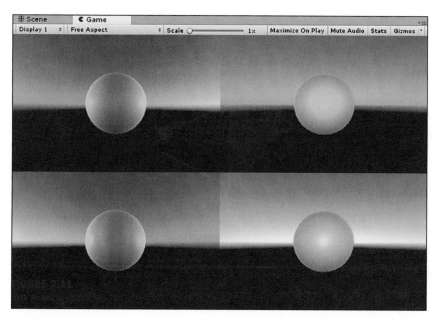

FIGURE 5.13
The completed exercise.

Game 1: *Amazing Racer*

What You'll Learn in This Hour:

▶ How to design a basic game
▶ How to apply your knowledge of terrains to build a game-specific world
▶ How to add objects to a game to provide interactivity
▶ How to playtest and tweak a finished game

In this hour, you'll use what you have learned so far to build your first Unity game. This lesson starts by covering the basic design elements of the game. From there, you will build the world in which the game will take place. Then you'll add some interactivity objects to make the game playable. You'll finish by playing the game and making any necessary tweaks to improve the experience.

TIP

Completed Project

Be sure to follow along in this hour to build the complete game project. If you get stuck, look for the completed copy of the game in the book assets for Hour 6. Take a look at it if you need help or inspiration!

Design

The design portion of game development is where you plan ahead of time all the major features and components of a game. You can think of it as laying down the blueprint so that the actual construction process is smoother. When making a game, a lot of time is normally spent working through the design. Because the game you are making in this hour is fairly basic, the design phase will go quickly. You need to focus on three areas of planning to make this game: the concept, the rules, and the requirements.

The Concept

The idea behind this game is simple: You start at one end of an area and run quickly to the other side. There are hills, trees, and obstacles in your path. Your goal is to see how fast you can make it to the finish zone. This game concept was chosen for your first game because it highlights everything you have worked on so far in this book. Also, because you have not learned scripting in Unity yet, you cannot add very elaborate interactions. Games you make in later hours will be more complex.

The Rules

Every game must have a set of rules. The rules serve two purposes. First, they say how the player will actually play the game. Second, because software is a process of permission (see the "Process of Permission" note), the rules dictate the actions available to the players to overcome challenges. The rules for *Amazing Racer* are as follows:

▶ There is no win or loss condition, only a completed condition. The game is completed when the player enters the finish zone.

▶ The player always spawns in the same spot. The finish zone is always in the same spot.

▶ There are water hazards, and whenever the player falls into one of them, the player is moved back to the spawn point.

▶ The objective of the game is to try to get the fastest time possible. This is an implicit rule and is not specifically built into the game. Instead, cues are built into the game as hints to the player that this is the goal. The idea is that the players will intuit the desire for a faster time based on the signals given to them.

NOTE

Process of Permission

Something to always remember when making a game is that software is a process of permission. What this means is that unless you specifically allow something, it is unavailable to the player. For instance, if the player wants to climb a tree, but you have not created any way for the player to climb a tree, that action is not permitted. If you do not give players the ability to jump, they can't jump. Everything that you want the player to be able to do must be explicitly built in. Remember that you cannot assume any action and must plan for everything! Also remember that players can combine actions in inventive ways—for example, stacking blocks and then jumping from the top block—if you make them possible.

NOTE

Terminology

Some new terms are used in this hour:

▶ **Spawn:** Spawning is the process by which a player or an entity enters a game.

▶ **Spawn point:** A spawn point is the place where a player or an entity spawns. There can be one or many of these. They can be stationary or moving around.

▶ **Condition:** A condition is a form of a trigger. A win condition is the event that causes the player to win the game (such as accumulating enough points). A loss condition is an event that causes the player to lose the game (such as losing all health points).

▶ **Game manager:** The game manager dictates the rules and flow of a game. It is responsible for knowing when the game is won or lost (or just over). Any object can be designated as the game manager, as long as it is always in the scene. Often, an empty object or the Main Camera is designated as the game manager.

▶ **Playtesting:** Playtesting is the process of having actual players play a game that is still in development to see how they react to the game so it can be improved accordingly.

The Requirements

An important step in the design process is determining which assets will be required for the game. Generally speaking, a game development team is made up of several individuals. Some of them handle designing, others work with programming, and others make art. Every member of the team needs something to do to be productive during every step of the development process. If everyone waited until something was needed to begin working, there would be a lot of starting and stopping. Instead, you determine your assets ahead of time so that things can be created before they are needed. Here is a list of all the requirements for *Amazing Racer*:

▶ A piece of rectangular terrain. The terrain needs to be big enough to present a challenging race. The terrain should have obstacles built in as well as a designated spawn and finish point (see Figure 6.1).

▶ Textures and environment effects for the terrain. These are provided in the Unity standard assets.

▶ A spawn point object, a finish zone object, and a water hazard object. These will be generated in Unity.

▶ A character controller. This is provided by the Unity standard assets.

▶ A graphical user interface (GUI). This will be provided for you in the book assets. Note that this hour uses the old-style GUI, which works purely from script, for simplicity. In your projects, use the new UI system introduced in Hour 14, "User Interfaces."

▶ A game manager. This will be created in Unity.

Spawn Point   Water Hazard   Finish Zone

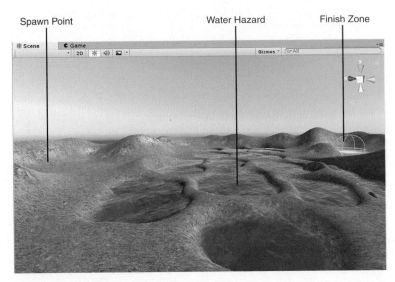

FIGURE 6.1
The general terrain layout for the game *Amazing Racer*.

Creating the Game World

Now that you have a basic idea of the game, it is time to start building it. There are many places to begin building a game. For this project, you'll begin with the world. Because this is a linear racing game, the world will be longer than it is wide (or wider than it is long, depending on how you look at it). You will use many of the Unity standard assets to rapidly create the game.

Sculpting the World

There are many ways you can create the terrain for *Amazing Racer*. Everyone will probably have a different vision for it in his or her head. To streamline the process and ensure that everyone will have the same experiences during this hour, a heightmap has been provided for you. To sculpt the terrain, follow these steps:

1. Create a new project and name it **Amazing Racer**. Add a terrain to the project and position its transform at (0, 0, 0) in the Inspector.

2. Locate the file TerrainHeightmap.raw in the book assets for Hour 6. Import the TerrainHeightmap.raw file as a heightmap for the terrain (by clicking **Import Raw** in the Heightmap section under Terrain Settings in the Inspector).

3. Leave the Depth, Width, and Height settings as they are. Change Byte Order to **Mac** and set Terrain Size to **200** wide by **100** long by **100** tall.

4. Create a **Scenes** folder under Assets and save the current scene as **Main**.

The terrain should now be sculpted to match the world in the book. Feel free to make minor tweaks and changes to your liking.

CAUTION

Building Your Own Terrain

In this hour, you are building a game based on a heightmap that has been provided for you. The heightmap has been prepared for you so that you can quickly get through the process of game development. You may, however, choose to build your own custom world to make this game truly unique and yours. If you do that, however, be warned that some of the coordinates and rotations provided for you in this hour might not match up. If you want to build your own world, pay attention to the intended placement of objects and position them in your world accordingly.

Adding the Environment

At this point, you can begin texturing and adding the environment effects to your terrain. You need to import the Environment package (by selecting **Assets > Import Package > Environment**).

You now have a bit of freedom to decorate the world however you would like. The suggestions in the following steps are guidelines. Feel free to do things in a manner that looks good to you:

1. Rotate the directional light to suit your preference.

2. Texture the terrain. The sample project uses the following textures: **GrassHillAlbedo** for flat parts, **CliffAlbedoSpecular** for steep parts, **GrassRockyAlbedo** for the areas in between, and **MudRockyAlbedoSpecular** for inside the pits.

3. Add trees to your terrain. Trees should be placed sparsely and mostly on flat surfaces.

4. Add some water to your scene from the Environment assets. Locate the **Water4Advanced** prefab in the folder Assets\Standard Assets\Environment\Water\Water4\Prefabs and drag it into your scene. (You'll learn more info about prefabs in Hour 11, "Prefabs.") Position the water at (100, 29, 100) and scale it to (2, 1, 2).

The terrain should now be prepared and ready to go. Be sure to spend a good amount of time on texturing to make sure you have a good blend and a realistic look.

Fog

In Unity, you can add fog to a scene to simulate many different natural occurrences, such as haze, actual fog, or the fading of objects over great distances. You can also use fog to give new and alien appearances to your world. In the *Amazing Racer* game, you can use fog to obscure the distant parts of the terrain and add an element of exploration.

Adding fog is quite simple:

1. Select **Window** > **Lighting** > **Settings**. The Lighting window opens.

2. Turn on fog by checking the **Fog** check box under Other Settings.

3. Change the color to **white** and set the density to **0.005**. (*Note:* These are arbitrary values and can be changed (or omitted) based on your preferences.)

4. Experiment with the different fog densities and colors. Table 6.1 describes the various fog properties.

Several properties impact how fog looks in a scene. Table 6.1 describes these properties.

TABLE 6.1 Fog Properties

Setting	Description
Fog Color	Specifies the color of the fog effect.
Fog Mode	Controls how the fog is calculated. The three modes are Linear, Exponential, and Exponential Squared. For mobile, Linear works best.
Density	Determines how strong the fog effect is. This property is used only if the fog mode is set to Exponential or Exponential Squared.
Start and End	Control how close to the camera the fog starts and how far from the camera it ends. These properties are used only in Linear mode.

Skyboxes

You can add some punch to a game by adding a skybox. A skybox is a large box that goes around a world. Even though it is a cube consisting of six flat sides, it has inward-facing textures to make it look round and infinite. You can create your own skyboxes or use Unity's standard skybox, which comes enabled in every 3D scene. For the most part, in this book, you will use the built-in ones.

The standard skybox is called a "procedural skybox." This means the color is not fixed but is instead calculated and can change. You can see this by rotating your scene's directional light. Notice how the color of the sky, and even the simulated sun, changes as the light is rotated. Procedural skyboxes key off a scene's main directional light by default.

Creating and applying your own custom procedural skybox is quite simple:

1. Right-click the Project view and select **Create** > **Material**. (Skyboxes are really just materials applied to a "giant box in the sky.")

2. In the Inspector for this new material, click the Shader drop-down and select **Skybox** > **Procedural**. Note that this is where you can also choose to create 6 Sided, Cubemap, or Panoramic skyboxes.

3. Apply the skybox to the scene through the Lighting settings window (which you open by selecting **Window** > **Lighting** > **Settings**). Alternatively, you can just drag your skybox material into any empty space in the scene view. When you apply the skybox to your scene, you don't immediately see any change. The skybox you just created has the same properties as the default skybox and thus will look exactly the same.

4. Experiment with the different skybox properties. You can modify how the sun looks, experiment with how light scatters in the atmosphere, and change the sky color and exposure. Feel free to make something truly alien and unique for your game.

Skyboxes don't have to be procedural. They can use six textures to create highly detailed skies (often called *cubemaps*). They could even contain HDR or panorama images. All these settings are available depending on the type of skybox shader you choose. For the most part, though, you will be working with procedural skyboxes in this book because they are easy to get up and running quickly.

The Character Controller

At this stage of development, add a character controller to your terrain:

1. Import the standard character controllers by selecting **Assets** > **Import Package** > **Characters**.

2. Locate the **FPSController** asset in the folder Assets\Standard Assets\Characters\ FirstPersonCharacter\Prefabs and drag it into your scene.

3. Position the controller (which is named FPSController and is blue in the Hierarchy view) at (165, 32, 125). If the controller doesn't seem to be positioned correctly on the terrain, ensure that the terrain is positioned at (0, 0, 0), as per the previous exercise. Now rotate the controller to 260 on the y axis so that it faces the correct direction. Rename the controller object **Player**.

4. Experiment with the First Person Controller and Character Controller components on the Player game object. These two components control much of how the player will be able to behave in your game. For instance, if your character is able to climb over hills that you want to be impassable, you could lower the **Slope Limit** property on the Character Controller component.

5. Because the Player controller has its own camera, delete the Main Camera from the scene.

Once the character controller is in your scene and positioned, play the scene. Be sure to move around and look for any areas that need to be fixed or smoothed. Pay attention to the borders. Look for any areas where you are able to escape the world. Those places need to be raised, or the controller needs to be modified, so that the player cannot fall off the map. This is the stage at which you generally fix any basic problems with your terrain.

TIP

Falling Off the World

Generally, game levels have walls or some other obstacle in place to prevent the player from exiting the developed area. If a game employs gravity, the player may fall off the side of the world. You always want to create some way to prevent players from going somewhere they shouldn't. This game project uses a tall berm to keep the players in the play area. The heightmap provided to you in the book's assets for Hour 6 intentionally has a few places where the player can climb out. See if you can find and correct them. You can also set a slope limit for FPSController in the Inspector, as explained earlier in this hour.

Gamification

You now have a world in which your game can take place. You can run around and experience the world to an extent. The piece that is missing is the game itself. Right now, what you have is considered a toy. It is something that you can play with. What you want is a game, which is a toy that has rules and a goal. The process of turning something into a game is called *gamification*, and that's what this section is all about. If you followed the previous steps, your game project should now look something like Figure 6.2 (though your choices for fog, skybox, and vegetation may create some differences). The next few steps are to add game control objects for interaction, apply game scripts to those objects, and connect them to each other.

FIGURE 6.2
The current state of the *Amazing Racer* game.

NOTE

Scripts

Scripts are pieces of code that define behaviors for game objects. You have not yet learned about scripting in Unity. To make an interactive game, however, scripts are a must. With this in mind, the scripts needed to make this game have been provided for you. These scripts are as minimal as possible so that you can understand most of this project. Feel free to open the scripts in a text editor and read them to see what they are doing. Scripts are covered in greater detail in Hour 7, "Scripting, Part 1," and Hour 8, "Scripting, Part 2."

Adding Game Control Objects

As defined earlier in this hour, in the section "The Requirements," you need four specific game control objects. The first object is a spawn point—a simple game object that exists solely to tell the game where to spawn the player. To create the spawn point, follow these steps:

1. Add an empty game object to the scene (by selecting **GameObject > Create Empty**).

2. Position the game object at (165, 32, 125) and give it a rotation of (0, 260, 0).

3. Rename the empty object **Spawn Point** in the Hierarchy view.

Next, you need to create the water hazard detector. This will be a simple plane that will sit just below the water. The plane will have a trigger collider (as covered in more detail in Hour 9, "Collision"), which will detect when a player has fallen in the water. To create the detector, follow these steps:

1. Add a plane to the scene (by selecting **GameObject > 3D Object > Plane**) and position it at (100, 27, 100). Scale the plane to (20, 1, 20).

2. Rename the plane **Water Hazard Detector** in the Hierarchy view.

3. Check the **Convex** and **Is Trigger** check boxes on the Mesh Collider component in the Inspector view (see Figure 6.3).

4. Make the object invisible by disabling its Mesh Renderer component. Do this by unchecking the box next to the Mesh Renderer component's name in the Inspector (see Figure 6.3).

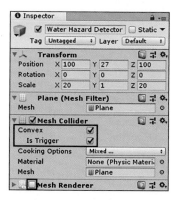

FIGURE 6.3
The Inspector view of the Water Hazard Detector object.

Next, you need to add the finish zone to your game. This zone will be a simple object with a point light on it so that the player knows where to go. The object will have a capsule collider attached to it so that it will know when a player enters the zone. To add the Finish Zone object, follow these steps:

1. Add an empty game object to the scene and position it at (26, 32, 37).

2. Rename the object **Finish Zone** in the Hierarchy view.

3. Add a light component to the Finish Zone object. (With the object selected, click **Component > Rendering > Light**.) Change the type to **Point** if it isn't already set to this and set the range to **35** and intensity to **3**.

4. Add a capsule collider to the Finish Zone object by selecting the object and clicking **Component > Physics > Capsule Collider**. Check the **Is Trigger** check box and change the Radius property to **9** in the Inspector view (see Figure 6.4).

FIGURE 6.4
The Inspector view of the Finish Zone object.

The final object you need to create is the Game Manager object. This object doesn't technically need to exist. You could instead just apply its properties to some other persistent object in the game world, such as the Main Camera. You generally create a dedicated game manager object to prevent any accidental deletion, though. During this phase of development, the game manager object is very basic. It will be used more later on. To create the Game Manager object, follow these steps:

1. Add an empty game object to the scene.

2. Rename the game object **Game Manager** in the Hierarchy view.

Adding Scripts

As mentioned earlier, scripts specify behaviors for game objects. In this section, you'll apply scripts to your game objects. At this point, it is not important for you to understand what these scripts do. You can add scripts to your project in one of two ways:

▶ Drag existing scripts into the Project view of your project.

▶ Create new scripts in your project by right-clicking in the Project view and selecting **Create > C# Script**.

Once scripts are in a project, applying them is easy. To apply a script, simply drag it from the Project view onto whatever object you want to apply it to in either the Hierarchy view or the Inspector view (see Figure 6.5).

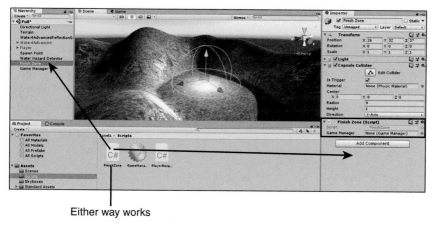

Either way works

FIGURE 6.5
Applying scripts by dragging them onto game objects.

You could also apply a script by dragging it onto an object in the Scene view, but if you do, you run the risk of missing and accidently putting the script on some other object. Therefore, applying scripts through the Scene view is not advisable.

TIP

The Special Script Icon

You may have noticed that the GameManager script has a different, gear-shaped, icon in the Project view. This is due to the script having a name that Unity automatically recognizes: GameManager. There are a few specific names that, when used for scripts, change the icon and make it easier to identify.

▼ TRY IT YOURSELF

Importing and Attaching Scripts

Follow these steps to import the scripts from the book files and attach them to the correct objects:

1. Create a new folder in your Project view and name it **Scripts**. Locate the three scripts in the Hour 6 book files—FinishZone.cs, GameManager.cs, and PlayerRespawn.cs—and drag them into your newly created Scripts folder.

2. Drag the FinishZone.cs script from the Project view onto the Finish Zone game object in the Hierarchy view.

3. Select the Game Manager object in the hierarchy. In the Inspector, select **Add Component > Scripts > GameManager**. (This is an alternative way of adding a script component to a game object.)

4. Drag the PlayerRespawn.cs script from the Project view onto the Water Hazard Detector game object in the hierarchy.

Connecting the Scripts

If you read through the scripts earlier, you may have noticed that they all have placeholders for other objects. These placeholders allow one script to talk to another script. For every placeholder in these scripts, there is a property in the component for that script in the Inspector view. Just as with scripts, you apply the objects to the placeholders by clicking and dragging (see Figure 6.6).

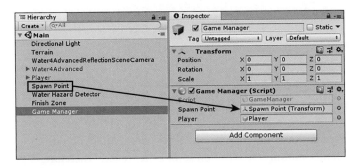

FIGURE 6.6
Moving game objects onto placeholders.

Connecting Scripts to Scripts

Follow these steps to give the scripts the game objects they need to function correctly:

1. Select the **Water Hazard Detector** object in the Hierarchy view. Notice that the Player Respawn component has a Game Manager property. This property is a placeholder for the Game Manager object you made previously.

2. Click and drag the **Game Manager** object from the Hierarchy view onto the Game Manager property of the Player Respawn (Script) component. Now, whenever players fall into the water hazard, the water hazard will let the Game Manager object know, and the player will get moved back to the spawn point at the beginning of the level.

3. Select the **Finish Zone** game object. Click and drag the **Game Manager** object from the Hierarchy view onto the Game Manager property of the Finish Zone (Script) component in the Inspector view. Now, whenever the player enters the finish zone, the game control will be notified.

4. Select the **Game Manager** object. Click and drag the **Spawn Point** object onto the Spawn Point property of the Game Manager (Script) component.

5. Click and drag the **Player** object (this is the character controller) onto the Player property of the Game Manager object.

That's all there is to connecting the game objects. Your game is now completely playable! Some of this might not make sense right now, but the more you study it and work with it, the more intuitive it becomes.

Playtesting

Your game is now done, but it is not time to rest just yet. Now you have to begin the process of playtesting. Playtesting involves playing a game with the intention of finding errors or things that just aren't as fun as you thought they would be. A lot of times, it can be beneficial to have other people playtest your games so that they can tell you what makes sense to them and what they found enjoyable.

If you followed all the steps previously described, there shouldn't be any errors (commonly called *bugs*) for you to find—at least, I hope so. The process of determining what parts are fun, however, is completely at the discretion of the person making the game. Therefore, this part is left up to you. Play the game and see what you don't like. Take notes of the things that aren't enjoyable to you. Don't just focus on the negative, though. Also find the things that you like. Your ability to change these things may be limited at the moment, so write them down. Plan on how you would change the game if you had the opportunity.

One simple thing you can tweak right now to make the game more enjoyable is the player's speed. If you have played the game a couple of times, you might have noticed that the character moves rather slowly, and that can make the game feel very long and drawn out. To make the character fast, you need to modify the First Person Controller (Script) component on the Player object. Expand the **Movement** property in the Inspector view and change the run speed (see Figure 6.7). The sample project has this set at 10. Try faster or slower speeds and pick one you enjoy. (You did notice that holding down **Shift** as you play makes you run, right?)

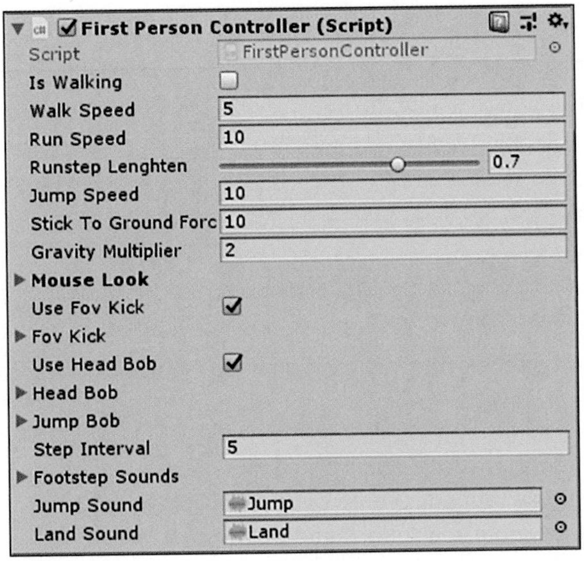

FIGURE 6.7
Changing the player's walk and run speeds.

TIP

Where's My Mouse?

To avoid having an annoying mouse cursor flying around while you are trying to play the game, the First Person Character Controller (the FPSController game object) hides and "locks" it. This is great when playing, except when you need your mouse to click a button or stop playing. If you need your mouse cursor back, you can simply press the **Escape** key to unlock and show it. Alternatively, if you need to leave play mode, you can do so by pressing **Ctrl+P** (**Command+P** on a Mac).

Summary

In this hour, you made your first game in Unity. You started by looking at the various aspects of the game's concept, rules, and requirements. From there, you built the game world and added environment effects. Then you added the game objects required for interactivity. You applied scripts to those game objects and connected them. Finally, you playtested your game and noted the things you liked and didn't like.

Q&A

Q. This lesson seems over my head. Am I doing something wrong?

A. Not at all! This process can feel very alien to someone who is not used to it. Keep reading and studying the materials, and it will all begin to come together. The best thing you can do is pay attention to how the objects connect through the scripts.

Q. You didn't cover how to build and deploy the game. Why not?

A. Building and deployment are covered later in this book, in Hour 23, "Polish and Deploy." There are many things to consider when building a game, and at this point, you should just focus on the concepts required to develop it.

Q. Why couldn't I make a game without scripts?

A. As mentioned earlier, scripts define the behavior of objects. It is very difficult to have a coherent game without some form of interactive behavior. The only reason you are building a game in Hour 6 before learning scripting in Hours 8 and 9 is to reinforce the topics you have already learned before moving on to something different.

Workshop

Take some time to work through the questions here to ensure that you have a firm grasp of the material.

Quiz

1. What are a game's requirements?

2. What is the win condition of the *Amazing Racer* game?

3. Which object is responsible for controlling the flow of the game?

4. Why is it important to playtest a game?

Answers

1. The requirements are the list of assets that will need to be created to make the game.

2. Trick question! There is no explicit win condition for this game. It is assumed that the player wins when he or she gets a better time than previous attempts. This is not built into the game in any way, though.

3. The game manager, which in the *Amazing Racer* game is called Game Manager

4. To discover bugs and determine what parts of the game work the way you want them to

Exercise

The best part about making games is that you get to make them the way you want. Following a guide can be a good learning experience, but you don't get the satisfaction of making a custom game. For this exercise, modify the *Amazing Racer* game a little to make it more unique. Exactly how you change the game is up to you. Some suggestions are listed here:

▶ Try to add multiple finish zones. See whether you can place them in a way that offers the players more choices.

▶ Modify the terrain to have more or different hazards. As long as the hazards are built like the water hazard (including the script), they will work just fine.

▶ Try having multiple spawn locations. Make it so some of the hazards move the player to a different spawn point.

▶ Modify the sky and textures to create an alien world. Make the world experience unique.

Scripting, Part 1

What You'll Learn in This Hour:

▶ The basics of scripts in Unity
▶ How to use variables
▶ How to use operators
▶ How to use conditionals
▶ How to use loops

You have so far in this book learned how to make objects in Unity. However, those objects have been a bit boring. How useful is a cube that just sits there? It would be much better to give the cube some custom action to make it interesting in some way. For this you need scripts. *Scripts* are files of codes that are used to define complex or nonstandard behaviors for objects. In this hour, you'll learn about the basics of scripting. You'll begin by looking at how to start working with scripts in Unity. You'll learn how to create scripts and use the scripting environment. Then you'll learn about the various components of a scripting language, including variables, operators, conditionals, and loops.

TIP

Sample Scripts

Several of the scripts and coding structures mentioned in this hour are available in the book assets for Hour 7. Be sure to check them out for additional learning.

CAUTION

New to Programming

If you have never programmed before, this lesson might seem strange and confusing. As you work through this hour, try your best to focus on how things are structured and why they are structured that way. Remember that programming is purely logical. If a program is not doing something you want it to, it is because you have not told it how to do it correctly. Sometimes it is up to you to change the way you think. Take this hour slowly and be sure to practice.

Scripts

As mentioned earlier in this hour, using scripts is a way to define behavior. Scripts attach to objects in Unity just like other components and give them interactivity. There are generally three steps involved in working with scripts in Unity:

1. Create the script.

2. Attach the script to one or more game objects.

3. If the script requires it, populate any properties with values or other game objects.

The rest of this lesson discusses these steps.

Creating Scripts

Before creating scripts, it is best to create a Scripts folder under the Assets folder in the Project view. Once you have a folder to contain all your scripts, simply right-click the folder and select **Create > C# Script**. Then give your script a name before continuing.

NOTE

Scripting Language

Unity allows you to write scripts in C# or JavaScript. This book uses the C# language for all scripts because it is a little more versatile and powerful in Unity. It is worth noting that JavaScript is being phased out, and the option to create new JavaScript files doesn't even appear in the editor anymore. At some point in the future, support for the language will be dropped entirely.

Once a script is created, you can view and modify it. Clicking a script in the Project view enables you to see the contents of the script in the Inspector view (see Figure 7.1). Double-clicking the script in the Project view opens your default editor, where you can add code to the script. Assuming that you have installed the default components and haven't changed anything, double-clicking a file opens the Visual Studio development environment (see Figure 7.2).

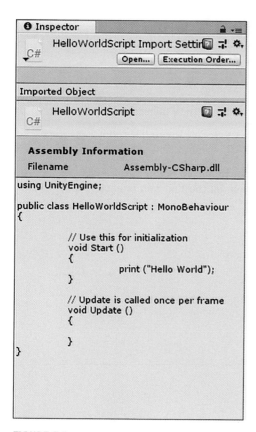

FIGURE 7.1
The Inspector view of a script.

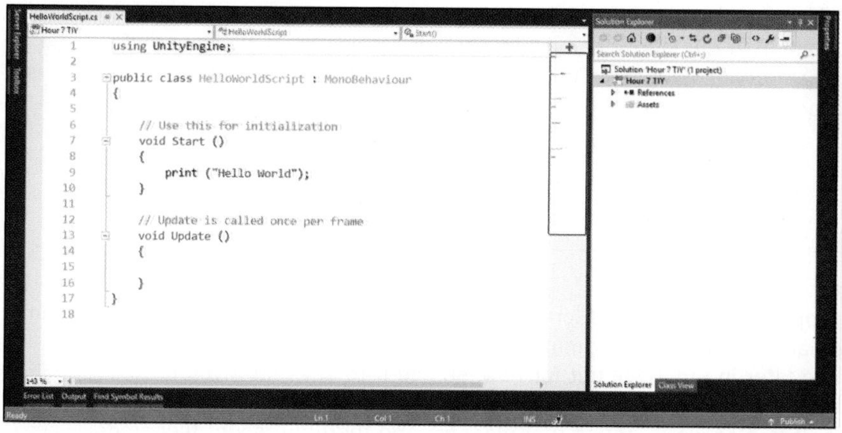

FIGURE 7.2
The Visual Studio software with the editor window showing.

▼ TRY IT YOURSELF

Creating a Script

Follow these steps to create a script for use in this section:

1. Create a new project or scene and add a **Scripts** folder to the Project view.

2. Right-click the Scripts folder and choose **Create > C# Script**. Name the script **HelloWorldScript**.

3. Double-click the new script file and wait for Visual Studio to open. In the editor window of Visual Studio (refer to Figure 7.2), erase all the text and replace it with the following code:

```
using UnityEngine;

public class HelloWorldScript : MonoBehaviour
{
    // Use this for initialization
    void Start ()
    {
        print ("Hello World");
    }

    // Update is called once per frame
    void Update ()
    {

    }
}
```

4. Save your script by selecting **File > Save** or by pressing **Ctrl+S** (**Command+S** on a Mac). Back in Unity, confirm in the Inspector view that the script has been changed and run the scene. Notice that nothing happens. The script was created, but it does not work until it is attached to an object, as discussed in the next section.

NOTE

Script Names

You just created a script named HelloWordScript; the name of the actual script file is important. In Unity and C#, the name of the file must match the name of the class that is inside it. Classes are discussed later in this hour, but for now, suffice it to say that if you have a script containing a class named MyAwesomeClass, the file that contains it will be named MyAwesomeClass.cs. It is also worth noting that classes, and therefore script filenames, cannot contain spaces.

IDEs

Visual Studio is a robust and complex piece of software that comes bundled with Unity. Editors like this are known as IDEs (integrated development environments), and they assist you with writing the code for games. Since IDEs are not actually part of Unity, this book does not cover them in any depth. The only part of Visual Studio you need to be familiar with right now is the editor window. If there is anything else you need to know about IDEs, it is covered in the hour where it is needed. (*Note:* Prior to Unity 2018.1, an IDE called MonoDevelop also came packaged with Unity. You can still acquire and use this software individually, but MonoDevelop is no longer shipped with the engine.)

Attaching a Script

To attach a script to a game object, just click the script in the Project view and drag it onto the object (see Figure 7.3). You can drag the script onto the object in the Hierarchy view, the Scene view, or the Inspector view (assuming that the object is selected). Once attached to an object, the script becomes a component of that object and is visible in the Inspector view.

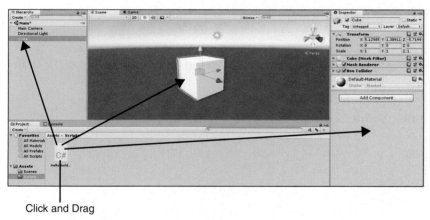

Click and Drag

FIGURE 7.3
Clicking and dragging the script onto the desired object.

To see this in action, attach the script HelloWorldScript that you created earlier to the Main Camera. You should now see a component named Hello World Script (Script) in the Inspector view. If you run the scene, you see Hello World appear at the bottom of the editor, underneath the Project view (see Figure 7.4).

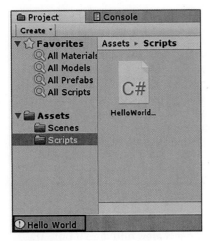

FIGURE 7.4
The words Hello World output when running the scene.

Anatomy of a Basic Script

In the preceding section, you modified a script to output some text to the screen, but the contents of the script were not explained. In this section, you'll look at the default template that is applied to every new C# script. (Note that scripts written in JavaScript have the same components even if they look a little different.) Listing 7.1 contains the full code that is generated for you by Unity when you make a new script named HelloWorldScript.

LISTING 7.1   Default Script Code

```
using UnityEngine;
using System.Collections;

public class HelloWorldScript : MonoBehaviour
{
    // Use this for initialization
    void Start () {

    }

    // Update is called once per frame
    void Update () {

    }
}
```

This code can be broken down into three parts: the using section, the class declaration section, and the class contents.

The Using Section

The first part of the script lists the libraries that the script will be using. It looks like this:

```
using UnityEngine;
using System.Collections;
```

Generally speaking, you don't change this section too often and should just leave it alone for the time being. These lines are usually added for you when you create a script in Unity. The System. Collections library is optional and is often omitted if the script doesn't use any functionality from it.

The Class Declaration Section

The next part of the script is called a *class declaration*. Every script contains a class that is named after the script. It looks like this:

```
public class HelloWorldScript : MonoBehaviour { }
```

All the code in between the opening bracket { and closing bracket } is part of this class and therefore is part of the script. All your code should go between these brackets. As with the using section, you rarely change the class declaration section and should just leave it alone for now.

The Class Contents

The section in between the opening and closing brackets of the class is considered to be "in" the class. All your code goes here. By default, a script contains two methods inside the class, Start and Update:

```
// Use this for initialization
void Start () {

}
 // Update is called once per frame
void Update () {

}
```

Methods are covered in greater detail in Hour 8, "Scripting, Part 2." For now, just know that any code inside the Start method runs when a scene first starts. Any code inside the Update method runs as fast as possible—even hundreds of times a second.

TIP

Comments

Programming languages enable code authors to leave messages for those who read the code later. These messages are called *comments*. Any words that follow two forward slashes (//) are "commented out." This means that the computer will skip over them and not attempt to read them as code. You can see an example of commenting in the Try It Yourself "Creating a Script," earlier in this hour.

NOTE

The Console

There is another window in the Unity editor that has not been mentioned until now: the Console. Basically, the Console is a window that contains text output from your game. Often, when there is an error or output from a script, messages get written to the Console. Figure 7.5 shows the Console. If the Console window isn't visible, you can access it by selecting **Window > Console**.

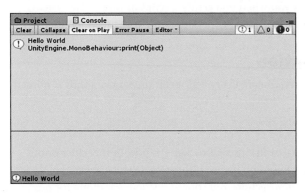

FIGURE 7.5
The Console window.

▼ TRY IT YOURSELF

Using the Built-in Methods

Now you're ready to try out the built-in methods `Start` and `Update` and see how they work. The completed ImportantFunctions script is available in the book assets for Hour 7. Try to complete the exercise that follows on your own, but if you get stuck, refer to the book assets:

1. Create a new project or scene. Add a script to the project named **ImportantFunctions**. Double-click the script to open it in your code editor.

2. Inside the script, add the following line of code to the `Start` method:

   ```
   print ("Start runs before an object Updates");
   ```

3. Save the script, and in Unity, attach it to the Main Camera. Run the scene and notice the message that appears in the Console window.

4. Back in Visual Studio, add the following line of code to the `Update` method:

   ```
   print ("This is called once a frame");
   ```

5. Save the script and quickly start and stop the scene in Unity. Notice how, in the Console, there is a single line of text from the `Start` method and there are a bunch of lines from the `Update` method.

Variables

Sometimes you want to use the same bit of data more than once in a script. In such a case, you need a placeholder for data that can be reused. Such placeholders are called *variables*. Unlike in traditional math, variables in programming can contain more than just numbers. They can hold words, complex objects, or other scripts.

Creating Variables

Every variable has a name and a type that are given to the variable when it is created. You create a variable with the following syntax:

```
<variable type> <name>;
```

So, to create an integer named num1, you type the following:

```
int num1;
```

Table 7.1 lists all the primitive (or basic) variable types and the types of data they can hold.

NOTE

Syntax

The term *syntax* refers to the rules of a programming language. Syntax dictates how things are structured and written so that the computer knows how to read them. You may have noticed that every statement, or command, in a script so far has ended with a semicolon. This is also a part of the C# syntax. Forgetting the semicolon causes your script to not work. If you want to know more about the syntax of C#, check out the C# Guide at https://docs.microsoft.com/en-us/dotnet/csharp/.

TABLE 7.1   C# Variable Types

Type	Description
int	Short for integer, int stores positive or negative whole numbers.
float	float stores floating-point data (such as 3.4) and is the default number type in Unity. float numbers in Unity are always written with an f after them, such as 3.4f, 0f, .5f, and so on.
double	double also stores floating-point numbers; however, it is not the default number type in Unity. It can generally hold bigger numbers than float.
bool	Short for Boolean, bool stores true or false (actually written in code as true or false).
char	Short for character, char stores a single letter, space, or special character (such as a, 5, or !). char values are written with single quotes ('A').
string	The string type holds entire words or sentences. String values are written with double quotes ("Hello World").

Variable Scope

Variable scope refers to where a variable is able to be used. As you have seen in scripts, classes and methods use open and close brackets to denote what belongs to them. The area between the two brackets is often referred to as a *block*. The reason this is important is that variables are only able to be used in the blocks in which they are created. So if a variable is created inside the `Start` method of a script, it is not available in the `Update` method because they are two different blocks. Attempting to use a variable where it is not available results in an error. If a variable is created in a class but outside a method, it will be available to both methods because both methods are in the same block as the variable (the class block). Listing 7.2 demonstrates this.

LISTING 7.2   **Demonstration of Class and Local Block Levels**

```
// This is in the "class block" and will
// be available everywhere in this class
private int num1;

void Start ()
{
    // this is in a "local block" and will
    // only be available in the Start method
    int num2;
}
```

Public and Private

In Listing 7.2, you can see that the keyword `private` appears before num1. This is called an *access modifier*, and it is needed only for variables declared at the class level. There are two access modifiers you need to use: `private` and `public`. A lot can be said about the two access modifiers, but what you really need to know at this point is how they affect variables. Basically, a private variable (a variable with the word `private` before it) is usable only inside the file in which it is created. Other scripts and the editor cannot see it or modify it in any way. Private variables are intended for internal use only. Public variables, in contrast, are visible to other scripts and even the Unity editor. This makes it easy for you to change the values of your variables on-the-fly within Unity. If you do not mark a variable as public or private, it defaults to private.

Modifying Public Variables in Unity

Follow these steps to see how public variables are visible in the Unity editor:

1. Create a new C# script and in Visual Studio add the following line in the class above the `Start` method:

   ```
   public int runSpeed;
   ```

2. Save the script and then, in Unity, attach it to the Main Camera.

3. Select the Main Camera and look in the Inspector view. Notice the script you just attached as a component. Now notice that the component has a new property: Run Speed. You can modify that property in the Inspector view, and the change will be reflected in the script at runtime. Figure 7.6 shows the component with the new property. This figure assumes that the script created was named ImportantFunctions.

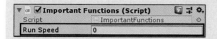

FIGURE 7.6
The new Run Speed property of the script component.

Operators

All the data in variables is worthless if you have no way of accessing or modifying it. Operators are special symbols that enable you to perform modifications on data. They generally fall into one of four categories: arithmetic operators, assignment operators, equality operators, and logical operators.

Arithmetic Operators

Arithmetic operators perform some standard mathematical operation on variables. They are generally used only on number variables, although a few exceptions exist. Table 7.2 describes the arithmetic operators.

TABLE 7.2 Arithmetic Operators

Operator	Description
+	Addition. Adds two numbers together. In the case of strings, the + sign concatenates, or combines, them. The following is an example: `"Hello" + "World"; // produces "HelloWorld"`
-	Subtraction. Reduces the number on the left by the number on the right.
*	Multiplication. Multiplies two numbers together.
/	Division. Divides the number on the left by the number on the right.

%	Modulus. Divides the number on the left by the number on the right but does not return the result. Instead, the modulus returns the remainder of the division. Consider the following examples:
	
	`10 % 2; // returns 0`
	`6 % 5;  // returns 1`
	`24 % 7; // returns 3`

Arithmetic operators can be cascaded together to produce more complex math strings, as in this example:

```
x + (5 * (6 - y) / 3);
```

Arithmetic operators work in the standard mathematic order of operations. Math is done left to right, with anything in parentheses calculated first, multiplication and division done second, and addition and subtraction done third.

Assignment Operators

Assignment operators are just what they sound like: They assign values to variables. The most notable assignment operator is the equals sign, but there are more assignment operators that combine multiple operations. All assignment in C# is right to left. This means that whatever is on the right side gets moved to the left. Consider these examples:

```
x = 5; // This works. It sets the variable x to 5.
5 = x; // This does not work. You cannot assign a variable to a value (5).
```

Table 7.3 describes the assignment operators.

TABLE 7.3   Assignment Operators

Operator	Description
=	Assigns the value on the right to the variable on the left.

+ =, – =, *=, /=	Shorthand assignment operator that performs some arithmetic operation based on the symbol used and then assigns the result to whatever is on the left. Consider these examples:
	
	`x = x + 5; // Adds 5 to x and then assigns it to x`
	`x += 5;    // Does the same as above, only shorthand`

++, –	Shorthand operators called the increment and decrement operators. They increase or decrease a number by 1. Consider these examples:
	
	`x = x + 1; // Adds 1 to x and then assigns it to x`
	`x++;       // Does the same as above, only shorthand`

Equality Operators

Equality operators compare two values. The result of an equality operator is always either `true` or `false`. Therefore, the only variable type that can hold the result of an equality operator is a Boolean. (Remember that Booleans can only contain `true` or `false`.) Table 7.4 describes the equality operators.

TABLE 7.4   Equality Operators

Operator	Description

==	Not to be confused with the assignment operator (=), this operator returns `true` only if the two values are equal. Otherwise, it returns `false`. Consider these examples:
	
	`5 == 6; // Returns false`
	`9 == 9; // Returns true`

>, <	These are the "greater than" and "less than" operators. Consider these examples:
	
	`5 > 3; // Returns true`
	`5 < 3; // Returns false`

>=, <=	These are similar to "greater than" and "less than" except that they are the "greater than or equal to" and "less than or equal to" operators. Consider these examples:
	
	`3 >= 3; // Returns true`
	`5 <= 9; // Returns true`

!=	This is the "not equal" operator, and it returns `true` if the two values are not the same. Otherwise, it returns `false`. Consider these examples:
	
	`5 != 6; // Returns true`
	`9 != 9; // Returns false`

TIP

Additional Practice

In the book assets for Hour 7 is a script called EqualityAndOperations.cs. Be sure to look through it for some additional practice with the various operators.

Logical Operators

Logical operators enable you to combine two or more Boolean values (true or false) into a single Boolean value. They are useful for determining complex conditions. Table 7.5 describes the logical operators.

TABLE 7.5 Logical Operators

Operator	Description
&&	Known as the AND operator, this compares two Boolean values and determines whether they are both true. If either, or both, of the values is false, this operator returns false. Consider these examples:
| | ```
true && false;  // Returns false
false && true;  // Returns false
false && false; // Returns false
true && true;   // Returns true
``` |
| \|\| | Known as the OR operator, this compares two Boolean values and determines whether either of them is true. If either or both of the values are true, this operator returns true. Consider these examples: |
| | ```
true || false;  // Returns true
false || true;  // Returns true
false || false; // Returns false
true || true;   // Returns true
``` |
| ! | Known as the NOT operator, this returns the opposite of a Boolean value. Consider these examples: |
| | ```
!true;  // Returns false
!false; // Returns true
``` |

Conditionals

Much of the power of a computer lies in its ability to make rudimentary decisions. At the root of this power lie the Boolean true and false. You can use these Boolean values to build conditionals and steer a program on a unique course. As you are building your flow of logic through code, remember that a machine can only make a single, simple decision at a time. Put enough of those decisions together, though, and you can build complex interactions.
```

The `if` Statement

The basis of conditionals is the `if` statement, which is structured like this:

```
if ( <some Boolean condition> )
{
  // do something
}
```

The `if` structure can be read as "if this is true, do this." So, if you want to output "Hello World" to the Console if the value of x is greater than 5, you could write the following:

```
if (x > 5)
{
  print("Hello World");
}
```

Remember that the contents of the `if` statement condition must evaluate to either `true` or `false`. Putting numbers, words, or anything else in there will not work:

```
if ("Hello" == "Hello") // Correct
```

```
if (x + y) // Incorrect
```

Finally, any code that you want to run if the condition evaluates to `true` must go inside the opening and closing brackets that follow the `if` statement.

TIP

Odd Behavior

Conditional statements use a specific syntax and can give you strange behaviors if you don't follow that syntax exactly. You may have an `if` statement in your code and notice that something isn't quite right. Maybe the condition code runs all the time, even when it shouldn't. You may also notice that it never runs, even if it should. You should be aware of two common causes of this. First, the `if` condition may not have a semicolon after it. If you write an `if` statement with a semicolon, the code following it will always run. Second, be sure that you are using the equality operator (==) and not the assignment operator (=) inside the `if` statement. Doing otherwise leads to bizarre behavior:

```
if (x > 5); // Incorrect
if (x = 5)  // Incorrect
```

Being mindful of these two common mistakes will save you heaps of time in the future.

The `if / else` Statement

The `if` statement is nice for conditional code, but what if you want to diverge your program down two different paths? The `if / else` statement enables you to do that. The `if / else` is the same basic premise as the `if` statement, except it can be read more like "if this is true do this; otherwise (else), do this other thing." The `if / else` statement is written like this:

```
if ( <some Boolean condition> )
{
    // Do something
}
else
{
    // Do something else
}
```

For example, if you want to print "X is greater than Y" to the Console if the variable x is larger than the variable y, or you want to print "Y is greater than X" if x isn't bigger than y, you could write the following:

```
if (x > y)
{
    print("X is greater than Y");
}
else
{
    print("Y is greater than X");
}
```

The `if / else if` Statement

Sometimes you want your code to diverge down one of many paths. You might want the user to be able to pick from a selection of options (such as a menu, for example). An `if / else if` is structured in much the same way as the previous two structures, except that it has multiple conditions:

```
if( <some Boolean condition> )
{
    // Do something
}
else if ( <some other Boolean condition> )
{
    // Do something else
}
else
```

```
{
    // The else is optional in the IF / ELSE IF statement
    // Do something else
}
```

For example, if you want to output a person's letter grade to the Console based on his percentage, you could write the following:

```
if (grade >= 90) {
    print ("You got an A");
} else if (grade >= 80) {
    print ("You got a B");
} else if(grade >= 70) {
   print ("You got a C");
} else if (grade >= 60) {
    print ("You got a D");
} else {
    print ("You got an F");
}
```

TIP

The Great Bracket Crusade

You may have noticed that sometimes I place opening brackets (also called curly braces) on their own lines and sometimes I put the opening bracket on the same line as a class name, a method name, or an `if` statement. The truth is that either is completely fine, and the choice is up to personal preference. That being said, great online debates and code wars have been waged (and still rage on) over which method is superior. Truly, this is a topic of great importance. There are no bystanders. Everyone must choose a side....

TIP

Single-line `if` Statements

Strictly speaking, if your `if` statement code is only a single line, you do not need to have the curly braces (also called brackets). Therefore, your code that looks like this:

```
if (x > y)
{
    print("X is greater than Y");
}
```

could also be written as follows:

```
if (x > y)
    print("X is greater than Y");
```

However, I recommend that you include the curly braces for now. This can save a lot of confusion later, as your code gets more complex. Code inside curly braces is referred to as a *code block* and is executed together.

Iteration

You have so far seen how to work with variables and make decisions. This is certainly useful if you want to do something like add two numbers together. But what if you want to add all the numbers between 1 and 100 together? What about between 1 and 1000? You definitely would not want to type all of that redundant code. Instead, you can use something called *iteration* (commonly referred to as *looping*). There are two primary types of loops to work with: the while loop and the for loop.

The while Loop

The while loop is the most basic form of iteration. It follows a structure similar to that of an if statement:

```
While ( <some Boolean condition> )
{
    // do something
}
```

The only difference is that an if statement runs its contained code only once, whereas a loop runs the contained code over and over until the condition becomes false. Therefore, if you want to add together all the numbers between 1 and 100 and then output them to the Console, you could write something like this:

```
int sum = 0;
int count = 1;

while (count <= 100)
{
    sum += count;
    count++;
}

print(sum);
```

As you can see, the value of count starts at 1 and increases by 1 every iteration—or execution of the loop—until it equals 101. When count equals 101, it is no longer less than or equal to 100, so the loop exits. Omitting the count++ line results in the loop running infinitely—so be sure it's there. During each iteration of the loop, the value of count is added to the variable sum. When the loop exits, the sum is written to the Console.

In summation, a while loop runs the code it contains over and over as long as its condition is true. When its condition becomes false, it stops looping.

The `for` Loop

The `for` loop follows the same idea as the `while` loop, except it is structured a bit differently. As you saw in the code for the `while` loop, you had to create a `count` variable, you had to test the variable (as the condition), and you had to increase the variable all on three separate lines. The `for` loop condenses that syntax down to a single line. It looks like this:

```
for (<create a counter>; <Boolean conditional>; <increment the counter >)
{
    // Do something
}
```

The `for` loop has three special *compartments* for controlling the loop. Notice the semicolons, not commas, in between the sections in the `for` loop header. The first compartment creates a variable to be used as a counter. (A common name for the counter is i, short for *iterator*.) The second compartment is the conditional statement of the loop. The third compartment handles increasing or decreasing the counter. The previous `while` loop example can be rewritten using a `for` loop. It would look like this:

```
int sum = 0;

for (int count = 1; count <= 100; count++)
{
    sum += count;
}

print(sum);
```

As you can see, the different parts of the loop get condensed and take up less space. You can see that the `for` loop is really good at things like counting.

Summary

In this hour, you took your first steps into video game programming. You started by looking at the basics of scripting in Unity. You learned how to make and attach scripts. You also looked at the basic anatomy of a script. From there, you studied the basic logical components of a program. You worked with variables, operators, conditionals, and loops.

Q&A

Q. How much programming is required to make a game?

A. Most games use some form of programming to define complex behaviors. The more complex the behaviors need to be, the more complex the programming needs to be. If you want to make games, you should definitely become comfortable with the concepts of programming. This is true even if you don't intend to be the primary developer for a game. With that in mind, rest assured that this book provides everything you need to know to make your first few simple games.

Q. Is this all there is to scripting?

A. Yes and no. Presented in this text are the fundamental blocks of programming. They never really change but just get applied in new and unique ways. That said, a lot of what is presented here is simplified because of the complex nature of programming in general. If you want to learn more about programming, you should read books or articles specifically on the subject.

Workshop

Take some time to work through the questions here to ensure that you have a firm grasp of the material.

Quiz

1. What two languages does Unity allow you to use for programming?

2. True or False: The code in the `Start` method runs at the start of every frame.

3. Which variable type is the default floating-point number type in Unity?

4. Which operator returns the remainder of division?

5. What is a conditional statement?

6. Which loop type is best suited for counting?

Answers

1. C# and JavaScript

2. False. The `Start` method runs at the beginning of the scene. The `Update` method runs every frame.

3. `float`

4. Modulus

5. A code structure that allows the computer to choose a code path based on a simple decision

6. The `for` loop

Exercise

It can often be helpful to view coding structures as building blocks. Alone, each piece is simple. Put together, however, they can build complex entities. In the following steps, you will encounter multiple programming challenges. Use the knowledge you have gained in this hour to build a solution to each problem. Put each solution in its own script and attach the scripts to the Main Camera of a scene to ensure that they work. You can find the solution to this exercise in the book assets for Hour 7.

1. Write a script that adds together all the even numbers from 2 to 499. Output the result to the Console.

2. Write a script that outputs all the numbers from 1 to 100 to the Console except for multiples of 3 or 5. In place of multiples of 3 or 5, output "Programming is awesome!" (*Hint:* You can tell whether a number is a multiple of another number if the result of a modulus operation is 0; for example, `12 % 3 == 0` because 12 is a multiple of 3.)

3. In the Fibonacci sequence, you determine a number by adding the two previous numbers together. The sequence starts with 0, 1, 1, 2, 3, 5....Write a script that determines the first 20 places of the Fibonacci sequence and outputs them to the Console.

Scripting, Part 2

What You'll Learn in This Hour:

▶ How to write methods

▶ How to capture user input

▶ How to work with local components

▶ How to work with game objects

In Hour 7, "Scripting, Part 1," you learned about the basics of scripting in Unity. In this hour, you'll use what you have learned to complete more meaningful tasks. First, you'll examine what methods are, how they work, and how to write them. Then you'll get some hands-on practice with user input. After that, you'll examine how to access components from scripts. You'll wrap up the hour by learning how to access other game objects and their components with code.

TIP

Sample Scripts

Several of the scripts and coding structures mentioned in this hour are available in the book assets for Hour 8. Be sure to check them out for additional learning.

Methods

Methods, often called *functions*, are modules of code that can be called and used independently of each other. Each method generally represents a single task or purpose, and often many methods can work together to achieve complex goals. Consider the two methods you have seen so far: Start and Update. Each represents a single and concise purpose. The Start method contains all the code that is run for an object when the scene first begins. The Update method contains the code that is run every update frame of the scene (which is different from a render frame, or "frames per second").

NOTE

Method Shorthand

You have seen so far that whenever the `Start` method is mentioned, the word *method* has followed it. It can become cumbersome to always have to specify that a word used is a method. You can't write just `Start`, though, because people wouldn't know if you meant the word, a variable, or a method. A shorter way of handling this is to use parentheses with the word. So, the method `Start` can be rewritten as just `Start()`. If you ever see something written like `SomeWords()`, you know instantly that the writer is talking about a method named `SomeWords`.

Anatomy of a Method

Before working with methods, you should look at the different parts that compose them. The following is the general format of a method:

```
<return type> <name> (<parameter list>)
{
    <Inside the method's block>
}
```

Method Name

Every method must have a unique name (sort of...see the "Method Signature" section below). Though the rules that govern proper names are determined by the language used, good general guidelines for method names include the following:

▶ Make a method name descriptive. It should be an action or a verb.

▶ Spaces are not allowed.

▶ Avoid using special characters (for example, !, @, *, %, $) in method names. Different languages allow different characters. By not using any, you avoid risking problems.

Method names are important because they allow you to both identify and use them.

Return Type

Every method has the ability to return a variable back to whatever code called it. The type of this variable is called the *return type*. If a method returns an integer (a whole number), the return type is an `int`. Likewise, if a method returns a `true` or a `false`, the return type is `bool`. If a method doesn't return any value, it still has a return type. In that instance, the return type is `void` (meaning nothing). Any method that returns a value will do so with the keyword `return`.

Parameter List

Just as methods can pass a variable back to whatever code called it, the calling code can pass variables in. These variables are called *parameters*. The variables sent into the method are identified in the parameter list section of the method. For example, a method named `Attack` that takes an integer called `enemyID` would look like this:

```
void Attack(int enemyID)
{}
```

As you can see, when specifying a parameter, you must provide both the variable type and the name. Multiple parameters are separated with commas.

Method Signature

The combination of a method's return type, name, and parameters list is often referred to as a method's *signature*. Earlier in this hour I mentioned that a method must have a unique name, but that isn't exactly true. What is true is that a method must have a unique signature. Therefore, consider these two methods:

```
void MyMethod()
{}

void MyMethod(int number)
{}
```

Even though these two methods have the same name, they have different parameter lists and thus are different. This practice of having different methods with the same name can also be called *overloading* a method.

Method Block

The method block is where the code of the method goes. Every time a method is used, the code inside the method block executes.

TRY IT YOURSELF ▼

Identifying Method Parts

Take a moment to review the different parts of a method and then consider the following method:

```
int TakeDamage(int damageAmount)
{
    int health = 100;
    return health - damageAmount;
}
```

Can you identify the following pieces?

1. What is the method's name?

2. What variable type does the method return?

3. What are the method's parameters? How many are there?

4. What code is in the method's block?

Methods as Factories

The concept of methods can be confusing for someone who is new to programming. Often, mistakes are made regarding method parameters and what methods return. A good way to keep it straight is to think of a method as a factory. Factories receive raw materials that they use to make products. Methods work the same way. The parameters are the materials you are passing in to the "factory," and the return is the final product of that factory. Just think of methods that don't take parameters as factories that don't require raw goods. Likewise, think of methods that don't return anything as factories that don't produce final products. By imagining methods as little factories, you can work to keep the flow of logic straight in your head.

Writing Methods

When you understand the components of a method, writing them is easy. Before you begin writing methods yourself, take a moment to answer three main questions:

▶ What specific task will the method achieve?

▶ Does the method need any outside data to achieve its task?

▶ Does the method need to give back any data?

Answering these questions will help you determine a method's name, parameters, and return data.

Consider this example: A player has been hit with a fireball. You need to write a method to simulate this by removing 5 health points. You know what the specific task of this method is. You also know that the task doesn't need any data (because you know it takes 5 points) and should probably return the new health value back. You could write the method like this:

```
int TakeDamageFromFireball()
{
    int playerHealth = 100;
    return playerHealth - 5;
}
```

As you can see in this method, the player's health is 100, and 5 is deducted from it. The result (which is 95) is passed back. Obviously, this can be improved. For starters, what if you want the fireball to do more than 5 points of damage? You would then need to know exactly how much damage a fireball is supposed to do at any given time. You would need a variable, or in this case a parameter. Your new method could be written as follows:

```
int TakeDamageFromFireball(int damage)
{
    int playerHealth = 100;
    return playerHealth - damage;
}
```

Now you can see that the damage is read in from the method and applied to the health. Another place where this can be improved is with the health itself. Currently, players can never lose because their health will always refresh back to 100 before having damage deducted. It would be better to store the player's health elsewhere so that its value is persistent. You could then read it in and remove the damage appropriately. Your method could then look like this:

```
int TakeDamageFromFireball(int damage, int playerHealth)
{
    return playerHealth - damage;
}
```

By examining your needs, you can build better, more robust methods for your game.

NOTE

Simplification

In the preceding example, the resulting method simply performs basic subtraction. This is oversimplified for instruction's sake. In a more realistic environment, there are many ways to handle this task. A player's health could be stored in a variable belonging to a script. In this case, it would not need to be read in. Another possibility would be to use a complex algorithm in the TakeDamageFromFireball method to reduce the incoming damage by some armor value, a player's dodging ability, or a magical shield. If the examples here seem silly, just bear in mind that they are meant to demonstrate various elements of the topic.

Using Methods

Once a method is written, all that is left is to use it. Using a method is often referred to as *calling* or *invoking* the method. To call a method, you just need to write the method's name followed by parentheses and any parameters. So, if you were trying to use a method named SomeMethod, you would write the following:

```
SomeMethod();
```

If SomeMethod() requires an integer parameter, you call it like this:

```
// Method call with a value of 5
SomeMethod(5);
// Method call passing in a variable
int x = 5;
SomeMethod(x); // do not write "int x" here.
```

Note that when you call a method, you do not need to supply the variable type with the variable you are passing in. If SomeMethod() returns a value, you want to *catch* it in a variable. The code could look something like this (with a Boolean return type assumed; in reality, it could be anything):

```
bool result = SomeMethod();
```

Using this basic syntax is all there is to calling methods.

▼ TRY IT YOURSELF

Calling Methods

Let's work further with the `TakeDamageFromFireball` method described in the previous section. This exercise shows how to call the various forms of the method. (You can find the solution for this exercise as FireBallScript in the book assets for Hour 8.) Follow these steps:

1. Create a new project or scene. Create a C# script called FireBallScript and enter the three `TakeDamageFromFireball` methods described earlier. These should go inside the class definition, at the same level of indent as the `Start()` and `Update()` methods, but outside those two methods.

2. In the `Start` method, call the first `TakeDamageFromFireball()` method by typing the following:

```
int x = TakeDamageFromFireball();
print ("Player health: " + x);
```

3. Attach the script to the Main Camera and run the scene. Notice the output in the Console. Now call the second `TakeDamageFromFireball()` method in `Start()` by typing the following (placing it below the first bit of code you typed; no need to remove it):

```
int y = TakeDamageFromFireball(25);
print ("Player health: " + y);
```

4. Again, run the scene and note the output in the Console. Finally, call the last `TakeDamageFromFireball()` method in `Start()` by typing the following:

```
int z = TakeDamageFromFireball(30, 50);
print ("Player health: " + z);
```

5. Run the scene and note the final output. Notice how the three methods behave a little differently from one another. Also notice that you called each one specifically, and the correct version of the `TakeDamageFromFireball()` method was used based on the parameters you passed in.

TIP

Help Finding Errors

If you are getting errors when you try to run your script, pay attention to the reported line number and character number in the Console, at the end of the error message. Furthermore, you can "build" your code inside Visual Studio by using **Ctrl+Shift+B** (**Command+Shift+B** on a Mac). When you do this, Visual Studio checks your code and points out any errors in context, showing you exactly where the troublesome line is. Try it.

Input

Without player input, *video games* would just be *video*. Player input can come in many different varieties. Inputs can be physical—for example, gamepads, joysticks, keyboards, and mice. There are capacitive controllers such as the relatively new touch screens in modern mobile devices. There are also motion devices like the Wii Remote, the PlayStation Move, and the Microsoft Kinect. Rarer is the audio input that uses microphones and a player's voice to control a game. In this section, you'll learn all about writing code to allow the player to interact with your game by using physical devices.

Input Basics

With Unity (as with most other game engines), you can detect specific key presses in code to make it interactive. However, doing so makes it difficult to allow players to remap the controls to their preference, so it is a good idea to avoid doing that. Thankfully, Unity has a simple system for generically mapping controls. With Unity, you look for a specific *axis* to know whether a player intends a certain action. Then, when the player runs the game, he can choose to make different controls mean different axes.

You can view, edit, and add different axes by using the Input Manager. To access the Input Manager, click **Edit > Project Settings > Input**. In the Input Manager, you can see the various axes associated with different input actions. By default, there are 18 input axes, but you can add your own if you want. Figure 8.1 shows the default Input Manager with the horizontal axis expanded.

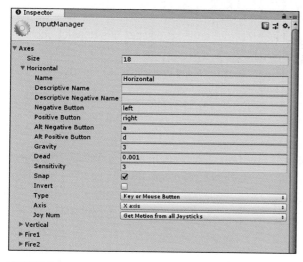

FIGURE 8.1
The Input Manager.

While the horizontal axis doesn't directly control anything (you will write scripts to do that later), it represents that player going sideways. Table 8.1 describes the properties of an axis.

TABLE 8.1   **Axis Properties**

Property	Description
Name	The name of the axis. This is how you reference it in code.
Descriptive Name/ Descriptive Negative Name	A verbose name for the axis that will appear to the player in the game configuration. The negative is the opposite name. For example: "Go left" and "Go right" would be a name and negative name pair.
Negative Button/ Positive Button	The buttons that pass negative and positive values to the axis. For the horizontal axis, these are the left arrow and the right arrow keys.
Alt Negative Button/ Alt Positive Button	Alternate buttons to pass values to the axis. For the horizontal axis, these are the A and D keys.
Gravity	How quickly the axis returns to 0 once the key is no longer pressed.
Dead	The value below which any input will be ignored. This helps prevent jittering with joystick devices.
Sensitivity	How quickly the axis responds to input.
Snap	When checked, Snap causes the axis to immediately go to 0 when the opposite direction is pressed.
Invert	Checking this property inverts the controls.
Type	The type of input. The types are keyboard/mouse buttons, mouse movement, and joystick movement.
Axis	The corresponding axis from an input device. This doesn't apply to buttons.
Joy Num	Which joystick to get input from. By default, this property gets input from all joysticks.

Input Scripting

Once your axes are set up in the Input Manager, working with them in code is simple. To access any of the player's input, you will be using the `Input` object. More specifically, you will be using the `GetAxis` method of the `Input` object. `GetAxis()` reads the name of the axis as a string and returns the value of that axis. So, if you want to get the value of the horizontal axis, you type the following:

```
float hVal = Input.GetAxis("Horizontal");
```

In the case of the horizontal axis, if the player is pressing the left arrow key (or the A key), `GetAxis()` returns a negative number. If the player is pressing the right arrow key (or the D key), the method returns a positive value.

Reading in User Input

Follow these steps to work with the vertical and horizontal axes and get a better idea of how to use player input:

1. Create a new project or scene. Add a script named PlayerInput to the project and attach the script to the Main Camera.

2. Add the following code to the Update method in the PlayerInput script:

```
float hVal = Input.GetAxis("Horizontal");
float vVal = Input.GetAxis("Vertical");
if(hVal != 0)
    print("Horizontal movement selected: " + hVal);
if(vVal != 0)
    print("Vertical movement selected: " + vVal);
```

This code must be in Update so that it continuously reads the input.

3. Save the script and run the scene. Notice what happens on the Console when you press the arrow keys. Now try out the W, A, S, and D keys. If you don't see anything, click in the Game window with the mouse and try again.

Specific Key Input

Although you generally want to deal with the generic axes for input, sometimes you want to determine whether a specific key has been pressed. To do so, you will again be using the Input object. This time, however, you will use the GetKey method, which reads in a special code that corresponds to a specific key. It then returns true if the key is currently down or false if the key is not currently down. To determine whether the K key is currently pressed, you type the following:

```
bool isKeyDown = Input.GetKey(KeyCode.K);
```

TIP

Finding Key Codes

Each key has a specific key code. You can determine the key code of the specific key you want by reading the Unity documentation. Alternatively, you can use the built-in tools of Visual Studio to find it. Whenever you are working on a script in Visual Studio, you can always type in the name of an object followed by a period. When you do, a menu with all the possible options pops up. Likewise, if you type an open parenthesis after typing a method name, the same menu pops up, showing you the various options. Figure 8.2 illustrates using this pop-up menu to find the key code for the Esc key.

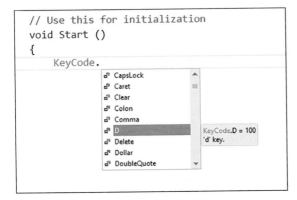

FIGURE 8.2
The automatic pop-up in Visual Studio.

▼ TRY IT YOURSELF

Reading in Specific Key Presses

Follow these steps to write a script that determines whether a specific key is pressed:

1. Create a new project or scene. Add to the project a script named PlayerInput (or modify the existing one) and attach it to the Main Camera.

2. Add the following code to the Update method in the PlayerInput script:

```
if(Input.GetKey(KeyCode.M))
    print("The 'M' key is pressed down");
if(Input.GetKeyDown(KeyCode.O))
    print("The 'O' key was pressed");
```

3. Save the script and run the scene. Notice what happens when you press the M key versus what happens when you press the O key. In particular, note that the M key causes output the entire time it is held, while the O key outputs only when it is first pressed.

TIP

"Gotta Gotta Get Up to Get Down"

In the Try It Yourself exercise "Reading in Specific Key Presses," you checked for key input in two different ways. Namely, you used Input.GetKey() to test whether a key was pressed at all. You also used Input.GetKeyDown() to test whether a key was pressed during this frame. This second version only registered the first time the key was pressed and ignored you holding down the key. Generally speaking, Unity looks for three types of key press events: GetKey(), GetKeyDown(), and GetKeyUp(). This is consistent across the other similar methods as well: GetButton(), GetButtonDown(), GetButtonUp(), GetMouseButton(), GetMouseButtonDown(), and so on. Knowing when to look for a first key press versus a held button is important. Whichever type of input you need, though, there's a method for it.

Mouse Input

Besides capturing key presses, you want to capture mouse input from the user. There are two components to mouse input: mouse button presses and mouse movement. Determining whether mouse buttons are pressed is much like detecting key presses, covered earlier this hour. In this section, you will again be using the `Input` object. This time you'll use the `GetMouseButtonDown` method, which takes an integer between 0 and 2 to dictate which mouse button you are asking about. The method returns a Boolean value indicating whether the button is pressed. The code to get the mouse button presses looks like this:

```
bool isButtonDown;
isButtonDown = Input.GetMouseButtonDown(0); // left mouse button
isButtonDown = Input.GetMouseButtonDown(1); // right mouse button
isButtonDown = Input.GetMouseButtonDown(2); // center mouse button
```

Mouse movement is only along two axes: x and y. To get the mouse movement, you use the `GetAxis` method of the input object. You can use the names Mouse X and Mouse Y to get the movement along the x axis and the y axis, respectively. The code to read in the mouse movement would look like this:

```
float value;
value = Input.GetAxis("Mouse X"); // x axis movement
value = Input.GetAxis("Mouse Y"); // y axis movement
```

Unlike button presses, mouse movement is measured by the amount the mouse has moved since the last frame only. Basically, holding a key causes a value to increase until it maxes out at -1 or 1 (depending on whether it is positive or negative). The mouse movement, however, generally has smaller numbers because it is measured and reset each frame.

TRY IT YOURSELF ▼

Reading Mouse Movement

In this exercise, you'll read in mouse movement and output the results to the Console:

1. Create a new project or scene. Add to the project a script named PlayerInput (or modify the existing one) and attach it to the Main Camera.

2. Add the following code to the `Update` method in the PlayerInput script:

   ```
   float mxVal = Input.GetAxis("Mouse X");
   float myVal = Input.GetAxis("Mouse Y");
   if(mxVal != 0)
       print("Mouse X movement selected: " + mxVal);
   if(myVal != 0)
       print("Mouse Y movement selected: " + myVal);
   ```

3. Save the script and run the scene. Read through the Console to see the output when you move the mouse around.

Accessing Local Components

As you have seen numerous times in the Inspector view, objects are composed of various components. There is always a transform component, and there may optionally be any number of other components, such as a Renderer, Light, and Camera. Scripts are also components, and together these components give a game object its behavior.

Using `GetComponent`

You can interact with components at runtime through scripts. The first thing you must do is get a *reference* to the component you want to work with. You should do this in `Start()` and save the result in a variable. This way, you won't have to waste time repeating this relatively slow operation.

The `GetComponent<Type>()` method has a slightly different syntax than you've seen to this point, using chevrons to specify the type you are looking for (for example, Light, Camera, script name).

`GetComponent()` returns the first component of the specified type that is attached to the same game object as your script. As mentioned earlier in this hour, you should then assign this component to a local variable so you can access it later. Here's how you do this:

```
Light lightComponent; // A variable to store the light component.
Start ()
{
    lightComponent = GetComponent<Light> ();
    lightComponent.type = LightType.Directional;
}
```

Once you have a reference to a component, you can then easily modify its properties through code. You do so by typing the name of the variable storing the reference followed by a dot followed by whatever property you want to modify. In the example above, you change the `type` property of the light component to be `Directional`.

Accessing the Transform

The component you'll most commonly work with is the transform component. By editing it, you can make objects move around the screen. Remember that an object's transform is made up of its translation (or position), its rotation, and its scale. Although you can modify those directly, it is easier to use some built-in options called the `Translate()` method, the `Rotate()` method, and the `localScale` variable, as shown here:

```
// Moves the object along the positive x axis.
// The '0f' means 0 is a float (floating point number). It is the way Unity reads
floats
transform.Translate(0.05f, 0f, 0f);
```

```
// Rotates the object along the z axis
transform.Rotate(0f, 0f, 1f);
// Scales the object to double its size in all directions
transform.localScale = new Vector3(2f, 2f, 2f);
```

NOTE

Finding the Transform

Because every game object has a transform, there's no need to do an explicit find operation; you can access the transform directly as above. This is the only component that works this way; the rest must be accessed using a `GetComponent` method.

Because `Translate()` and `Rotate()` are methods, if the preceding code were put in `Update()`, the object would continually move along the positive x axis while being rotated along the z axis.

TRY IT YOURSELF ▼

Transforming an Object

Follow these steps to see the previous code in action by applying it to an object in a scene:

1. Create a new project or scene. Add a cube to the scene and position it at (0, -1, 0).

2. Create a new script and name it **CubeScript**. Place the script on the cube. In Visual Studio, enter the following code to the `Update` method:

```
transform.Translate(.05f, 0f, 0f);
transform.Rotate(0f, 0f, 1f);
transform.localScale = new Vector3(1.5f, 1.5f, 1.5f);
```

3. Save the script and run the scene. You may need to move to Scene view to see the full motion. Notice that the effects of the `Translate()` and `Rotate()` methods are cumulative, and the variable `localScale` is not; `localScale` does not keep growing.

Accessing Other Objects

Many times, you want a script to be able to find and manipulate other objects and their components. Doing so is simply a matter of finding the object you want and calling on the appropriate component. There are a few basic ways to find objects that aren't local to the script or to the object the script is attached to.

Finding Other Objects

The first and easiest way to find other objects to work with is to use the editor. By creating a public variable on the class level of type GameObject, you can simply drag the object you want onto the script component in the Inspector view. The code to set this up looks like this:

```
// This is here for reference
public class SomeClassScript : MonoBehaviour
{
    // This is the game object you want to access
    public GameObject objectYouWant;
    // This is here for reference
    void Start() {}
}
```

After you have attached the script to a game object, you see a property in the Inspector called Object You Want (see Figure 8.3). Just drag any game object you want onto this property to have access to it in the script.

Drag Game Object You Want Here

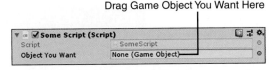

FIGURE 8.3
The new Object You Want property in the Inspector.

Another way to find a game object is by using one of the Find methods. As a rule of thumb, if you want a designer to be able to connect the object, or if it's optional, then connect via the Inspector. If disconnecting would break the game, then use a Find method. There are three major ways to find using a script: by name, by tag, and by type.

One option is to search by the object's name. The object's name is what it is called inside the Hierarchy view. If you were looking for an object named Cube, the code would look like this:

```
// This is here for reference
public class SomeClassScript : MonoBehaviour
{
    // This is the game object you want to access
    private GameObject target; //  Note this doesn't need to be public if using find.
    // This is here for reference
    void Start()
    {
        target = GameObject.Find("Cube");
    }
}
```

The shortcoming of this method is that it just returns the first item it finds with the given name. If you have multiple Cube objects, you won't know which one you are getting.

TIP

Finding Efficiency

Be aware that using a `Find()` method is extremely slow as it searches every game object in the scene, in order, until it finds a match. In very large scenes, the amount of time this method takes can cause a noticeable framerate drop in your game. It is advisable to *never* use `Find()` if you can avoid it. That being said, there are many times when it is necessary. In these instances, however, it is very beneficial to call the method in `Start()` and save the results of the find in a variable for future use to minimize the impact.

Another way to find an object is by its tag. An object's tag is much like its layer (discussed earlier in this hour). The only difference is semantics. The *layer* is used for broad categories of interaction, whereas the *tag* is used for basic identification. You create tags using the Tag Manager (click **Edit > Project Settings > Tags & Layers**). Figure 8.4 shows how to add a new tag to the Tag Manager.

FIGURE 8.4
Adding a new tag.

Once a tag is created, simply apply it to an object by using the Tag drop-down list in the Inspector view (see Figure 8.5).

FIGURE 8.5
Selecting a tag.

After a tag is added to an object, you can find it by using the `FindWithTag()` method:

```
// This is here for reference
public class SomeClassScript : MonoBehaviour
{
    // This is the game object you want to access
    private GameObject target;
    // This is here for reference
    void Start()
    {
        target = GameObject.FindWithTag("MyNewTag");
    }
}
```

There are additional `Find()` methods available, but the ones covered here should work for you in most situations.

Modifying Object Components

Once you have a reference to another object, working with the components of that object is almost exactly the same as using local components. The only difference is that now, instead of simply writing the component name, you need to write the object variable and a period in front of it, like so:

```
// This accesses the local component, not what you want
transform.Translate(0, 0, 0);
// This accesses the target object, what you want
targetObject.transform.Translate(0, 0, 0);
```

▼ TRY IT YOURSELF

Transforming a Target Object

Follow these steps to modify a target object by using scripts:

1. Create a new project or scene. Add a cube to the scene and position it at (0, -1, 0).

2. Create a new script and name it **TargetCubeScript**. Place the script on the Main Camera. In Visual Studio, enter the following code in TargetCubeScript:

```
// This is the game object you want to access
private GameObject target;
// This is here for reference
void Start()
{
    target = GameObject.Find("Cube");
}
```

```
void Update()
{
    target.transform.Translate(.05f, 0f, 0f);
    target.transform.Rotate(0f, 0f, 1f);
    target.transform.localScale = new Vector3(1.5f, 1.5f, 1.5f);
}
```

3. Save the script and run the scene. Notice that the cube moves around even though the script is applied to the Main Camera.

Summary

In this hour, you have explored more scripting in Unity. You have learned all about methods and looked at some ways to write your own. You have also worked with player inputs from the keyboard and mouse. You learned about modifying object components with code, and you finished the hour by learning how to find and interact with other game objects via scripts.

Q&A

Q. How do I know how many methods a task requires?

A. A method should perform a single, concise function. You don't want to have too few methods with a lot of code because each method would then have to do more than one thing. You also don't want to have too many small methods because that defeats the purpose of modularizing blocks of code. As long as each process has its own specific method, you have enough methods.

Q. Why didn't we learn more about gamepads in this hour?

A. The problem with gamepads is that all are unique. In addition, different operating systems treat them differently. The reason they aren't covered in detail in this hour is that they are too varied, and discussing some of them wouldn't allow for a consistent reader experience. (In addition, not everyone has a gamepad.)

Q. Is every component editable by script?

A. Yes, at least all of the built-in ones are.

Workshop

Take some time to work through the questions here to ensure that you have a firm grasp of the material.

Quiz

1. True or False: Methods can also be referred to as functions.

2. True or False: Not every method has a return type.

3. Why is it a bad thing to map player interactions to specific buttons?

4. In the Try It Yourself exercises in the sections on local and target components, the cube was translated along the positive x axis and rotated along the z axis. This caused the cube to move around in a big circle. Why?

Answers

1. True

2. False. Every method has a return type. If a method returns nothing, the type is void.

3. If you map player interactions to specific buttons, the players will have a much harder time remapping the controls to meet their preferences. If you map controls to generic axes, players can easily change which buttons map to those axes.

4. Transformations happen on the local coordinate system (refer to Hour 2, "Game Objects"). Therefore, the cube did move along the positive x axis. The direction that axis was facing relative to the camera, however, kept changing.

Exercise

It is a good idea to combine each hour's lessons together to see them interact in a more realistic way. In this exercise, you'll write scripts to allow the player directional control over a game object. You can find the solution to this exercise in the book assets for Hour 8 if needed.

1. Create a new project or scene. Add a cube to the scene and position it at (0, 0, -5).

2. Create a new folder called Scripts and create a new script called CubeControlScript. Attach the script to the cube.

3. Try to add the following functionality to the script. If you get lost, check the book assets for Hour 8 for help:

▶ Whenever the player presses the left or right arrow key, move the cube along the x axis negatively or positively, respectively. Whenever the player presses the down or up arrow key, move the cube along the z axis negatively or positively, respectively.

▶ When the player moves the mouse along the y axis, rotate the *camera* about the x axis. When the player moves the mouse along the x axis, rotate the *cube* about the y axis.

▶ When the player presses the M key, have the cube double in size. When the player presses the M key again, have the cube go back to its original size. The M key should act as a toggle switching between the two scale sizes.

HOUR 9
Collision

What You'll Learn in This Hour:

- ▶ The basics of rigidbodies
- ▶ How to use colliders
- ▶ How to script with triggers
- ▶ How to raycast

In this hour, you'll learn to work with the most prevalent physics concept in video games: collision. Collision, simply put, involves knowing when the border of one object has come into contact with another object. You'll begin by learning what rigidbodies are and what they can do for you. After that, you'll experiment with Unity's powerful built-in physics engines—Box2D and PhysX. From there, you'll learn some more subtle uses of collision with triggers. You'll end the hour by learning to use a raycast to detect collisions.

Rigidbodies

For objects to take advantage of Unity's built-in physics engines, they must include a component called a *rigidbody*. Adding a rigidbody component makes an object behave like a real-world physical entity. To add a rigidbody component, simply select the object that you want (make sure you choose the version without 2D on the end) and click **Component > Physics > Rigidbody**. The new rigidbody component is added to the object in the Inspector (see Figure 9.1).

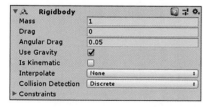

FIGURE 9.1
The rigidbody component.

The rigidbody component has several properties that you have not seen yet. Table 9.1 describes them.

TABLE 9.1   Rigidbody Properties

Property	Description
Mass	Specifies the mass of the object, in arbitrary units. Use 1 unit = 1 kg unless you have a good reason to deviate. Higher mass requires more force to move.
Drag	Indicates how much air resistance is applied to the object when moving. Higher drag means more force is required to move an object and stops a moving object more quickly. A drag of 0 applies no air resistance.
Angular Drag	Much like drag, indicates air resistance applied when spinning.
Use Gravity	Determines whether Unity's gravity calculations are applied to this object. Gravity affects an object more or less depending on its drag.
Is Kinematic	Allows you to control the movement of a rigidbody yourself. If an object is kinematic, it will not be affected by forces.
Interpolate	Determines how and whether motion for an object is smoothed. By default, this property is set to None. With Interpolate, smoothing is based on the previous frame, whereas with Extrapolate, it is based on the next assumed frame. It is recommended to turn this on only if you notice a lagging or stutter, and you want your physical objects to have smoother motion.
Collision Detection	Determines how collision is calculated. Discrete is the default setting, and it is how all objects test against each other. The Continuous setting can help if you are having trouble detecting collisions with very fast objects. Be aware, though, that Continuous can have a large impact on performance. The Continuous Dynamic setting uses discrete detection against other discrete objects and continuous detection against other continuous objects.
Constraints	Specifies movement limitations that a rigidbody enforces on an object. By default, these limitations are turned off. Freezing a position axis prevents the object from moving along that axis, and freezing a rotation axis prevents an object from rotating about that axis.

▼ TRY IT YOURSELF

Using Rigidbodies

Follow these steps to see a rigidbody in action:

1. Create a new project or scene. Add a cube to the scene and place it at (0, 1, –5).

2. Run the scene. Notice how the cube floats in front of the camera.

3. Add a rigidbody to the object (by selecting **Components > Physics > Rigidbody**).

4. Run the scene. Notice that the object now falls due to gravity.

5. Experiment with the drag and constraints properties and note their effects.

Enabling Collision

Now that you have objects moving around, it is time to start getting them to crash into each other. For objects to detect collision, they need a component called a collider. A *collider* is a perimeter that is projected around an object that can detect when other objects enter it.

Colliders

Geometric objects such as spheres, capsules, and cubes already have collider components on them when they are created. You can add a collider to an object that doesn't have one by selecting **Component > Physics** and then choosing the collider shape you want from the menu. Figure 9.2 shows the various collider shapes you can choose from.

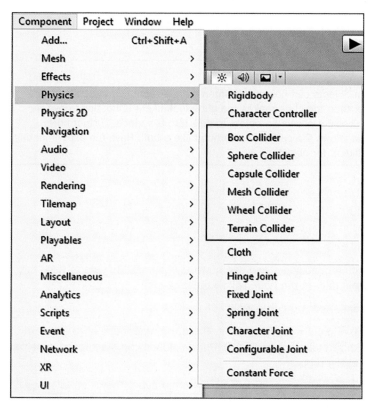

FIGURE 9.2
The available colliders.

Once a collider is added to an object, the collider object appears in the Inspector. Table 9.2 describes the collider properties. In addition to these, if a collider is a sphere or capsule, you might have an additional property, such as Radius. These geometric properties behave exactly as you would expect them to.

TABLE 9.2   Collider Properties

Property	Description
Edit Collider	Allows you to graphically adjust the collider size (and in some cases shape) in the Scene view.
Is Trigger	Determines whether the collider is a physical collider or a trigger collider. Triggers are covered in greater detail later in this hour.
Material	Allows you to apply physics materials to objects to change the way in which they behave. You can make an object behave like wood, metal, or rubber, for instance. Physics materials are covered later in this hour.
Center	Indicates the center point of the collider relative to the containing object.
Size	Specifies the size of the collider.

TIP

Mix-and-Match Colliders

Using different-shaped colliders on objects can have some interesting effects. For instance, making the collider on a cube much bigger than the cube makes the cube look like it is floating above a surface. Likewise, using a smaller collider allows an object to sink into a surface. Furthermore, putting a sphere collider on a cube allows the cube to roll around like a ball. Have fun experimenting with the various ways to make colliders for objects.

▼ TRY IT YOURSELF

Experimenting with Colliders

It's time to try out some of the different colliders and see how they interact. Be sure to save this exercise because you'll use it again later in the hour. Follow these steps:

1. Create a new project or scene. Add two cubes to it.

2. Place one cube at (0, 1, –5) and put a rigidbody on it. Place the other cube at (0, –1, –5) and scale it to (4, .1, 4) with a rotation of (0, 0, 15). Put a rigidbody on the second cube as well but uncheck the **Use Gravity** property.

3. Run the scene and notice how the top cube falls onto the other cube. They then fall away from the screen.

4. Now, on the bottom cube, under the constraints of the rigidbody component, freeze all three axes for both position and rotation.

5. Run the scene and notice how the top cube now falls and stops on the bottom cube.

6. Remove the box collider from the top cube (by right-clicking the Box Collider component and selecting **Remove Component**). Add a sphere collider to the top cube (by selecting **Component > Physics > Sphere Collider**). Give the bottom cube a rotation of (0, 0, 350).

7. Run the scene. Notice how the box rolls off of the ramp like a sphere, even though it is a cube.

8. Experiment with various colliders. Another fun experiment is to change the constraints on the bottom cube. Try freezing the y axis position and unfreezing everything else. Try out different ways of making the boxes collide.

TIP

Complex Colliders

You may have noticed a collider called the mesh collider. This collider is specifically not discussed in this book because it is quite difficult to make and very easy to get wrong. Basically, a *mesh collider* is a collider that uses a mesh to define its shape. In actuality, the other colliders (box, sphere, and so on) are mesh colliders; they are just simple built-in ones. While mesh colliders can provide for very accurate collision detection, they can also hurt performance. A good habit to get into (at least at this stage in your learning) is to compose a complex object with several basic colliders. If you have a humanoid model, for example, try spheres for the head and hands and capsules for the torso, arms, and legs. You will save on performance and still have some very sharp collision detection.

Physics Materials

Physics materials can be applied to colliders to give objects varied physical properties. For instance, you can use a rubber material to make an object bouncy or an ice material to make it slippery. You can even make your own physics materials to emulate specific materials of your choosing.

There are some premade physics materials in the Characters standard assets pack. To import them, select **Assets > Import Package > Characters**. In the Import screen, click the **None** button to deselect all and then scroll down. Check the box next to Physics Materials near the bottom and click **Import**. This adds an **Assets\Standard Assets\PhysicsMaterials** folder in your project that contains physics materials for Bouncy, Ice, Metal, Rubber, and Wood. To create a new physics material, right-click the Assets folder in the Project view and select **Create > Physic Material** or **Create > Physics Material 2D** (if you're working with 2D physics, covered in Hour 12, "2D Game Tools").

A physics material has a set of properties that determine how it behaves on a physical level (see Figure 9.3). Table 9.3 describes the physics material properties. You can apply a physics material to an object by dragging it from the Project view onto an object with a collider.

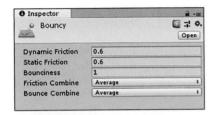

FIGURE 9.3
The properties of physics materials.

TABLE 9.3 Physics Material Properties

Property	Description
Dynamic Friction	Specifies the friction applied when an object is already moving. Lower numbers make an object more slippery.
Static Friction	Specifies the friction applied when an object is stationary. Lower numbers make an object more slippery.
Bounciness	Specifies the amount of energy retained from a collision. A value of 1 causes the object to bounce without any loss of energy; it will bounce forever. A value of 0 prevents the object from bouncing.
Friction Combine	Determines how the friction of two colliding objects is calculated. The friction can be averaged, the smallest or largest can be used, or they can be multiplied.
Bounce Combine	Determines how the bounce of two colliding objects is calculated. The bounce can be averaged, the smallest or largest can be used, or they can be multiplied.

The effects of a physics material can be as subtle or as distinct as you like. Try it out for yourself and see what kinds of interesting behaviors you can create.

Triggers

So far, you have seen physical colliders—colliders that react in a positional and rotational fashion using Unity's built-in physics engine. If you think back to Hour 6, "Game 1: *Amazing Racer*," however, you can probably remember using another type of collider. Remember how the game detected when the player entered the water hazards and finish zone? That was the trigger collider at work. A trigger detects collision just like normal colliders do, but it doesn't do anything specific about it. Instead, triggers call three specific methods that allow you, the programmer, to determine what the collision means:

```
void OnTriggerEnter(Collider other) // is called when an object enters the trigger
void OnTriggerStay(Collider other) // is called while an object stays in the trigger
void OnTriggerExit(Collider other) // is called when an object exits the trigger
```

Using these methods, you can define what happens whenever an object enters, stays in, or leaves the collider. For example, if you want to write a message to the Console whenever an object enters the perimeter of a cube, you can add a trigger to the cube. Then you attach a script to the cube with the following code:

```
void OnTriggerEnter(Collider other)
{
    print("Object has entered collider");
}
```

You might notice the one parameter to the trigger methods: the variable `other` of type `Collider`. This is a reference to the object that entered the trigger. Using that variable, you can manipulate the object however you want. For instance, to modify the preceding code to write to the Console the name of the object that enters the trigger, you can use the following:

```
void OnTriggerEnter(Collider other)
{
    print(other.gameObject.name + " has entered the trigger");
}
```

You could even go so far as to destroy the object entering the trigger with some code like this:

```
void OnTriggerEnter(Collider other)
{
    Destroy(other.gameObject);
}
```

TRY IT YOURSELF ▼

Working with Triggers

In this exercise, you'll get a chance to build an interactive scene with a functioning trigger:

1. Create a new project or scene. Add a cube and a sphere to the scene.

2. Place the cube at (–1, 1, –5) and place the sphere at (1, 1, 5).

3. Create two scripts named TriggerScript and MovementScript. Place TriggerScript on the cube and MovementScript on the sphere.

4. On the cube's collider, check **Is Trigger**. Add a rigidbody to the sphere and uncheck **Use Gravity**.

5. Add the following code to the `Update()` method of MovementScript:

```
float mX = Input.GetAxis("Mouse X") / 10;
float mY = Input.GetAxis("Mouse Y") / 10;
transform.Translate(mX, mY, 0);
```

6. Add the following code to TriggerScript:

```
void OnTriggerEnter (Collider other)
{
    print(other.gameObject.name + " has entered the cube");
}
void OnTriggerStay (Collider other)
{
    print(other.gameObject.name + " is still in the cube");
}
void OnTriggerExit (Collider other)
{
    print(other.gameObject.name + " has left the cube");
}
```

Be sure to place this code outside any methods but inside the class—that is, at the same level of indentation as the `Start()` and `Update()` methods.

7. Run the scene. Notice how the mouse moves the sphere. Collide the sphere with the cube and pay attention to the Console output. Notice how the two objects don't physically react, but they still interact. Can you work out which cell of Figure 9.4 this interaction falls into?

	Static Collider	Rigidbody Collider	Kinematic Rigidbody Collider	Static Trigger Collider	Rigidbody Trigger Collider	Kinematic Rigidbody Trigger Collider
Static Collider		collision			trigger	trigger
Rigidbody Collider	collision	collision	collision	trigger	trigger	trigger
Kinematic Rigidbody Collider		collision		trigger	trigger	trigger
Static Trigger Collider		trigger	trigger		trigger	trigger
Rigidbody Trigger Collider	trigger	trigger	trigger	trigger	trigger	trigger
Kinematic Rigidbody Trigger Collider	trigger	trigger	trigger	trigger	trigger	trigger

FIGURE 9.4
Collider interaction matrix.

NOTE

Collisions Not Working

Not all collision scenarios result in collisions actually happening. Refer to Figure 9.4 to look up whether the interaction between two objects will create a collision, a trigger method in code, or neither.

Static colliders are simply colliders on any game object that doesn't have a rigidbody component. They become rigidbody colliders when you add a rigidbody component, and these become kinematic rigidbody colliders when you check the Is Kinematic box. For each of these three colliders, you can also select Is Trigger if desired. These options lead to the six types of colliders shown in Figure 9.4.

Raycasting

Raycasting is the act of sending out an imaginary line, called a *ray*, and seeing what it hits. Imagine, for instance, looking through a telescope. Your line of sight is the ray, and whatever you can see at the other end is what your ray hits. Game developers use raycasting all the time for things like aiming, determining line of sight, gauging distance, and more. There are a few `Raycast` methods in Unity. The two most common uses are laid out here. The first `Raycast` method looks like this:

```
bool Raycast(Vector3 origin, Vector3 direction, float distance, LayerMask mask);
```

Notice that this method takes quite a few parameters. Also notice that it uses a variable called `Vector3` (which you've used before). `Vector3` is a variable type that holds three floats inside it. Using it is a great way to specify x, y, and z coordinates without requiring three separate variables. The first parameter, `origin`, is the position at which the ray starts. The second, `direction`, is the direction in which the ray travels. The third parameter, `distance`, determines how far out the ray will go, and the final variable, `mask`, determines what layers will be hit. You can omit both the `distance` and the `mask` variables. If you do, the ray will travel an infinite (or very far, in this case) distance and hit all object layers.

As mentioned earlier, there are many things you can do with rays. If you want to determine whether something is in front of the camera, for example, you can attach a script with the following code:

```
void Update()
{
    // cast the ray from the camera's position in the forward direction
    if (Physics.Raycast(transform.position, transform.forward, 10))
        print("There is something in front of the camera!");
}
```

Another way you can use this method is to find the object that the ray collided with. This version of the method uses a special variable type called `RaycastHit`. Many versions of the `Raycast` method use `distance` (or don't) and `layer mask` (or don't). The most basic way to use this version of the method, though, looks something like this:

```
bool Raycast(Vector3 origin, Vector3 direction, out Raycast hit, float distance);
```

There is one new interesting thing about this version of the method. You might have noticed that it uses a new keyword that you have not seen before: `out`. This keyword means that when the method is done running, the variable `hit` will contain whatever object was hit. The method effectively sends the value back *out* when it is done. It works this way because the `Raycast()` method already returns a Boolean variable that indicates whether it hit something. Since a method cannot return two variables, you use `out` to get more information.

▼ TRY IT YOURSELF

Casting Some Rays

In this exercise, you will create an interactive "shooting" program. This program will send a ray from the camera and destroy whatever objects it comes into contact with. Follow these steps:

1. Create a new project or scene and add four spheres to it.

2. Place the spheres at (–1, 1, –5), (1, 1.5, –5), (–1, –2, 5), and (1.5, 0, 0).

3. Create a new script called RaycastScript and attach it to the Main Camera. Inside the `Update()` method for the script, add the following:

```
float dirX = Input.GetAxis ("Mouse X");
float dirY = Input.GetAxis ("Mouse Y");
// opposite because we rotate about those axes
transform.Rotate (dirY, dirX, 0);
CheckForRaycastHit (); // this will be added in the next step
```

4. Add the method `CheckForRaycastHit()` to your script by adding the following code outside a method but inside the class:

```
void CheckForRaycastHit() {
    RaycastHit hit;
    if (Physics.Raycast (transform.position, transform.forward, out hit)) {
    print (hit.collider.gameObject.name + " destroyed!");
    Destroy (hit.collider.gameObject);
  }
}
```

5. Run your scene. Notice how moving the mouse moves the camera. Try to center the camera on each sphere. Notice how the sphere is destroyed and the message is written to the Console.

Summary

In this hour, you have learned about object interactions through collision. First, you learned about the basics of Unity's physics capabilities with rigidbodies. Then you worked with various types of colliders and collision. From there, you learned that collision is more than just stuff bouncing around, and you got hands-on with triggers. Finally, you learned to find objects by using raycasting.

Q&A

Q. Should all my objects have rigidbodies?

A. Rigidbodies are useful components that serve largely physical roles. That said, adding rigidbodies to every object can have strange side effects and may reduce performance. A good rule of thumb is to add components only when they are needed and not preemptively.

Q. There are several colliders we didn't talk about. Why not?

A. Most colliders either behave the same way as the ones covered here or are beyond the scope of this text (and are, therefore, omitted). Suffice it to say that this text still provides what you need to know to make some very fun games.

Workshop

Take some time to work through the questions here to ensure that you have a firm grasp of the material.

Quiz

1. What component is required on an object if you want it to exhibit physical traits such as falling?

2. True or False: An object can have only a single collider on it.

3. What sorts of things are raycasts useful for?

Answers

1. Rigidbody

2. False. An object can have many, and varied, colliders on it.

3. Determining what an object can see and finding objects along line of sight as well as finding distances between objects

Exercise

In this exercise, you'll create an interactive application that uses motion and triggers. The exercise requires you to creatively determine a solution (because one is not presented here). If you get stuck and need help, you can find the solution to this exercise, called Hour 9 Exercise, in the book assets for Hour 9.

1. Create a new project or scene. Add a cube to the scene and position it at (−1.5, 0, −5). Scale the cube to (.1, 2, 2) and rename it **LTrigger**.

2. Duplicate the cube (by right-clicking the cube in the Hierarchy view and selecting **Duplicate**). Name the new cube **RTrigger** and place it at (1.5, 0, −5.)

3. Add a sphere to your scene and place it at (0, 0, −5). Add a rigidbody to the sphere and uncheck **Use Gravity**.

4. Create a script named TriggerScript and place it on both LTrigger and RTrigger. Create a script called **MotionScript** and place it on the sphere.

5. Now comes the fun part. You need to create the following functionality in your application:

   ▶ The player should be able to move the sphere with the arrow keys.

   ▶ When the sphere enters, exits, or stays in either of the triggers, the corresponding message should be written to the Console. The message should indicate which of the three it is and the name of the trigger that the sphere collided with (LTrigger or RTrigger).

   ▶ There is a hidden "gotcha" built into this exercise that you need to overcome in order to make this work.

Good luck!

HOUR 10
Game 2: *Chaos Ball*

What You'll Learn in This Hour:

▶ How to design the game *Chaos Ball*

▶ How to build the *Chaos Ball* arena

▶ How to build the *Chaos Ball* entities

▶ How to build the *Chaos Ball* control objects

▶ How to further improve *Chaos Ball*

It is time once again to use what you have learned to make another game. In this hour, you'll make the game *Chaos Ball*, which is a fast-paced arcade-style game. You'll start by learning about the basic design elements of the game. From there, you'll build arena and game objects. Each object type will be made unique and given special collision properties. Then you'll add interactivity to make the game playable. You'll finish this hour by playing the game and making any necessary tweaks to improve the experience.

TIP

Completed Project

Be sure to follow along in this hour to build the complete game project. In case you get stuck, you can find a completed copy of the game in the book assets for Hour 10. Take a look at it if you need help or inspiration!

Design

In Hour 6, "Game 1: *Amazing Racer*," you learned a lot about game design elements. This time, you'll get right into them.

The Concept

This is a game slightly akin to *Pinball* or *Breakout*. The player will be in an arena. Each of the four corners will have a color, and four balls with corresponding colors will be floating around. Amid the four colored balls, there will be several yellow balls, called *chaos balls*. Chaos balls exist solely to get in the player's way and make the game challenging. They are smaller than the four colored balls, but they also move faster. Players will have a flat surface with which they will attempt to knock the colored balls into the correct corners.

The Rules

The rules for this game state how to play and also allude to some of the properties of the objects. The rules for *Chaos Ball* are as follows:

▶ The player wins when all four balls are in the correct corners. There is no loss condition.

▶ Hitting the correct corner causes a ball to disappear and the corner light to go out.

▶ All objects in the game are super-bouncy and lose no energy on impact.

▶ No ball (or player) can leave the arena.

The Requirements

The requirements for this game are simple. This is not a graphically intense game; rather, it relies on scripting and interaction for its entertainment value. The requirements for *Chaos Ball* are as follows:

▶ A walled arena to play the game in.

▶ Textures for the arena and game objects. These are provided in the Unity standard assets.

▶ Several colored balls and chaos balls. These will be generated in Unity.

▶ A character controller. This is provided by the Unity standard assets.

▶ A game manager. This will be created in Unity.

▶ A bouncy physics material. This will be created in Unity.

▶ Colored corner indicators. These will be generated in Unity.

▶ Interactive scripts. These will be written in MonoDevelop.

The Arena

The first thing you want to create is an area where the action will take place. The term *arena* is used here to give the idea that this level is quite small and also walled in. Neither the player nor any balls should be able to leave the arena. Otherwise, the arena is quite simple, as shown in Figure 10.1.

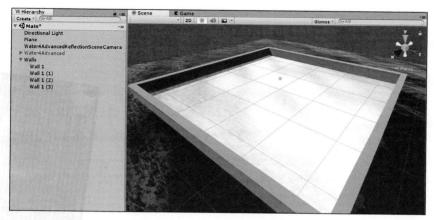

FIGURE 10.1
The arena.

Creating the Arena

As mentioned earlier, creating the arena is going to be easy because of the simplicity of the basic arena map. To create the arena, follow these steps:

1. Create a new project called Chaos Ball.

2. Click **Assets** > **Import Package** and select the **Characters** and **Environment** packages.

3. Add a plane to the scene (by selecting **GameObject** > **3D** > **Plane**). Position the plane at (0, 0, 0) and give it a scale of (5, 1, 5).

4. Delete the Main Camera.

5. Add a cube to the scene. Place the cube at (–25, 1.5, 0) and scale it to (1.5, 3, 51). Notice how it becomes a side wall for the arena. Rename the cube **Wall 1**.

6. Save the scene as **Main** in a Scenes folder.

TIP

Consolidating Objects

You might be wondering why you created only a single wall when the arena will obviously need four. The idea is that you want to do as little redundant, tedious work as possible. Often, if you require several objects that are very similar, you can create one object and then duplicate it multiple times. In this instance, you set up a single wall with its materials and properties and then simply copy it three times. You repeat the same process for the corner nodes, the chaos balls, and the colored balls. Hopefully you can see that a little planning can save you a fair bit of time. It's also worth noting that this entire process can be made even easier with the use of prefabs. Since somebody (I won't mention names) doesn't cover prefabs until the next hour, you can just do it this way for now.

Texturing

Right about now, the arena is looking pretty pitiful and bland. Everything is white, and there is only a single wall. The next step is to add some textures to liven the place up. You need to texture two objects specifically: the wall and the ground. Feel free to experiment with the texturing as you complete this step. You can make it more interesting if you'd like, but begin by following these steps:

1. Create a new folder called Materials under Assets in the Project view. Add a material to the folder (by right-clicking the folder and selecting **Create > Material**). Name the material **Wall**.

2. Apply the Sand Albedo texture to the Wall material in the Inspector view. You can do this by dragging the material onto the Albedo property or by clicking the circle selector next to the word Albedo in the Inspector (see Figure 10.2).

3. Drag the Smoothness slider to a value of **0**.

4. Set the X axis tiling to **10**.

5. Click and drag the wall material onto the wall object in the Scene view.

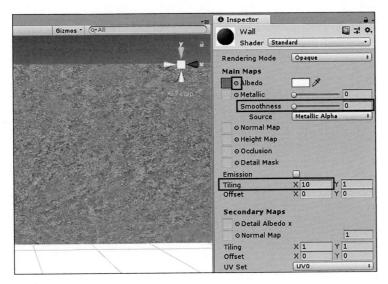

FIGURE 10.2
The wall material.

Next, you need to make the ground more interesting. Unity comes with some great water shaders, and you can use them again here:

1. In the Project view, navigate to the folder Standard Assets\Environment\ Water\Water4\ Prefabs. Drag the Water4Advanced asset into the scene.

2. Position the water centrally, at (0, .5, 0).

Creating a Super-Bouncy Material

You want objects to bounce off the walls without losing any energy, and what you need for this is a super-bouncy material. If you recall, Unity has a set of physics materials available. The bouncy material provided, however, is not quite bouncy enough for your needs. Therefore, you need to create a new material, as follows:

1. Right-click the **Materials** folder and select **Create > Physic Material**. Name the new material **SuperBouncy**.

2. Set the properties for the super-bouncy material as shown in Figure 10.3. Basically, you want to ensure that the balls are 100% bouncy, so they keep moving at the same speed.

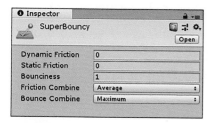

FIGURE 10.3
SuperBouncy material settings.

At this point, you could place the SuperBouncy physics material directly onto the collider of your wall. The problem, however, is that you will need to add this material onto all the walls, all the balls, and the player. Basically, everything that collides in this game needs this material. You can therefore apply the SuperBouncy material as the default material for all colliders by using the Physics Settings menu. Follow these steps:

1. Select **Edit > Project Settings > Physics**. The Physics Manager menu opens in the Inspector view (see Figure 10.4).

2. Apply the SuperBouncy material to the Default Material property.

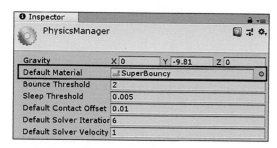

FIGURE 10.4
The Physics Manager menu.

This menu is also where you can modify the fundamentals of how physics (collision, gravity, and so on) behave. For now though, you should resist the urge to be all-powerful and leave reality as it is.

Finishing the Arena

Now that the wall and ground are complete, you can finish the arena. The hard work has been done, and all you need to do at this point is duplicate the walls (by right-clicking in the Hierarchy view and selecting **Duplicate**). The exact steps are as follows:

1. Duplicate the wall once. Place the new instance at (25, 1.5, 0).

2. Duplicate the wall again. Place it at (0, 1.5, 25) with a rotation of (0, 90, 0).

3. Duplicate the wall created in step 2 (the one that's turned) and place it at (0, 1.5, –25).

4. Create an empty game object called **Walls**. Set the position of the new object to (0, 0, 0). Group the four walls you created under this new placeholder object.

Your arena should now have four walls without any gaps or seams (refer to Figure 10.1).

Game Entities

In this section you'll create the various game objects required for playing the game. Just as with the arena wall, it is easier to create one instance of each entity and then duplicate it.

The Player

The player in this game will be a modified First Person character controller. When you created this project, you should have imported the character controller's package. You will also want to raise the controller's camera up so that the player has a better field of vision while playing. Follow these steps:

1. Drag an FPSController character controller into the scene, from the folder Assets\Characters\FirstPersonCharacter\Prefabs.

2. Position the controller at (0, 1, 0).

3. Expand the FPSController object in the Hierarchy view and locate the FirstPersonCharacter child object (which has a camera on it).

4. Position the FirstPersonCharacter at (0, 5, –3.5) with a rotation of (43, 0, 0). The camera should now be above, behind, and slightly looking down on the controller.

The next thing to do is to add a bumper to the controller. The bumper will be the flat surface off which the player will bounce balls. To do this, follow these steps:

1. Add a cube to the scene and rename the cube **Bumper**. Scale the bumper to (3.5, 3, 1).

2. In the Hierarchy view, click and drag the bumper onto the FPSController object to nest the bumper onto the controller.

3. Change the position of the bumper to (0, 0, 1) with a rotation of (0, 0, 0). The bumper is now slightly in front of the controller.

4. Give the bumper color by creating a new material (*not* a physics material) called BumperColor. Set the albedo color to something of your choosing and drag the material onto the bumper.

The last thing to do is to tweak the FPSController's default settings to make it more suitable for this game. Carefully set everything as per Figure 10.5, noting that the settings that differ from the defaults are bold.

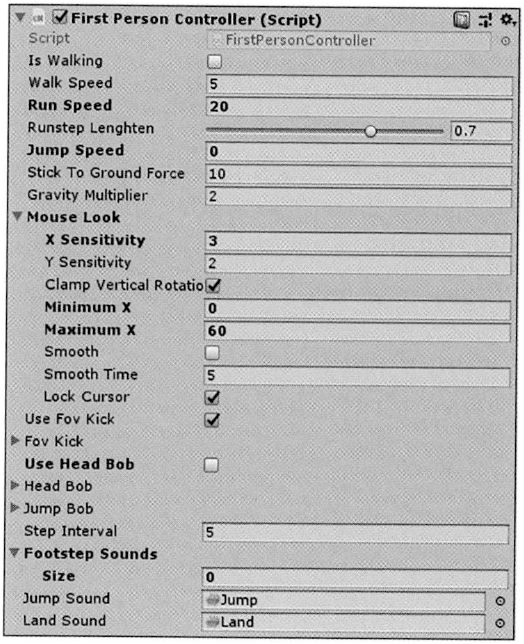

FIGURE 10.5
The FPSController script settings.

The Chaos Balls

The chaos balls will be the fast and wild balls flying around the arena and disrupting the player. In many ways, they are similar to the colored balls, so you will be working to give them universally applicable assets. To create the first chaos ball, follow these steps:

1. Add a sphere to the scene. Rename the sphere **Chaos** and position it at (12, 2, 12) with a scale of (.5, .5, .5).

2. Create a new material (*not* a physics material) for the chaos ball called ChaosBall and set the albedo color to a bright yellow color. Click and drag the material onto the sphere.

3. Add a rigidbody to the sphere. As shown in Figure 10.6, uncheck **Use Gravity**. Change the Collision Detection property to **Continuous Dynamic**. Under the Constraints property, freeze the y position because you don't want the balls to be able to go up or down.

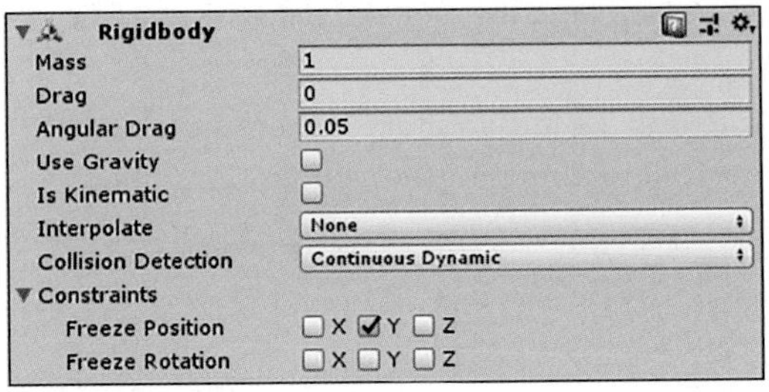

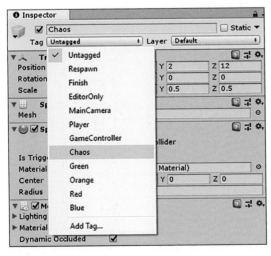

FIGURE 10.6
The chaos ball rigidbody component.

4. Open the Tag Manager (by selecting **Edit > Project Settings > Tags & Layers**), expand the **Tags** section by clicking the arrow next to Tags, and add the tag **Chaos**. While you're here, go ahead and add the tags **Green**, **Orange**, **Red**, and **Blue** as well, as they are all used later.

5. Select the Chaos sphere and change its tag to **Chaos** in the Inspector view (see Figure 10.7).

FIGURE 10.7
Choosing the Chaos tag.

The ball is now complete, but it still doesn't do anything. You need to create a script to move the ball all around the arena. In this case, create a script called VelocityScript and attach it to the chaos ball. Move the script into a Scripts folder. Listing 10.1 contains the full code for VelocityScript.

LISTING 10.1   VelocityScript.cs

```
using UnityEngine;
public class VelocityScript : MonoBehaviour
{
    public float startSpeed = 50f;
    void Start ()
    {
        Rigidbody rigidBody = GetComponent<Rigidbody> ();
        rigidBody.velocity = new Vector3 (startSpeed, 0, startSpeed);
    }
}
```

Run your scene and watch the ball begin to fly around the arena. At this point, the chaos ball is finished. In the Hierarchy view, duplicate the chaos ball four times. Scatter each ball around the arena (be sure to only change the x and z positions) and give each of them a random y axis rotation. Remember that movement along the y axis is locked, so make sure that each ball stays at a y position of 2. Finally, create an empty GameObject called Chaos Balls, position it at (0, 0, 0), and child the balls to it to keep your Hierarchy tidy.

The Colored Balls

Whereas the chaos balls are actually a color (yellow), they are not considered colored balls in this game; rather, the colored balls are the four specific balls needed to win the game. They should be red, orange, blue, and green. As with the chaos balls, you can make a single ball and then duplicate it to make the creation of the colored balls easier.

To create the first ball, follow these steps:

1. Add a sphere to the scene and rename it **Blue Ball**. Position the sphere somewhere near the middle of the arena and make sure the y position is **2**.

2. Create a new material called BlueBall and set its color to blue, the same way you set the color of the chaos balls to yellow. While you're at it, go ahead and create RedBall, GreenBall, and OrangeBall materials and set each one to the appropriate color. Click and drag the BlueBall material onto the sphere.

3. Add a rigidbody to the sphere. Uncheck **Use Gravity**, set the collision detection to **Continuous Dynamic**, and freeze the y position under Constraints.

4. Previously, you created the Blue tag. Now change the sphere's tag to Blue just as you set the tag for the chaos ball (refer to Figure 10.7).

5. Attach the velocity script to the sphere. In the Inspector, locate the Velocity Script (Script) component and change the Start Speed property to **25** (see Figure 10.8). This causes the sphere to initially move more slowly than the chaos balls.

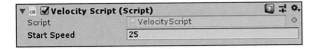

FIGURE 10.8
Changing the Start Speed property.

If you run the scene now, you should see the blue ball moving rapidly around the arena.

Now you need to create the other three balls. Each one will be a duplicate of the blue ball. To create the other balls, follow these steps:

1. Duplicate the Blue Ball object. Rename the new ball to its color: **Red Ball**, **Orange Ball**, or **Green Ball**.

2. Give the new ball a tag corresponding to its name. It is important for the name and the tag to be the same.

3. Drag the appropriate color material onto the new ball. It is important for the ball to be the same color as its name.

4. Give the ball a random location and rotation in the arena but ensure that its y position is **2**.

At this point, the game entities are complete. If you run the scene, you see all the balls bouncing around the arena.

The Control Objects

Now that you have all the pieces in place, it is time to gamify them. That is, it is time to turn them into a playable game. To do that, you need to create the four corner goals, the goal scripts, and the game controller. When you are done, you will have a game.

The Goals

Each of the four corners has a specific colored goal that corresponds with a colored ball. The idea is that when a ball enters a goal, the goal will check the ball's tag. If the tag matches the color of the goal, there is a match. When a match is found, the ball is destroyed and the goal is set to solved. As with the ball objects earlier, you can configure a single goal and then duplicate it to match your needs.

To set up the initial goal, follow these steps:

1. Create an empty game object (by selecting **GameObject > Create Empty**). Rename the game object **Blue Goal** and assign the tag Blue to it. Position the game object at (–22, 2, –22).

2. Attach a box collider to the goal and check the **Is Trigger** property. Change the size of the box collider to (3, 2, 3).

3. Attach a light to the goal (by selecting **Component > Rendering > Light**). Make it a point light and make it the same color as the goal (see Figure 10.9). Change the Intensity of the light to **3** and the Indirect Multiplier to **0**.

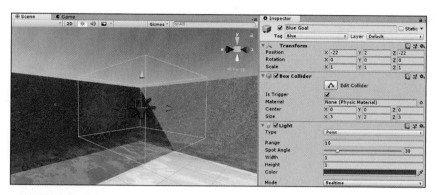

FIGURE 10.9
The blue goal.

Next, you need to create a script called GoalScript and attach it to the blue goal. Listing 10.2 shows the contents of the script.

LISTING 10.2   GoalScript.cs

```
using UnityEngine;
public class GoalScript : MonoBehaviour
{
    public bool isSolved = false;
    void OnTriggerEnter (Collider collider)
    {
        GameObject collidedWith = collider.gameObject;
        if (collidedWith.tag == gameObject.tag)
        {
            isSolved = true;
            GetComponent<Light>().enabled = false;
            Destroy (collidedWith);
        }
    }
}
```

As you can see in the script, the OnTriggerEnter() method checks the tag of every object that contacts it against its own tag. If they match, the object is destroyed, the goal is flagged as solved, and that goal's light is disabled.

When the script is complete and attached to the goal, it is time to duplicate it. To create the other goals, follow these steps:

1. Duplicate the Blue Goal. Name the new goal according to its color: **Red Goal**, **Green Goal**, or **Orange Goal**.

2. Change the tag of the goal to its corresponding color.

3. Change the color of the point light to the goal's corresponding color.

4. Position the goal. The colors can go in any corner as long as each goal gets its own corner. The three other corner positions are (22, 2, –22), (22, 2, 22), and (–22, 2, 22).

5. Organize the goals under a new empty game object called **Goals**.

All the goals should now be set up and operational.

The Game Manager

The last element needed to finish the game is the game manager. This controller will be responsible for checking each goal every frame and determining when all four goals are solved. For this particular game, the game manager is very simple. To create the game manager, follow these steps:

1. Add an empty game object to the scene. Move it someplace out of the way. Rename it **Game Manager**.

2. Create a script called GameManager and add the code from Listing 10.3 to it. Attach the script to the game manager.

3. With the game manager selected, click and drag each goal to its corresponding property on the Game Manager (Script) component (see Figure 10.10).

LISTING 10.3   Game Control Script

```
using UnityEngine;
public class GameManager : MonoBehaviour
{
    public GoalScript blue, green, red, orange;
    private bool isGameOver = true;
    void Update ()
    {
        // If all four goals are solved then the game is over
        isGameOver = blue.isSolved && green.isSolved && red.isSolved &&
        orange.isSolved;
    }
void OnGUI ()
```

```
    {
        if(isGameOver)
        {
            Rect rect = new Rect (Screen.width / 2 - 100, Screen.height / 2 - 50, 200, 75);
            GUI.Box (rect, "Game Over");
            Rect rect2 = new Rect (Screen.width / 2 - 30, Screen.height / 2 - 25, 60, 50);
            GUI.Label (rect2, "Good Job!");
        }
    }
}
```

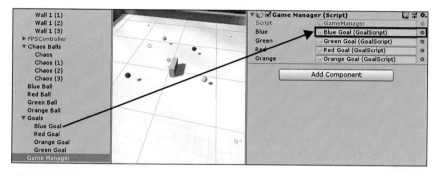

FIGURE 10.10
Adding the goals to the game controller.

As you can see in the script shown in Listing 10.3, the game manager has a reference to each of the four goals. Every frame, the manager checks to see if all the goals are solved. If they are, the manager sets the variable `isGameOver` to `true` and displays the "game over" message on the screen.

Congratulations. *Chaos Ball* is now complete!

Improving the Game

Even though *Chaos Ball* is a complete game, it is hardly as good as it could be. Several features that would greatly improve gameplay have been omitted. They were left out for brevity and to give you an opportunity to experiment with the game and make it better. In a way, you could say that *Chaos Ball* is now a complete prototype. It is a playable example of the game, but it lacks polish. You are encouraged to go back through this hour and look for ways to make the game better. Think about the following as you play it:

▶ Is the game too easy or hard?

▶ What would make it easier or harder?

> ► What would give it a "wow" factor?

> ► What parts of the game are fun? What parts of the game are tedious?

The exercise at the end of this hour gives you an opportunity to improve the game and add some features that will improve it. Note that if you get any errors, it means you missed a step. Be sure to go back through and double-check everything to resolve any errors that arise.

Summary

In this hour, you made the game *Chaos Ball*. You started by designing the game, based on the stated concept, rules, and requirements. From there, you sculpted the arena and learned that sometimes you can make a single object and duplicate it to save time. From there, you created the player, the chaos balls, the colored balls, the goals, and the game controller. You finished by playing the game and thinking of ways to improve it.

Q&A

Q. Why use Continuous Dynamic collision detection on the chaos balls? I thought this setting reduced performance.

A. Continuous collision detection can, in fact, reduce performance. In this instance, it is needed, however. The chaos balls are small and fast enough that sometimes they can pass right through the walls.

Q. Why did I need to create a Chaos tag if I never used it?

A. You now have this tag ready for making improvements in the following exercise.

Workshop

Take some time to work through the questions here to ensure that you have a firm grasp of the material.

Quiz

1. How does a *Chaos Ball* player lose the game?

2. What is the positional axis on which all the ball objects are constrained?

3. True or False: The goals in *Chaos Ball* use the method `OnTriggerEnter()` to determine whether an object is the correct ball.

4. Why are some basic features omitted from the game *Chaos Ball*?

Answers

1. This is a trick question. The player cannot lose the game.

2. The y axis

3. True

4. To give you a chance to add them

Exercise

One of the best parts of making games is that you get to make them the way you want. Following a guide can be a good learning experience, but you don't get the satisfaction of making a custom game. In this exercise, you have an opportunity to modify the game a little to make something more unique. Exactly how you change the game is up to you. Here are some suggestions:

▶ Try adding a button that allows the player to play again whenever the game is completed. (Graphical user interface elements haven't been covered yet, but this feature exists in the *Amazing Racer* game you created in Hour 6, so see if you can figure it out.)

▶ Try adding a timer so that the player knows how long it took to win.

▶ Try adding variations of the chaos balls.

▶ Try adding a chaos goal that you must bounce all the chaos balls into.

▶ Try changing the size or shape of the player's bumper.

▶ Try making a complex bumper out of many shapes.

▶ Try covering up the water with a terrain, plane, or other game objects around the border of the arena.

What You'll Learn in This Hour:

▶ The basics of prefabs

▶ How to work with custom prefabs

▶ How to instantiate prefabs in code

A *prefab* is a complex object that has been bundled up so that it can be re-created over and over with little extra work. In this hour, you'll learn all about them, starting with what they are and what they do. From there, you'll learn how to create prefabs in Unity. You'll learn about the concept of *inheritance*. You'll finish the lesson by learning how to add prefabs to a scene both through the editor and through code.

Prefab Basics

As mentioned earlier, a prefab is a special type of asset that bundles up game objects. Unlike normal game objects that exist only as a part of a single scene, prefabs are stored as assets. As such they can be seen in the Project view and reused over and over across many scenes. You can, for example, build a complex object, such as an enemy, turn it into a prefab, and then use that prefab to build an army. You can also create copies of prefabs with code. This allows you to generate a nearly infinite number of objects at runtime. The best part is that any game object or collection of game objects can be put in a prefab. The possibilities are endless!

NOTE

Thought Exercise

If you are having trouble understanding the importance of prefabs, consider this: In the preceding hour, you made the game *Chaos Ball*. When making that game, you had to make a single chaos ball and duplicate it four times. What if you want to make changes to all chaos balls at the same time, regardless of where they are in your scene or project? Doing so can be difficult—sometimes prohibitively so. Prefabs make it incredibly easy, though.

What if you have a game that uses an orc enemy type? Again, you could set up a single orc and then duplicate it many times, but what if you want to use the orc again in another scene? You have to completely remake the orc in the new scene. If the orc were a prefab, though, it would be a part of the project and could be reused again in any number of scenes. Prefabs are an important aspect of Unity game development.

Prefab Terminology

You need to know some particular terminology related to working with prefabs. If you are familiar with the concepts of object-oriented programming, you may notice some similarities:

▶ **Prefab:** The prefab is the base object. It exists only in the Project view. Think of it as the blueprint.

▶ **Instance:** An instance is an actual object of the prefab in a scene. If the prefab is a blueprint for a car, an instance is an actual car. If an object in the Scene view is referred to as a prefab, it is really a prefab instance. The phrase *instance of a prefab* is synonymous with *object of a prefab* or even *clone* of a prefab.

▶ **Instantiate:** Instantiation is the process of creating an instance of a prefab. Instantiate is a verb, used like this: "I need to instantiate an instance of this prefab."

▶ **Inheritance:** With prefabs, inheritance is not the same as standard programming inheritance. In this case, the term *inheritance* refers to the nature by which all instances of a prefab are linked to the prefab itself. This is covered in greater detail later in this hour.

Prefab Structure

Whether you know it or not, you have already worked with prefabs. Unity's character controllers are prefabs. To instantiate an object of a prefab into a scene, you only need to click and drag it into place in the Scene view or Hierarchy view (see Figure 11.1).

When looking at the Hierarchy view, you can always tell which objects are instances of prefabs because they appear blue. This can be a subtle color difference, so note that you can also tell that an object is a prefab by looking at the top of the Inspector (see Figure 11.2).

Just as with non-prefab complex objects, complex instances of prefabs also have an arrow that allows you to expand them and modify the objects inside.

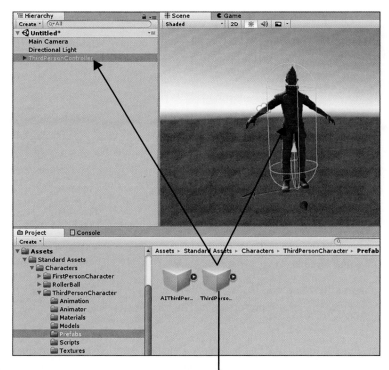

Drag into Scene or Hierarchy

FIGURE 11.1
Adding a prefab instance to a scene.

FIGURE 11.2
The appearance of prefab instances in the Inspector.

Because a prefab is an asset that belongs to a project and not to a particular scene, you can edit a prefab in the Project view or the Scene view. If you edit an instance of a prefab in the Scene view, you must save the changes back to the prefab by clicking the Apply button in the top right of the Inspector (refer to Figure 11.2).

Just like game objects, prefabs can be complex. You can edit the child elements of a prefab by clicking the arrow on the right side of the prefab (see Figure 11.3). Clicking this arrow expands the object for editing. Clicking again condenses the prefab again.

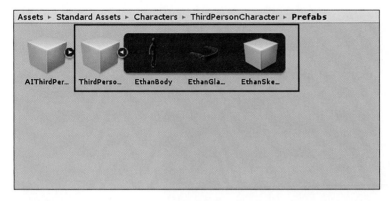

FIGURE 11.3
Expanding the contents of a prefab in the Project view.

Working with Prefabs

Using Unity's built-in prefabs is nice, but often you want to create your own. Creating a prefab is a two-step process. The first step is to create the prefab asset. The second step is to fill the asset with some content.

Creating a prefab is really easy. Simply right-click in the Project view and select **Create > Prefab** (see Figure 11.4). A new prefab appears, and you can name it whatever you want. Because the prefab is empty, it appears as an empty white box.

FIGURE 11.4
Creating a new prefab.

As with all other assets, it is generally a good idea to start by creating a folder under Assets in the Project view to contain your prefabs. Creating a folder to contain your prefabs is not required, but it is a great organization step and should be done to prevent confusion between prefabs and original assets (such as meshes or sprites).

The next step is to fill the prefab with something. Any game object can go into a prefab. You simply need to create the object once in the Scene view and then click and drag it onto the prefab asset.

Alternatively, you can shorten this process to a single step by simple dragging any game object from the Hierarchy view down into the project view. Doing so creates the prefab, names it, and fills it—all at the same time (see Figure 11.5).

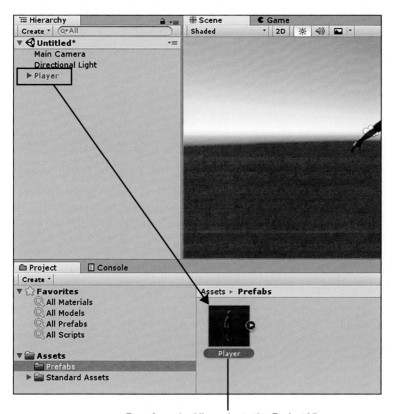

Drag from the Hierarchy to the Project View

FIGURE 11.5
A faster way to create prefabs.

▼ TRY IT YOURSELF

Creating a Prefab

Follow these steps to create a prefab of a complex game object, which you will use later in this hour (so don't delete it!):

1. Create a new project or scene. Add a cube and a sphere to the scene. Rename the cube **Lamp**.

2. Position the cube at (0, 1, 0) with a scale of (.5, 2, .5). Add a rigidbody to the cube. Position the sphere at (0, 2.2, 0). Put a point light component on the sphere.

3. Click and drag the sphere in the Hierarchy view onto the cube to nest the sphere under the cube (see Figure 11.6).

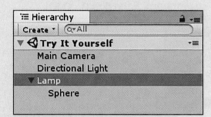

FIGURE 11.6
The sphere nested under the cube.

4. Create a new folder under the Assets folder in the Project view. Name the new folder **Prefabs**.

5. In the Hierarchy view, click and drag the Lamp game object (which contains the sphere) into the Project view (see Figure 11.7). Notice that this creates a prefab that looks like a lamp. Also notice that the cube and sphere in the Hierarchy view turn blue. At this point, you can delete the cube and sphere from the scene because they are now contained in the prefab.

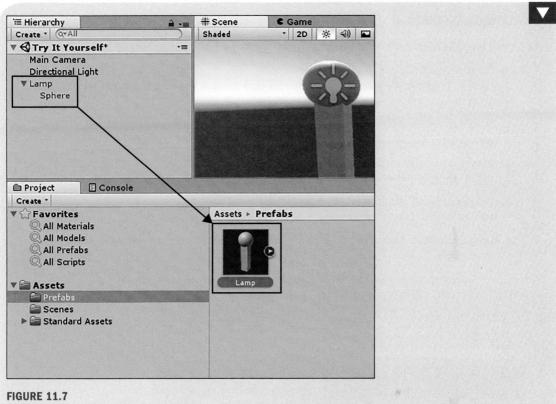

FIGURE 11.7
Adding an object to a prefab.

Adding a Prefab Instance to a Scene

Once a prefab asset is created, you can add it as many times as you want to a scene or any number of scenes in a project. To add a prefab instance to a scene, all you need to do is click and drag the prefab from the Project view into place in the Scene view, or Hierarchy view.

If you drag into the Scene view, the prefab is instantiated where you drag. If you drag into a blank part of the Hierarchy view, its initial position is whatever is set in the prefab. If you drag onto another object in the Hierarchy view, the prefab becomes a child of that object.

▼ TRY IT YOURSELF

Creating Multiple Prefab Instances

In the Try It Yourself "Creating a Prefab," you made a Lamp prefab. This time, you will be using that prefab to create many lamps in a scene. Be sure to save the scene created here because you will use it later in this hour. Follow these steps:

1. Create a new scene in the same project used for the Try It Yourself "Creating a Prefab," and call this scene **Lamps**.

2. Create a plane and ensure that it is positioned at (0, 0, 0). Rename the plane **Floor**. Optionally, give the floor a gray material so that shadows appear more clearly on it.

3. Drag your Lamp prefab onto the floor in the Scene view. Notice how the lamp tracks to the collider of the floor.

4. Drag three more Lamp prefabs onto the floor and position them near the corners (see Figure 11.8).

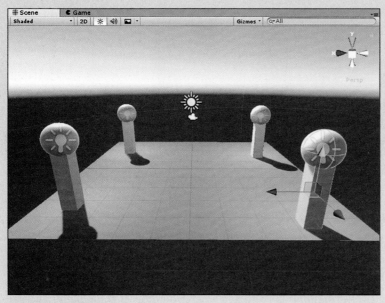

FIGURE 11.8
Placing lamps in the scene.

Inheritance

When the term *inheritance* is used in conjunction with prefabs, it refers to the link by which the instances of a prefab are connected to the actual prefab asset. That is, if you change the prefab asset, all objects of the prefab are also automatically changed. This is incredibly useful. You would be like many other game programmers if you put a large number of prefab objects into a scene only to realize that they all need a minor change. Without inheritance, you would have to change each one individually.

There are two ways you can change a prefab asset. The first is by making changes in the Project view. Just selecting the prefab asset in the Project view brings up its components and properties in the Inspector view. If you need to modify a child element, you can expand the prefab (as described earlier this hour) and change those objects in a similar fashion.

Another way you can modify a prefab asset is to drag an instance into the scene. From there, you can make any major modifications you would like. When you're finished, simply click **Apply** at the top right of the Inspector.

TRY IT YOURSELF ▼

Updating Prefabs

So far in this hour, you have created a prefab and added several instances of it to a scene. Now you have a chance to modify the prefab and see how it affects the assets already in the scene. For this exercise, you should use the scene created in the Try It Yourself "Creating Multiple Prefab Instances." If you have not completed that one yet, you need to do so before following these steps:

1. Open the Lamps scene from the Try It Yourself "Creating Multiple Prefab Instances."

2. Select the **Lamp** prefab from the Project view and expand it (by clicking the arrow on the right side). Select the **Sphere** child game object. In the Inspector, change the color of the light to red. Notice how the prefabs in the scene automatically change (see Figure 11.9).

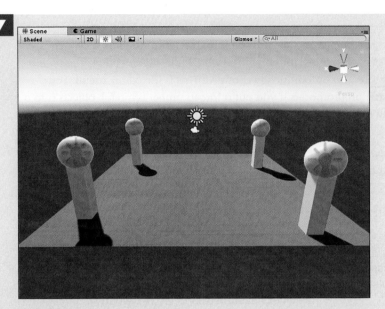

FIGURE 11.9
The modified lamp instances.

3. Select one of the lamp instances in the scene. Expand it by clicking the arrow to the left of its name in the Hierarchy view and then select the **Sphere** child object. Change the sphere's light back to white. Notice that the other prefab objects don't change.

4. With the lamp still selected, click **Apply** to update the prefab asset with the modified lamp instance's changes. Notice that all the instances change back to a white light.

Breaking Prefab Links

Sometimes you need to break a prefab instance's link to the prefab asset. You might want to do this if you need an object of the prefab but you don't want the object to change if the prefab ever changes. Breaking an instance's link to the prefab does not change the instance in any way. The instance still maintains all its objects, components, and properties. The only difference is that it is no longer an instance of the prefab and therefore is no longer affected by inheritance.

To break an object's link to the prefab asset, simply select the object in the Hierarchy view. After selecting it, click **GameObject > Break Prefab Instance**. The object does not change, but its name turns from blue to black. After the link is broken, it can be reapplied by clicking **Revert** in the Inspector view.

Instantiating Prefabs Through Code

Placing prefab objects into a scene is a great way to build a consistent and planned level. Sometimes, however, you want to create instances at runtime. Maybe you want enemies to respawn, or you want them to be randomly placed. It is also possible that you need so many instances that placing them by hand is no longer feasible. Whatever the reason, instantiating prefabs through code is a good solution.

There are two ways to instantiate prefab objects in a scene, and they both use the `Instantiate()` method. The first way is to use `Instantiate()` like this:

```
Instantiate(GameObject prefab);
```

As you can see, this method simply reads in a `GameObject` variable and makes a copy of it. The location, rotation, and scale of the new object are the same as those of the one being cloned. The second way to use the `Instantiate()` method is like this:

```
Instantiate(GameObject prefab, Vector3 position, Quaternion rotation);
```

This method requires three parameters. The first is still the object to copy. The second and third parameters are the desired position and rotation of the new object. You might have noticed that the rotation is stored in something called a *quaternion*. Just know that this is how Unity stores rotation information. (The true application of the quaternion is beyond the scope of this hour.)

The exercise at the end of this hour shows an example of the two methods of instantiating objects in code.

Summary

In this hour, you have learned all about prefabs in Unity. You started by learning the basics of prefabs: the concept, terminology, and structure. From there, you learned to make your own prefabs. You explored how to create them, add them to a scene, modify them, and break their links. Finally, you learned how to instantiate prefab objects through code.

Q&A

Q. Prefabs seem a lot like classes in object-oriented programming (OOP). Is that accurate?

A. Yes. There are many similarities between classes and prefabs. Both are like blueprints, objects of both are created through instantiation, and objects of both are linked to the original.

Q. How many objects of a prefab can exist in a scene?

A. As many as you want. Be aware, though, that after you get above a certain number, the performance of the game will be impacted. Every time you create an instance, it is permanent until it is destroyed. Therefore, if you create 10,000 instances, there will be 10,000 of them just sitting in your scene.

Workshop

Take some time to work through the questions here to ensure that you have a firm grasp of the material.

Quiz

1. What is the term for creating an instance of a prefab asset?

2. What are two ways to modify a prefab asset?

3. What is inheritance?

4. How many ways can you use the `Instantiate()` method?

Answers

1. Instantiation

2. You can modify a prefab asset through the Project view or by modifying an instance in the Scene view and clicking **Apply** in the Inspector.

3. It is the link that connects the prefab asset to its instances. It basically means that when the asset changes, the objects change as well.

4. Two. You can specify just the prefab or you can also specify the position and rotation.

Exercise

In this exercise, you'll work once again with the prefab you made earlier in this hour. This time, you will instantiate objects of the prefab through code and hopefully have some fun with it:

1. Create a new scene in the same project where you're storing the Lamp prefab. Click the **Lamp** prefab in the Project view and change its position to (–1, 0, –5).

2. Delete the Directional Light game object from the scene.

3. Add an empty game object to the scene and rename it **Spawn Point**. Position it at (1, 1, –5). Add a plane to your scene and position it at (0, 0, –4) with a rotation of (270, 0, 0).

4. Add a script to your project. Name the script **PrefabGenerator** and attach it to the spawn point object. Listing 11.1 shows the complete code for the PrefabGenerator script.

LISTING 11.1 PrefabGenerator.cs

```
using UnityEngine;

public class PrefabGenerator : MonoBehaviour
{
    public GameObject prefab;

    void Update()
    {
        // Whenever we hit the B key we will generate a prefab at the
        // position of the original prefab
        // Whenever we hit the space key, we will generate a prefab at the
        // position of the spawn object that this script is attached to
        if (Input.GetKeyDown(KeyCode.B))
        {
            Instantiate(prefab);
        }

        if (Input.GetKeyDown(KeyCode.Space))
        {
            Instantiate(prefab, transform.position, transform.rotation);
        }
    }
}
```

5. With the spawn point selected, drag the Lamp prefab onto the Prefab property of the Prefab Generator component. Now run the scene. Notice how pressing the **B** key creates a lamp at its default prefab position and how pressing the **spacebar** creates an object at the spawn point.

HOUR 12
2D Game Tools

What You'll Learn in This Hour:

▶ How orthographic cameras work

▶ How to position sprites in 3D space

▶ How to move and collide sprites

Unity is a powerhouse at creating both 2D and 3D games. A pure 2D game is one in which all the assets are simple flat images called *sprites*. In a 3D game, the assets are 3D models with 2D textures applied to them. Typically, in a 2D game, the player can move in only two dimensions (for example, left, right, up, down). This hour is devoted to helping you understand the basics of creating 2D games in Unity.

The Basics of 2D Games

The principles of design for a 2D game are the same as for a 3D game. You still need to consider the concepts, rules, and requirements of the game. There are pros and cons to making a game 2D. On one hand, a 2D game can be simple and much cheaper to produce. On the other hand, the limitations of 2D can make some types of games impossible. 2D games are built from images called sprites. These are a bit like cardboard cutouts in a kids' stage show. You can move them around, place them in front of each other, and cause them to interact to create a rich environment.

When you create a new Unity project, you have the choice of 2D or 3D (see Figure 12.1). Selecting 2D defaults the Scene view to 2D mode and makes the camera orthographic (as discussed later this hour). Another thing you will notice about a 2D project is that there's no directional light or skybox in the scene. In fact, 2D games are generally unlit because sprites are drawn by a simple type of renderer called a "sprite renderer." Unlike a texture, lighting does not generally affect the way a sprite is drawn.

FIGURE 12.1
Setting a project to 2D.

TIP

2D Game Challenges

2D games bring unique design challenges. Examples include the following:

▶ The lack of depth makes immersion harder to achieve.

▶ A lot of game types don't translate well to 2D.

▶ 2D games are generally unlit, so the sprites have to be carefully drawn and arranged.

The 2D Scene View

A project with 2D defaults will already be in the 2D Scene view. To change between 2D and 3D view, click the 2D button at the top of the Scene view (see Figure 12.2). The 3D gizmo disappears when you enter 2D mode.

You can move around in 2D mode by right-clicking (or middle-clicking) and dragging in the scene. You can use the mouse wheel to zoom, or you can use the scroll gesture on a trackpad. You can use the background grid to orient yourself. You no longer have the scene gizmo, but you don't need it. Your scene orientation in 2D mode doesn't change.

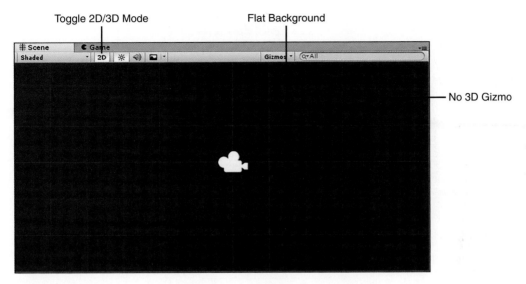

FIGURE 12.2
The 2D Scene view.

Creating and Placing a Sprite

You'll look at importing and using sprites later. For now, you will just create a simple sprite and add it to the scene:

1. Create a new project, this time selecting 2D (refer to Figure 12.1). The project defaults are now set up for a 2D game. (Note that there is no directional light in a 2D game.)

2. Add a new folder to the project and name it **Sprites**. Right-click in the Project view and select **Create > Sprites > Hexagon**.

3. Drag the newly created Hexagon sprite into the Scene view. Notice the Sprite Renderer component in the Inspector.

4. While the sprite asset is white, you can change its color by using the Sprite Renderer component, so choose a different color for the sprite (see Figure 12.3).

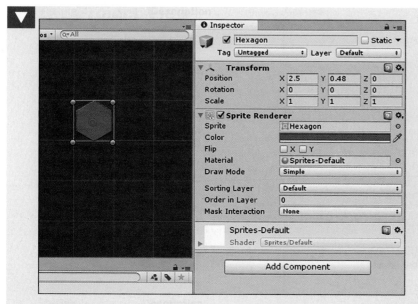

FIGURE 12.3
The Hexagon sprite.

TIP

The Rect Tool

As explained in Hour 2, "Game Objects," the Rect transform tool is ideal for manipulating rect(angular) sprites. You can access this tool at the top left of the Unity editor or by pressing the **T** key. Try playing with it while you have a sprite onscreen.

Orthographic Cameras

Because you set up your project as a 2D project, the camera defaults to the orthographic type. This means the camera doesn't show perspective distortion; rather, all objects appear the same size and shape, regardless of distance. This type of camera is suitable for 2D games, where you control the apparent depth of sprites by their size and sorting layer.

A *sorting layer* allows you to determine which sprites and groups of sprites draw in front of each other. Imagine that you are setting up a stage. You would want the background props behind the foreground props. If you sort the sprites from front to back properly and choose appropriate sizes, you can give the impression of depth.

You can see the camera type for yourself by clicking **Main Camera** and noticing that Projection is set to **Orthographic** in the Inspector (see Figure 12.4). (The rest of the camera settings are covered in Hour 5, "Lights and Cameras.")

TIP

The Size of an Orthographic Camera

Often you want to change the relative sizes of sprites in your scene all at once, without resizing them. If the camera doesn't take depth into account, you may be wondering how you do this, as you can't just move them closer to the camera.

In this case, you need to use the Size property in the Inspector (see Figure 12.4), which appears only for orthographic projection cameras. This is the number of world units from the center to the top of the camera's view. That might seem odd, but it has to do with measurements such as aspect ratio. In essence, though, bigger numbers "zoom out," while smaller numbers "zoom in."

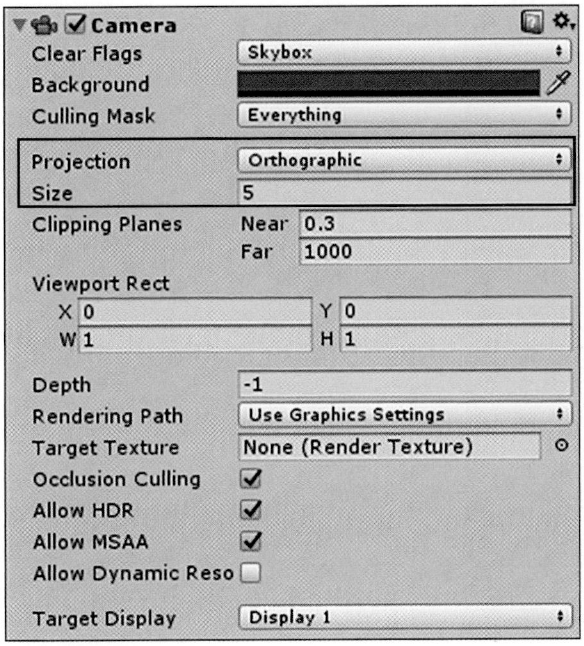

FIGURE 12.4
Setting the size of an orthographic camera.

Adding Sprites

Adding a sprite to a scene is a very easy process. Once a sprite image is imported into a project (again, super simple), you simply need to drag it into your scene.

Importing Sprites

If you wish to use your own image as a sprite, you need to make sure Unity knows that it is a sprite. Here's how you import a sprite:

1. Locate the ranger.png file in the book assets (or use your own).

2. Drag the image into the Project view in Unity. If you created a 2D project, it imports as a sprite. If you made a 3D project, you need to tell Unity to use it as a sprite by setting Texture Type to **Sprite** (see Figure 12.5).

3. Simply drag the sprite into the Scene view. It's that simple! Note that if your Scene view is not in 2D mode, the sprite that is created won't necessarily be at a z axis position of 0 (like the rest of the sprites).

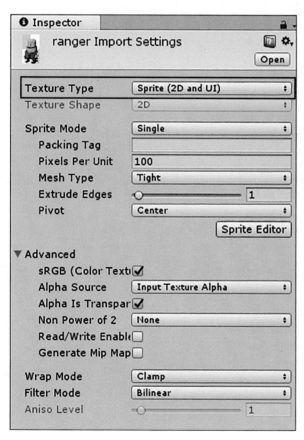

FIGURE 12.5
Making an image texture into a sprite.

Sprite Mode

Single sprites are fine, but the fun really starts when you start animating. Unity provides some powerful tools for using sprite sheets. A *sprite sheet* is an image with multiple frames of an animation laid out in a grid.

The Sprite Editor (which you will explore in a moment) helps you automatically extract tens or hundreds of different animation frames from a single image.

Exploring Sprite Modes

Follow these steps to explore the difference between the Single and Multiple sprite modes:

1. Create a new 2D project or a new scene in your existing 2D project.

2. Import rangerTalking.png from the book asset files or source your own sprite sheet.

3. Ensure that Sprite Mode is set to **Single** and expand the sprite tray in the Project view to make sure Unity is treating this image as a single sprite (see Figure 12.6).

FIGURE 12.6
Importing a sprite in Single mode.

4. Now change the Sprite Mode to **Multiple** and click **Apply** at the bottom of the Inspector. Note that there is temporarily no tray to expand.

5. Click the **Sprite Editor** button in the Inspector; a window pops up. Click the **Slice** drop-down, set Type to **Automatic**, and click **Slice** (see Figure 12.7). Notice how the outlines are automatically detected but are different for each frame.

6. Set Type to **Grid by Cell Size** and adjust the grid to fit your sprite. For the supplied image, the grid values are x = 62 and y = 105. Leave the other settings as they are and click **Slice**. Notice that the borders are now more even.

7. Click **Apply** to save the changes and close the Sprite Editor.

8. Look at your sprite in the Project view and note that the tray now contains all the individual frames, ready for animation.

Click to Start Slicing

Select Type   Perform Slice   Sprite Outlines

Apply Changes

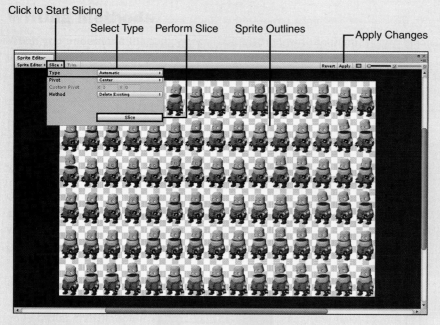

FIGURE 12.7
The Sprite Editor window.

NOTE

Sprite Sheet Animation

The Try It Yourself "Exploring Sprite Modes" shows how to import and configure a sprite sheet. As mentioned earlier, sprite sheets are often used for 2D animations. You will learn about sprite-based animations in Hour 17, "Animations."

Imported Sprite Sizes

If you need to scale sprite images so that their sizes match, you have a couple options. The best way to fix sprite sizing issues is to open the sprites in image editing software such as Photoshop and make the corrections. You may not always have that capability (or time), though. Another option is to use the scale tool in the scene. Doing that, however, adds inefficiencies and potentially "odd" scaling behavior in the future.

If you need to consistently scale a sprite—for example, SpriteA always needs to be half as big, consider instead using the Pixels per Unit import setting. This setting determines how many world units a sprite of a given resolution occupies. For example, a 640 × 480 image imported with a Pixels per Unit setting of **100** would occupy 6.4 × 4.8 world units.

Draw Order

To determine what sprites draw in front of each other, Unity has a sorting layer system. It is controlled by two settings on the Sprite Renderer component: Sorting Layer and Order in Layer (see Figure 12.8).

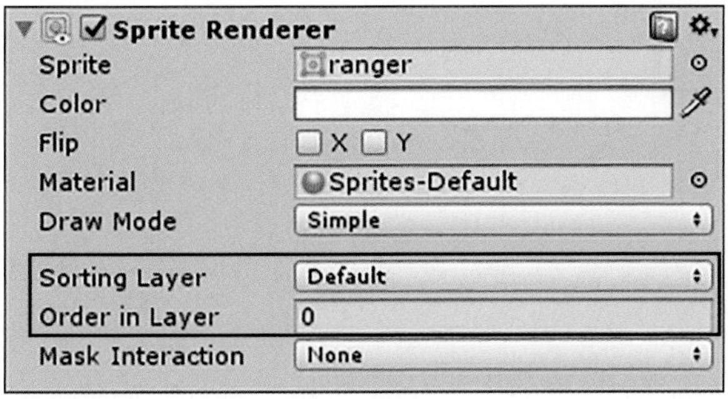

FIGURE 12.8
The default sprite layer properties.

Sorting Layers

You can use sorting layers to group major categories of sprites by depth. When you first create a new project, there is only one sorting layer, called Default (refer to Figure 12.8). Imagine that you have a simple 2D platform game with a background consisting of hills, trees, and clouds. In this case, you would want to create a sorting layer called Background.

▼ TRY IT YOURSELF

Creating Sorting Layers

Follow these steps to create and assign a new sorting layer to a sprite:

1. Create a new project and import the entire 2D asset pack (by selecting **Assets > Import Package > 2D**).

2. Locate the sprite BackgroundGreyGridSprite in the folder Standard Assets\2D\Sprites and drag it into the scene. Set its position to (–2.5, –2.5, 0) and scale it to (2, 2, 1).

3. Add a new sorting layer by clicking the **Sorting Layer** drop-down of the Sprite Renderer component and then clicking **Add Sorting Layer** (see Figure 12.9).

FIGURE 12.9
Adding new sorting layers.

4. Add two new layers called Background and Player. Do this by clicking the + button under Sorting Layers (see Figure 12.10). Note that the lowest layer in the list, currently Player, will be drawn last and will thus appear in front of all others in the game. It is a good idea to move the default layer to the bottom so that new items are drawn on top of other layers.

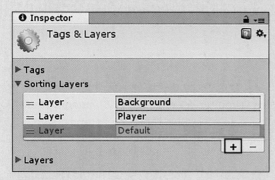

FIGURE 12.10
Managing sorting layers.

5. Re-select the BackgroundGreyGridSprite game object and set its sorting layer to the newly created **Background**.

6. In the Project view, search for the sprite RobotBoyCrouch00 and drag it into the scene. Position it at (0, 0, 0).

7. Set Sorting Layer for this sprite to **Player** (see Figure 12.11). Note that the player is drawn on top of the background. Now try going back into the Tags & Layers Manager (by selecting **Edit > Project Settings > Tags and Layers**) and rearranging the layers so that the background is drawn on top of the player.

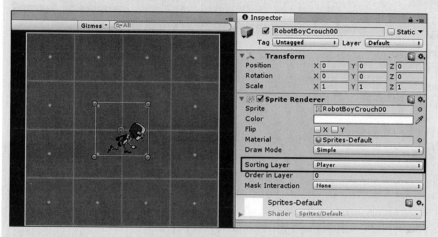

FIGURE 12.11
Setting a sprite's sorting layer.

You would likely want another layer for power-ups, bullets that may spawn, and so on. The ground or platform may be on another layer. Finally, if you want to add more sense of depth with subtle foreground sprites, they could go in a Foreground layer.

Order in Layer

Once you have your major layers defined and assigned to your sprites, you can fine-tune the draw order with the Order in Layer setting. This is a simple priority system, with higher numbers drawing on top of lower numbers.

Sprites Going Missing

When you are starting out, it is quite common for sprites to go missing altogether. This is usually either because a sprite is behind a larger element or behind the camera.

You may also find that if you forget to set the Sorting Layer and Order in Layer properties, the z depth can affect the draw order. This is why it is important to always set the layer for every sprite.

2D Physics

Now that you understand how static sprites work in your game, it's time to add some spice by making them move. Unity has some fantastic tools to help with this. There are two main ways of animating sprites in Unity, as detailed in the following sections. Let's dive in and explore them. Unity has a powerful 2D physics system that integrates a system called Box2D. Just as in 3D games, you can use rigidbodies with gravity, various colliders, and physics specific to 2D platform and driving games.

Rigidbody 2D

Unity has a different type of rigidbody for 2D purposes. This physics component shares many of the same properties with its 3D counterpart, which you have already met. It is a common mistake to choose the wrong type of rigidbody or collider for a game, so be careful to ensure that you are using items from **Add Component > Physics 2D**.

Mixing Physics Types

2D and 3D physics can exist in the same scene together, but they will not interact with each other. Also, you can put 2D physics on 3D objects and vice versa!

2D Colliders

Just like 3D colliders, 2D colliders allow game objects to interact with one another when they touch. Unity comes with a range of 2D colliders (see Table 12.1).

TABLE 12.1   2D Colliders

Collider	Description
Circle Collider 2D	A circle with a fixed radius and an offset.
Box Collider 2D	A rectangle with an adjustable width, height, and offset.
Edge Collider 2D	A segmented line that does not need to be closed.

Collider	Description
Capsule Collider 2D	A capsule shape with offset, size, and direction.
Composite Collider 2D	A special collider that is a composite of several primitive colliders, turning several into one.
Polygon Collider 2D	A closed polygon with three or more sides.

TRY IT YOURSELF ▼

Making Two Sprites Collide

Follow these steps to see the effects of 2D colliders by playing with some 2D squares:

1. Create a new 2D scene and ensure that the 2D package is imported.

2. Find the sprite RobotBoyCrouch00 in the folder Assets\Standard Assets\2D\Sprites and drag it into your Hierarchy view. Ensure that the sprite is at (0, 0, 0).

3. Add a polygon collider (by selecting **Add Component > Physics 2D > Polygon Collider 2D**). Note that this collider roughly fits the outline of the sprite.

4. Duplicate this sprite and move the duplicate down and to the right to (.3, −1, 0). This gives the top sprite something to fall onto.

5. So that the top sprite responds to gravity, select it and add a rigidbody 2D (by selecting **Add Component > Physics 2D > Rigidbody 2D**). See Figure 12.12 for the final setup.

6. Play the scene and notice the behavior. See? Just like 3D physics.

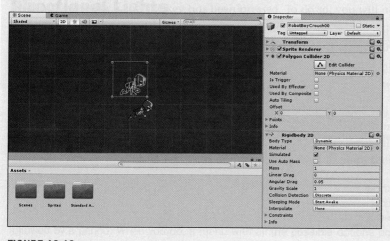

FIGURE 12.12
The finished setup with the top robot selected.

TIP
_____

2D Colliders and Depth

One thing you may find a little odd about 2D colliders, if you look at them in a 3D Scene view, is that they don't need to be at the same z depth in order to collide. They work only on the x and y positions of the collider.

_____

Summary

In this hour, you have learned about the basics of 2D games in Unity. You started by increasing your understanding of orthographic cameras and how depth works in 2D. You went on to make a simple 2D object move and collide, which is the basis of many 2D games.

Q&A

Q. Is Unity a good choice for creating 2D games?

A. Yes. Unity has a fantastic set of tools for creating 2D games.

Q. Can Unity deploy 2D games to mobile and other platforms?

A. Absolutely. One of Unity's core strengths is its capability to deploy to many platforms with relative ease. 2D games are no exception to this, and many very successful 2D games have been made with Unity.

Workshop

Take some time to work through the questions here to ensure that you have a firm grasp of the material.

Quiz

1. What camera projection renders all objects without perspective distortion?

2. What does the size setting of an orthographic camera relate to?

3. Do two 2D sprites need to be at the same z depth in order to collide?

4. Will sprites render if they are behind the camera?

Answers

1. Orthographic

2. The size setting specifies half of the vertical height that the camera covers, specified in world units.

3. No. 2D collisions take account of only x and y positions.

4. No. This is a common cause of lost sprites when making 2D games.

Exercise

In this exercise, you are going to use some Unity standard assets so that you can see what can be achieved when you combine sprites with a little animation, some character control script, and some colliders.

1. Create a new 2D project or a new scene in an existing project.

2. Import the 2D asset pack (by selecting **Assets > Import Package > 2D**). Leave everything selected.

3. Find CharacterRobotBoy in Assets\Standard Assets\2D\Prefabs and drag it into the Hierarchy view. Set the position to (3, 1.8, 0). Note that this prefab comes with many components in the Inspector.

4. Find PlatformWhiteSprite in Assets\Standard Assets\2D\Sprites and drag it into the Hierarchy view. Set the position to (0, 0, 0) and scale to (3, 1, 1). Add a Box Collider 2D so that your player doesn't fall through the floor!

5. Duplicate this platform game object. Position the duplicate at (7.5, 0, 0), rotate it to (0, 0, 30) to make a ramp, and scale it to (3, 1, 1).

6. Move the Main Camera to (11, 4, –10) and adjust its size to 7. See Figure 12.13 for the final setup.

7. Click **Play**. Use the arrow keys to move and the spacebar to jump.

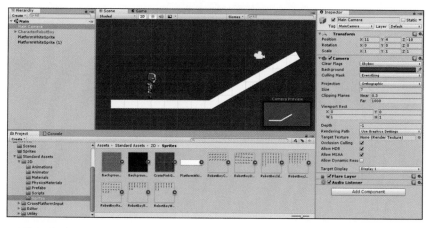

FIGURE 12.13
The final exercise setup.

HOUR 13
2D Tilemap

What You'll Learn in This Hour:

▶ What tilemaps are

▶ How to create palettes

▶ How to create and place tiles

▶ How to add physics to tilemaps

You learned to created 3D worlds using Unity's terrain system in Hour 4, "Terrain and Environments." Now it is time to extend that knowledge into 2D games, using Unity's new 2D Tilemap system. Using this system, you can create worlds quickly and easily for more interesting and compelling game experiences. In this hour you'll start by learning about tilemaps. From there you'll examine palettes, which you use to hold your tiles. Finally, you'll create tiles and paint them onto your tilemaps before adding collision to make your tilemaps interactable.

The Basics of Tilemaps

As the name implies, a *tilemap* is simply a "map" of tiles (in the same way old-school bitmaps are maps of bits). Tilemaps sit on a *grid* object that defines the tile sizes and spacing common to all tilemaps. *Tiles* are individual sprite elements used to draw a world. These tiles are placed on a *palette*, which is then used to draw the tiles onto the tilemap. It may seem like a lot, but it is basically a "paint, palette, brush, canvas" type of setup, and once you begin using it, it will seem very natural.

If it isn't already painfully obvious, it should be noted that tilemaps are meant to be used for 2D games. While they could technically be used for 3D, using them that way would not be very effective. It is also a good idea to use sprite sheets in conjunction with tilemaps. You can create a sheet of the various environment parts and then easily convert them into tiles.

Creating a Tilemap

You can have as many tilemaps in a scene as you like, and you will often find yourself creating several of them and layering them together. This method enables you to set up background, midground, and foreground tilemaps for things like parallax effects. To create a tilemap in a scene, you can select **GameObject > 2D Object > Tilemap**. Unity adds two game objects, named Grid and Tilemap, to your scene (see Figure 13.1).

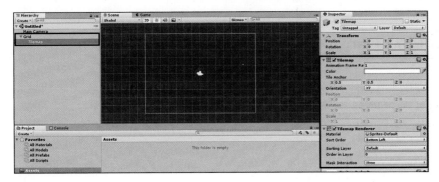

FIGURE 13.1
Adding a tilemap.

The Tilemap game object has two components worth noting: Tilemap and Tilemap Renderer. The Tilemap component has to do with tile placement, anchor positions, and overall color tinting. The Tilemap Renderer allows you to specify sorting orders so that you can ensure that your tilemaps draw in the correct order.

▼ TRY IT YOURSELF

Adding a Tilemap to a Scene

In this exercise, you will add a tilemap to a scene. Be sure to save this scene because you will be using it more later in this hour. Follow these steps:

1. Create a new 2D project. Create a new folder named **Scenes** and save your scene into it.

2. Add a tilemap to your scene by selecting **GameObject > 2D Object > Tilemap**.

3. Eventually, this tilemap will be the background of your scene, so rename the new Tilemap game object **Background**.

4. To create another tilemap without also creating another grid, right-click the Grid game object in the Hierarchy window and select **2D Object > Tilemap** (see Figure 13.2). Name the new tilemap **Platforms**.

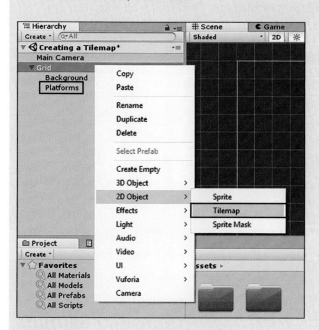

FIGURE 13.2
Adding a new tilemap from the Hierarchy view.

5. Add two new sorting layers to your project and name them **Background** and **Foreground**. (Review Hour 12, "2D Game Tools," if you do not remember how to add sorting layers to a project.)

6. Select the **Background** tilemap and set the Sorting Layer property of the Tilemap Renderer component to **Background**. Select the **Platforms** tilemap and set the Sorting Layer property of the Tilemap Renderer component to **Foreground**.

The Grid

As you saw earlier, when you add a tilemap to a scene, you also get a Grid game object (see Figure 13.3). The grid manages settings that are common across all similar tilemaps. Specifically, the grid manages the cell size and cell gap for your tilemaps. Therefore, if all your tilemaps need to be the same size, you need only a single grid for all of them to sit under. Otherwise, you can have multiple grids for multiple tilemap sizes. Notice that the default cell size is 1. This information will become important later, so be sure to remember that.

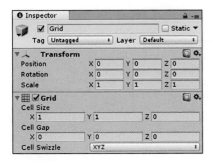

FIGURE 13.3
The Grid object.

TIP

Angled Tilemaps

Usually, tilemaps are aligned with each other. However, that doesn't have to be the case. If you want one of your background tilemaps to be at an angle, you can simply rotate it in the Scene view. You can even move tilemaps to offset their positions for staggered tiles or push them back on the z axis for a built-in parallax effect.

Palettes

In order to paint tiles onto tilemaps, you need to first assemble them on a palette. You can think of the palette as a painter's palette, where all your painting choices take place. The palette comes with many tools that help you sculpt worlds exactly as you see fit. You access the tile palette by going to **Window > Tile Palette**. The Tile Palette window, shown in Figure 13.4, appears.

FIGURE 13.4
The Tile Palette window.

Tile Palette Window

The Tile Palette window has several tools for painting and a main middle area where all your tiles are laid out. By default, a project doesn't have any palettes to work with, but a new one can be created by clicking the **Create New Palette** drop-down.

▼ TRY IT YOURSELF

Creating Palettes

Now it is time to add a couple palettes to your project. You will be using the project created in the Try It Yourself "Adding a Tilemap to a Scene," so if you haven't done that one yet, go ahead and complete it now. Be sure to save the scene because you will be using it more later in this hour. When you're ready to create a palette, follow these steps:

1. Open the scene you created in the Try It Yourself "Adding a Tilemap to a Scene." Open the Tile Palette window (by selecting **Window > Tile Palette**) and dock it next to the Inspector view (refer to Figure 13.4).

2. Add a palette by clicking **Create New Palette** and name the palette **Jungle Tiles**. Leave the rest of the palette settings at their defaults (see Figure 13.5). Click **Create**.

FIGURE 13.5
Creating a new palette.

3. In the Create Palette into Folder dialog that appears, create a new folder, name it **Palettes**, and click **Select Folder**.

4. Repeat steps 2 and 3 to create another palette named **Grass Tiles**. When you are done, you should have two palettes in the palette drop-down and two tilemaps in the Active Tilemap drop-down (see Figure 13.6).

FIGURE 13.6
The correct palettes and tilemaps.

Tiles

So far in this hour, you have been doing a lot of prep work that will allow you to use tiles. Now it is time to dig in and make the tiles to paint with. In essence, tiles are sprites that are specially configured to be used with tilemaps. Sprites that are being used as tiles can still be used as regular sprites if you happen to need them for both. Once sprites are imported and configured, they can be turned into tiles, added to a palette, and then painted onto tilemaps.

NOTE

Crazy Custom Tiles

In this hour you are going to be working with and painting basic tiles. While there is a ton of functionality in these built-in tile options, there are a lot of further customizations that can be done with the new 2D Tilemap feature. If you want to take your expertise even further—creating things like animated tiles, smart tiles, or even custom brushes with game object logic built into the tiles—you should check out Unity's 2D Extras package. At the time this book was published, this package was located at https://github.com/Unity-Technologies/2d-extras. Eventually, though, this package will be migrated into the Unity engine's package manager and will be available like all the other assets you've been using in this book. So much to do, so much to see!

Configuring Sprites

There isn't much you need to do to prepare sprites for use as tiles. There are two major steps:

1. Ensure that the Pixels per Unit property of your sprites is configured to be exactly the same size as the Cell Size property of your grid. (You'll learn more about this shortly.)

2. Slice up the sprites (assuming that they are in a sprite sheet) so that there is as little extra space around them as possible. Where possible, having no extra space around a tile is preferred.

The first step in preparing a sprite for use as a tile may seem complex, but it is really rather straightforward. For example, in this hour you will be using sprite sheets that have multiple tiles in them. These tiles are 64 pixels by 64 pixels (because that's how the artist made them). Since your grid's Cell Size property is 1 unit by 1 unit, you will want to set the Pixels per Unit property to 64. That way, every 64 pixels in your sprite will equal 1 unit, which is the cell size.

Creating Tiles

Once your sprites are prepared correctly, it is time to make some tiles. Doing so simply requires dragging the sprites onto the correct palette in the Tile Palette window and choosing where you'd like to save the resulting tiles. The original sprites remain where they are, unchanged. New tile assets are created that reference the original sprites.

▼ TRY IT YOURSELF

Configuring Sprites and Creating Tiles

This exercise shows you how to configure your sprites and use them to make tiles. You will be using the project created earlier in this hour, so if you haven't done the Try It Yourself "Creating Palettes," go ahead and get caught up. If you've forgotten how to complete any of these steps, you can go back and review Hour 12. Be sure to save this scene because you will be using it more later in this hour. Follow these steps:

1. Open the scene you created in the Try It Yourself "Creating Palettes." Create a new folder and name it **Sprites**. Locate the two sprites GrassPlatform_TileSet and Jungle_Tileset in the book files for this hour. Drag them into the newly created Sprites folder.

2. Select the **GrassPlatform_Tileset** sprite in the Project view and look at its properties in the Inspector view. Set Sprite Mode to **Multiple** and set Pixels per Unit to **64**. Click **Apply**.

3. Open the Sprite Editor and click **Slice** in the upper-left corner. Set Type to **Grid By Cell Size** and set the X and Y Pixel Size properties to **64** (see Figure 13.7).

4. Click **Slice** and then click **Apply**. Then close the Sprite Editor window.

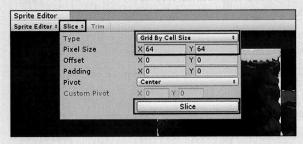

FIGURE 13.7
Slicing the sprite sheet.

5. Repeat steps 2 through 4 for the **Jungle_Tileset** sprite. This sprite is a bit larger than the grass tiles, though, so set Pixels per Unit and the X and Y Pixel Size properties to **128**.

6. Ensure that the Tile Palette window is open and docked next to the Inspector view. Also ensure that the Grass Tiles palette is currently active. Drag the **GrassPlatform_Tileset** sprite into the center area of the Tile Palette window (see Figure 13.8).

FIGURE 13.8
Turning sprites into tiles.

7. In the Generate Tiles into Folder dialog that appears, create a new folder, name it **Tiles**, and then click **Select Folder**.

8. In the Tile Palette window, change the active palette to Jungle Tiles and then repeat steps 6 and 7 for **Jungle_Tileset**.

Now that you have your sprites configured and your tiles created, it is time to start painting!

Painting Tiles

To paint tiles onto a tilemap, you need to pay attention to three things: the selected tile, the active tilemap, and the selected tool (see Figure 13.9). When selecting which tile to paint, you can click a single tile, or you can drag to grab a selection of tiles. This is useful if you want to paint a section of tiles that go together (like a complex roof piece).

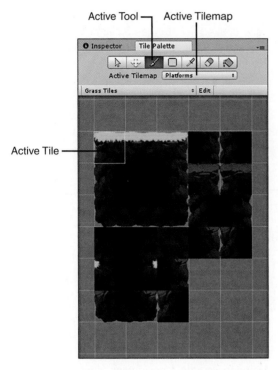

FIGURE 13.9
Preparing to paint.

When you're ready, click in the Scene view to begin painting on the tilemap. Table 13.1 lists the tools that appear in the Tile Palette window (from left to right).

TABLE 13.1 Tile Palette Window tools

Collider	Description
Select tool	Used to select a tile or group of tiles on a tilemap.
Move tool	Used to move a selection on a tilemap from one location to another.
Paint tool	Used to paint the currently highlighted tile (on the palette) onto the active tilemap. Clicking and dragging paints multiple tiles at once. Holding Shift while painting toggles this tool with the Erase tool. Holding Ctrl (Command on Mac) while painting toggles this tool with the Picker tool.
Rectangle tool	Used to paint a rectangular shape on the tilemap and fills it with the currently highlighted tile.
Picker tool	Used to select a tile from a tilemap to paint with (instead of highlighting it on the palette). This tool speeds up painting repeating complex tile groups.
Erase tool	Used to erase a tile or group of tiles from the active tilemap.
Fill tool	Used to fill an area with the currently highlighted tile.

Painting Tiles

It is time to start painting tiles. You will be using the project created earlier in this hour, so if you haven't done that yet, go ahead and get caught up with all the Try It Yourself exercises. Be sure to save this scene because you will be using it more later in this hour. Follow these steps:

1. Open the scene created in the Try It Yourself "Configuring Sprites and Creating Tiles."

2. With the Tile Palette window open, select the **Jungle Tiles** palette and ensure that the Active Tilemap is set to **Background**.

3. Begin selecting tiles and painting them in the Scene view (see Figure 13.10). Continue to select tiles and paint until you've created a jungle background that you like.

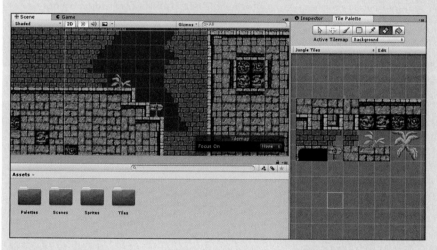

FIGURE 13.10
Painting the background.

4. Switch to the **Grass Tiles** palette and change Active Tilemap to **Platforms**.

5. Paint some grass platforms for your level. You will be using these platforms with a character controller soon, so be sure to make something a player can jump around on (see Figure 13.11).

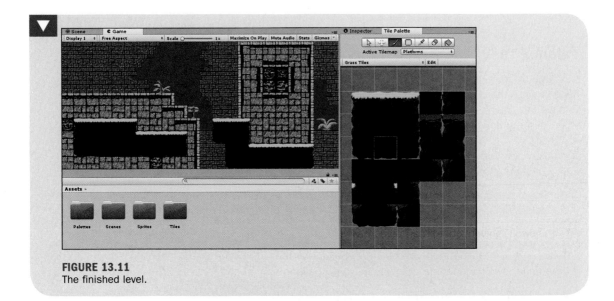

FIGURE 13.11
The finished level.

TIP

Enhanced Controls

Several hotkeys can assist you in finding and painting the correct tiles. First, the Tile Palette window uses the same controls for navigation as the 2D Scene view. This means you can use the scroll wheel to zoom as well as right-clicking and dragging to pan around. When painting tiles, you can rotate and flip them to generate new and interesting designs. Simply use the , (comma) and . (period) keys to rotate the tile before painting. Likewise, use **Shift+,** to flip the tiles horizontally and **Shift+.** to flip the tiles vertically.

Customizing the Palettes

You might have noticed that the palettes aren't exactly laid out in the most convenient manner. When you created the tiles by dragging sprites onto the palette, Unity placed them in a straightforward, but not necessarily intuitive, manner. Luckily, you can customize the palette to suit your needs. Simply click the **Edit** button in the Tile Palette window (see Figure 13.12) and use the palette tools to paint, move, or modify the tiles as you see fit. You can even create several copies of the same tile and rotate or flip them for convenient painting.

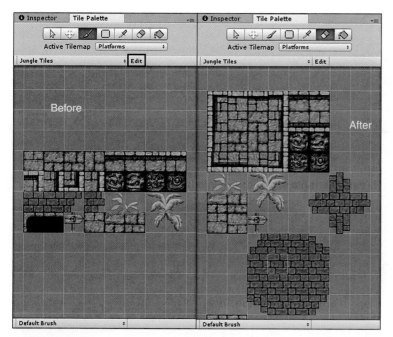

FIGURE 13.12
Editing the tile palette.

Tilemaps and Physics

You've now learned to paint on tilemaps to create brand-new 2D level designs. If you actually try to play with these levels, however, you'll find that your characters fall right through the floor. It's time to learn about using colliders with these new tilemaps.

Tilemap Colliders

You could add collision to your levels by placing box colliders around your tiles manually, but who wants to work that hard? I don't! Instead, you can use a Tilemap Collider 2D component to automatically handle collision. Besides working specifically for tilemaps, these colliders function just like any other colliders you've used in the previous hours. All you need to do is select the tilemap you want to have collision and select **Component > Tilemap > Tilemap Collider 2D** to add the collider as a component.

▼ TRY IT YOURSELF

Adding a Tilemap Collider 2D Component

In this exercise you are going to finish the scene you've been working with all throughout this hour by adding colliders to your platforms. You will be using the project created earlier in this hour, so if you haven't done that yet, go ahead and get caught up. Then follow these steps:

1. Open the scene you created in the Try It Yourself "Painting Tiles." Import the 2D standard assets (by selecting **Assets > Import Package > 2D**).

2. Locate the CharacterRobotBoy prefab (in the folder Assets\Standard Assets\2D\Prefabs) and drag it into your scene, above one of your platforms. You may need to change the scale of the prefab to (1, 1, 1).

3. Play your scene and notice that the robot falls right through the ground. Exit play mode.

4. Select the **Platforms** tilemap game object and then add a Tilemap Collider 2D component (by selecting **Add Component > Tilemap > Tilemap Collider 2D**). Notice that a collider is placed around each individual tile (see Figure 13.13).

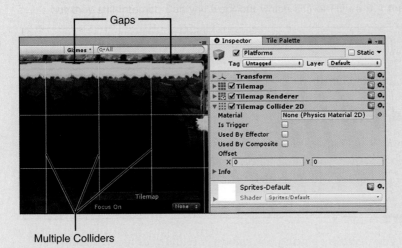

FIGURE 13.13
The Tilemap Collider 2D component.

5. Enter play mode again and notice that the robot lands on the platform now. If you zoom in, however, you will notice that because the collider fits around the tile, there are gaps between the grass platform and the collider (refer to Figure 13.13).

6. On the Tilemap Collider 2D component, set Y Offset to **−0.1** to lower the collider a little. Enter play mode again and notice that the robot now stands on the grass.

The colliders you now have on your tiles make the level complete and playable. One problem worth noting, however, is that placing a collider around each tile is very inefficient and can lead to performance issues. You can resolve this by using something called a Composite Collider 2D component.

TIP

Collision Accuracy

When you begin using colliders with tilemaps, you might need to make some changes to the rigidbody components of your moving objects. Because the edges of a Tilemap Collider 2D component and even a Composite Collider 2D component are very thin, you may notice that objects that have small colliders or that move quickly can tend to get stuck on them or even fall through them. If you notice this behavior, you should set the Collision Detection property of the problematic rigidbody to **Continuous**. That should prevent any more of the collider issues with your tilemaps.

Using a Composite Collider 2D Component

A *composite* collider is a collider that is composed of many other colliders. In a way, it allows you to merge all the individual tile colliders into a single larger collider. The really cool thing about doing this is that whenever you add or change tiles, the collider is automatically updated for you. You can add a Composite Collider 2D component by selecting **Add Component > Physics 2D > Composite Collider 2D**. When you do, a Rigidbody 2D component is also added; it is required for the Composite Collider 2D component to work (see Figure 13.14). Obviously, if you don't want all your tiles to fall due to gravity, you will want to change the Body Type property of the Rigidbody 2D component to Static.

After you add the composite collider, nothing really changes with the tilemap. Each tile still has its own individual collider. The reason is that you need to tell the collider that it should be used in the composite. To do that, simply check the **Used By Composite** check box. After you do this, all the colliders are merged into one large (and more efficient) collider.

One Collider

FIGURE 13.14
The Composite Collider 2D component.

Summary

In this hour, you have learned about creating 2D worlds using Unity's 2D Tilemap system. You began by learning about tilemaps in general. After that you created palettes and configured sprites to be added as tiles. Once your tiles were prepared, you painted a couple tilemaps to build a level. Finally, you learned how to add collision to your tilemaps to make them playable.

Q&A

Q. Can tilemaps be combined with regular sprites when building 2D worlds?

A. Yes, absolutely. A tile is really just a special kind of sprite.

Q. Are there any kinds of levels that tilemaps aren't good for?

A. Tilemaps are great for repetitive and modular levels. Scenes that involve a large number of different shapes or very unique and nonrepeating sprites would be difficult to create with tilemaps.

Workshop

Take some time to work through the questions here to ensure that you have a firm grasp of the material.

Quiz

1. What component defines properties (such as Cell Size) that tilemaps share?

2. Where are tiles placed prior to painting them onto a tilemap?

3. What collider type allows the combination of multiple colliders into one?

Answers

1. The Grid component

2. A palette

3. A Composite Collider 2D component

Exercise

In this exercise, you are going to experiment with the tilemaps you've created to enhance their appearance and usability. Here are some things to try:

▶ Try fully painting and modifying both of your tilemaps until you are satisfied with them.

▶ Try adding a Foreground tilemap to add more plant or rock elements to your scene.

▶ Try testing your full level by adding a 2D character and getting the camera to follow the character. The book files include a script called CameraFollow.cs to help get the camera to follow your player around.

▶ Try pushing your background tilemap away from the camera on the z axis. In this way, you can create a natural parallax effect. Remember that you will be able to see the effect only if you have a perspective camera.

▶ Try modifying the color property of the background's Tilemap component to make the background images look faded and distant.

HOUR 14
User Interfaces

What You'll Learn in This Hour:

▶ The elements of a user interface (UI)

▶ An overview of the UI elements

▶ The different UI render modes

▶ How to build a simple menu system

A *user interface* (UI) is a special set of components responsible for sending information to, and reading information from, the user. In this hour, you'll learn all about using Unity's built-in UI system. You'll start by examining the UI basics. From there, you'll get to try out the various UI elements, such as text, images, buttons, and more. You'll finish this lesson by creating a simple but complete menu system for your games.

Basic UI Principles

A user interface (commonly referred to as a UI) is a special layer that exists to give information to the user and to accept simple inputs from the user. This information and input could take the form of an HUD (heads up display) drawn over the top of your game or some object actually located within your 3D worlds.

In Unity, the UI is based on a *canvas* onto which all the UI elements are painted. This canvas needs to be the parent of all UI objects in order for them to work, and it is the main object driving your entire UI.

TIP

UI Design

As a general rule, you should sketch your UI ahead of time. A fair bit of thought needs to go into what to display on the screen, where it will be displayed, and how. Too much information will cause the screen to feel cluttered. Too little information will leave the players confused or unsure. Always look for ways to condense information and make information more meaningful. Your players will thank you.

TIP

New UI

Unity got a new UI in version 4.6. In older versions, you had to use many lines of confusing code to create UIs, but now it's much easier. The old UI system is still there. If you are familiar with that legacy system, you may be tempted to use it. Please don't. The legacy system is only still there for debugging, backward compatibility with old projects, and editor extensions. It is not nearly as efficient or powerful as the new system!

The Canvas

A canvas is the basic building block for a UI, and all the UI elements are contained within the canvas. All the UI elements you add to a scene will be child objects of the canvas in the Hierarchy view and must stay as children; otherwise, they'll disappear from the scene.

Adding a canvas to a scene is very easy. You can add one simply by selecting **GameObject > UI > Canvas**. Once the canvas is added to a scene, you are ready to begin building the rest of the UI.

▼ TRY IT YOURSELF

Adding a Canvas

Follow these steps to add a canvas to a scene and explore its unique features:

1. Create a new project (either 2D or 3D).

2. Add a UI canvas to the scene (by selecting **GameObject > UI > Canvas**).

3. Zoom out so you can see the whole canvas (by double-clicking it in Hierarchy view). Notice how big it is!

4. Note in the Inspector the odd transform component the canvas has. This is a *Rect transform*, and we will discuss it shortly.

NOTE

EventSystem

You may have noticed that when you added a canvas to your scene, you also got an EventSystem game object. This object is always added when you add a canvas. The event system is what allows users to interact with the UI by pressing buttons or dragging elements. Without the event system, a UI would never know if it was being used—so don't delete it!

Performance Woes

Canvases are very efficient because they turn the UI elements nested on them into a single static object behind the scenes. This allows them to be processed very quickly. The downside is that when one part of a UI changes, the whole thing needs to be rebuilt. This can be a very slow and inefficient process and can cause a noticeable stutter in a game. Therefore, it is a good idea to use canvas components to separate objects that move a lot onto their own canvas. That way, their movement will force a smaller set of your UI to rebuild and ultimately be much faster.

The Rect Transform

You will notice that a canvas (and every other UI element) has a *Rect transform* rather than the normal 3D transform you are familiar with. Rect, short for *rectangle*, transforms give you fantastic control over the positioning and rescaling of UI elements while remaining very flexible. This allows you to create a user interface and ensure that it works well on a wide range of devices.

For the canvas you created earlier in this hour, the Rect transform is entirely grayed out (see Figure 14.1). This is because, in its current form, the canvas derives its values entirely from the Game view (and, by extension, the resolution and aspect ratio of any devices your game runs on). This mean the canvas will always take up the entire screen. A good workflow is to make sure the first thing you do whenever building a UI is to select a target aspect ratio to work with. You can do this from the Aspect Ratio drop-down in the Game view (see Figure 14.2).

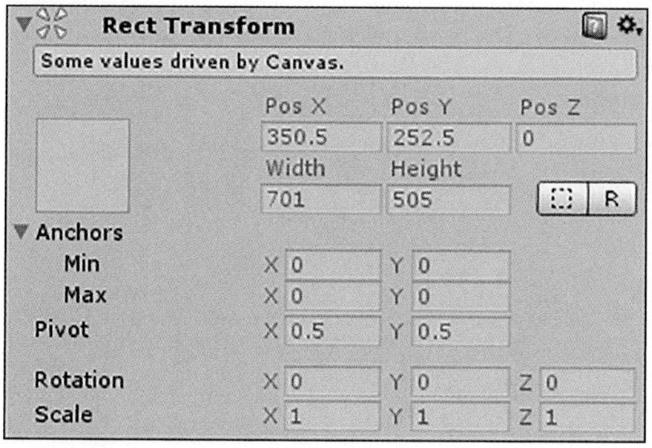

FIGURE 14.1
The Rect transform of a canvas.

FIGURE 14.2
Setting the game's aspect ratio.

Rect transforms work a little differently from traditional transforms. With normal 2D and 3D objects, the transform is concerned with determining how far (and with what alignment) an object is from the world origin. The UI, however, is unconcerned with world origin and instead needs to know how it's aligned in relation to its *anchor point*. (You will learn more about Rect transforms and anchors later, when you have a UI element that can actually use it.)

Anchors

A key concept in making UI elements work is anchors. Every UI element comes with an anchor and uses that anchor to find its place in the world in relation to the Rect transform of its parent. Anchors determine how elements are resized and repositioned when the Game window changes size and shape. In addition, an anchor has two "modes": together and split. When an anchor is together as a single point, the object knows where it is by determining the distance (in pixels) of its pivot from the anchor. When an anchor is split, however, the UI element bases its bounding box on how far (again in pixels) each of its corners is from each corner of the split anchor. Confusing? Let's try it out!

▼ TRY IT YOURSELF

Using a Rect Transform

Rect transforms and anchors can be confusing, so follow these steps to better understand them:

1. Create a new scene or project.

2. Add a UI image (by selecting **GameObject > UI > Image**). Note that if you add an image to a scene without a canvas, Unity automatically puts a canvas in your scene and then puts the image on it.

3. Zoom out so you can see the whole image and canvas. Note that it is much easier working with the UI when your scene is in 2D mode (which you enter by clicking the **2D** button at the top of Scene view) and you are using the Rect tool (hotkey: **T**).

4. Try dragging the image around the canvas. Also try dragging the anchor around the canvas. Notice that the lines show you how far the image's pivot is from the anchor. Also notice the properties of the Rect transform in the Inspector and how they change (see Figure 14.3).

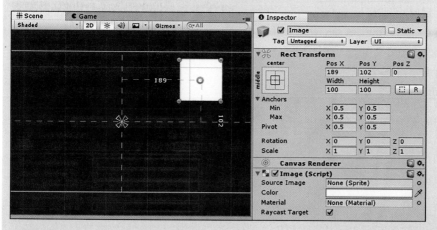

FIGURE 14.3
The anchor at a single point.

5. Now try splitting your anchor. You can do this by dragging any of the corners of the anchor away from the rest. With the anchor split, move your image around again. Notice how the properties of the Rect transform change (see Figure 14.4). (*Hint:* Where did Pos X, Pos Y, Width, and Height go?)

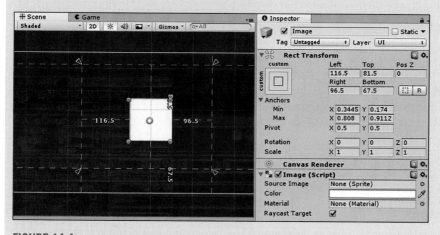

FIGURE 14.4
The anchor after being split.

So what exactly does splitting an anchor (or keeping it together) do? In simple terms, an anchor that is a single point fixes your UI element in place relative to that spot. So if the canvas changes size, the element doesn't. Splitting the anchor causes the element to fix its corners relative to the corners of the anchor. If the canvas resizes, so does the element. You can easily preview this behavior in the Unity editor. Using the preceding example, if you select the image and then click and drag the border of the canvas (or any other parent, if you have more elements), the word *Preview* appears, and you can see what will happen when using different resolutions (see Figure 14.5). Try it out with both a single anchor and a split anchor and notice how differently they behave.

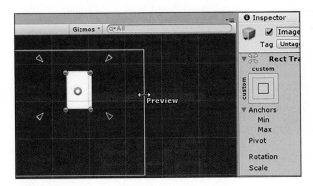

FIGURE 14.5
Previewing a canvas change.

TIP

Getting Anchors Right

Anchors may seem a little odd at first, but understanding them is the key to understanding the UI. Get the anchors, and everything else just falls into place. When working with UI elements, it is great to get into the habit of always placing the anchor and then placing the object because objects snap to their anchors but not vice versa.

When you get into that habit (place anchor, place object, place anchor, place object, and so on), everything becomes a lot easier. Invest some time in playing with anchors until you understand them.

TIP

The Anchor Button

You don't always have to manually drag anchors around your scene in order to place them. You can also type their values into the Anchors property in the Inspector (a value of 1 is 100%, .5 is 50%, and so on). If even that is too much work for you, you can use the convenient anchor button that enables you to place the anchor (and additionally the pivot and position) in one of 24 preset locations (see Figure 14.6). Sometimes it pays to be lazy!

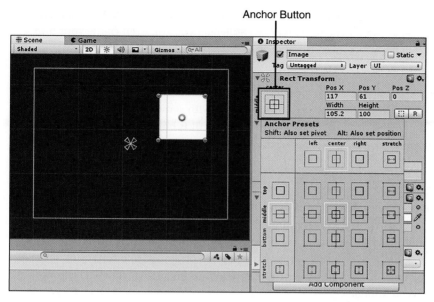

FIGURE 14.6
The anchor button.

Additional Canvas Components

So far, we've talked about the canvas a bit but still haven't even mentioned the actual Canvas component. Truth be told, there isn't much with the component itself that you need to concern yourself with. You do need to know about render modes, and we look at them in detail later in this hour.

Depending on what version of Unity you are using, you may have a couple extra components. Again, these are very simple to use, so they aren't covered in detail here (there's just too much other good stuff to get to). The Canvas Scaler component allows you to specify how, if at all, you would like your UI elements resized as the screen of your target device changes (for instance, seeing the same UI on a web page versus a high-DPI Retina iPad device). The Graphical Raycaster component, which works with the EventSystem object, allows your UI to receive button clicks and screen touches. It allows you to use raycasting without needing to drag in the entire physics engine to do it.

UI Elements

At this point, you're probably pretty tired of the canvas, so let's get working with some UI elements (also called *UI controls*). Unity has several built-in controls available for you to get started with. Don't worry if you don't see a control that you want, though. Unity's UI library is open source, and plenty of custom controls are being created by members of the community all the time. As a matter of fact, if you're up for the challenge, you can even create your own controls and share them with everyone else.

Unity has many controls that you can add to scenes. Most of them are simple combinations and variations of two basic elements: images and text. This makes sense if you think about it: A panel is just a full-sized image, a button is just an image with some text, and a slider is really three images stacked together. As a matter of fact, the whole UI is built to be a system of basic building blocks that are stackable to get the functionality you want.

Images

Images are the fundamental building pieces of a UI. They can range from background images, to buttons, to logos, to health bars, to everything in between. If you completed the Try It Yourself exercises earlier in this hour, then you already have some familiarity with images, but now you'll take a closer look. As you saw earlier, you can add an image to a canvas by selecting **GameObject > UI > Image**. Table 14.1 lists the properties of an image, which is just a game object with an **Image** component.

TABLE 14.1 Properties of the Image Component

Property	Description
Source Image	Specifies the image to be displayed. This must be a sprite. (For more on sprites, refer to Hour 12, "2D Game Tools.")
Color	Indicates any color tinting and opacity changes to be applied to the image.
Material	Specifies a material (if any) to be applied to the image.
Raycast Target	Determines whether the image is clickable.
Image Type	Specifies the type of sprite to be used for the image. This property affects how the image scales and tiles.
Preserve Aspect	Determines whether the image will maintain its original aspect ratio, regardless of scaling.
Set Native Size	Sets the size of the image object to the size of the image file being used.

Besides the basic properties, there isn't much more you need to know about using an image. Work through the following Try It Yourself to see how easy it is to use images.

Using an Image

Let's try creating a background image. This exercise uses the BackgroundSpace.png file from the book assets for Hour 14. Follow these steps:

1. Create a new scene or project.

2. Import BackgroundSpace.png into your project, ensuring that it is imported as a sprite. (Refer to Hour 12 if you don't remember how to do this.)

3. Add an image to your scene (by selecting **GameObject > UI > Image**).

4. Set the BackgroundSpace sprite as the Source Image property of the Image object.

5. Resize the image to fill the entire canvas. Switch over to the Game view and see what happens if you change the aspect ratio. Notice that the image may get cut off or fail to fill the screen.

6. Split the anchor of the image so that the four corners of the anchor reach the four corners of the canvas (see Figure 14.7). Now switch back to the Game view and see what happens when you change the aspect ratio. Notice that the image always fills the screen and is never cut off—although it may skew.

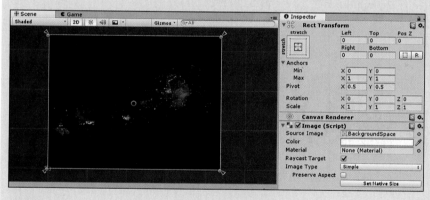

FIGURE 14.7
Expanding the image and anchors.

NOTE

UI Materials

As you can see In Figure 14.7, there is a Material property for the image component in the Try It Yourself "Using an Image." It's worth noting that the Material property is completely optional and not required for this UI. Furthermore, in the current canvas render mode (explained in more detail later in this hour), the Material property doesn't do a whole lot. In other modes, however, the Material property can allow you to apply lights and shader effects to UI elements.

Text

Text objects (which are really just text components) are elements you use to display text to the user. If you've ever used text formatting controls before (think blogging software, word processors like Word or WordPad, or anywhere else you would use and style text), the Text component will be very familiar. You can add a Text component to a canvas by selecting **GameObject > UI > Text**. Table 14.2 lists the properties of the Text component. Because most text properties are self-explanatory, only the new or unique properties are listed.

TABLE 14.2 Properties of the Text Component

Property	Description
Text	Specifies the text to display.
Rich Text	Indicates whether to support rich text tags within text.
Horizontal Overflow and Vertical Overflow	Specify how to handle a situation in which the text does not fit within the bounding box of the UI element that contains it. The value **Wrap** means text will wrap down to the next line. **Truncate** means that the text that doesn't fit will be removed. **Overflow** means that the text can spill out of the box. If text does not fit within the box and **Overflow** is not set, the text may disappear.
Best Fit	As an alternative to Overflow (which will not work if Overflow is used), resizes text to fit within the bounding box of the object. With Best Fit, you can choose a minimum and maximum size. The font then expands or shrinks between those two values to always fit within the text box.

It is worth taking a moment to try out the different settings, especially for Overflow and Best Fit. If you don't understand how to use these properties, you may be surprised to find your text mysteriously disappearing (because it has been truncated), and it may take time to figure out why.

Buttons

Buttons are elements that allow click input from the user. They may seem complex at first look, but remember that, as mentioned earlier, a button is really just an image with a text object child and a little more functionality. You can add buttons to your scene by selecting **GameObject > UI > Button**.

Where a button is different from either of the other controls you've seen so far is that it is interactable. Because of that, it has some interesting properties and features. For instance, buttons can have transitions, they can be navigated, and they can have OnClick event handlers. Table 14.3 lists the Button component properties.

TABLE 14.3   Properties of the Button Component

Property	Description
Interactable	Indicates whether the user can click the button.
Transition	Specifies how the button should respond to user interaction (see Figure 14.8). The available events to respond to are Normal (nothing happening), Highlighted (mouse over), Pressed, and Disabled. By default, the button simply changes color (Color Tint). You could also remove any transitions (None) or cause the button to change images (Sprite Swap). Finally, you can choose Animation to use full animations, which can make your buttons look very impressive.
Navigation	Specifies how users will navigate between buttons if they are using devices like controllers or joysticks (that is, no mouse or touch screen). Clicking Visualize allows you to see how buttons will be navigated; this works only if you have more than one button on the canvas.
On Click ()	Specifies what happens when you click the button (as discussed in more detail later in this hour).

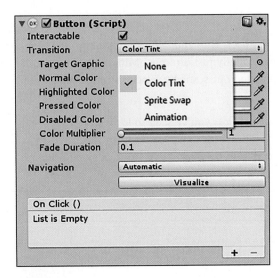

FIGURE 14.8
The transition type selector.

On Click ()

When users are done marveling at your various button transition effects, they may eventually click some buttons. You can use the On Click () property at the bottom of the Inspector to call a function from a script and to access many other components. You can pass parameters to any method you call, which means the designer can control the behavior without entering code. An advanced use of this functionality might be to call methods on a game object or make a camera look at a target directly.

▼ TRY IT YOURSELF

Using a Button

Follow these steps to put what you know so far to practice and create a button, give it some color transitions, and make it change its text when clicked:

1. Create a new scene or project.

2. Add a button to the scene (by selecting **GameObject > UI > Button**).

3. Under the Button (Script) component in the Inspector, set Highlighted Color to red and Pressed Color to green (see Figure 14.9 for the finished settings).

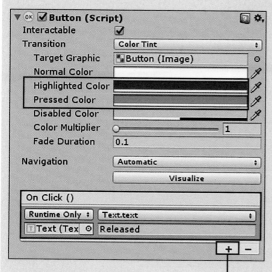

Click to Add On Click () Handler

FIGURE 14.9
The finished button settings.

4. Add a new On Click () handler by clicking the little **+** sign at the bottom of the Inspector (see Figure 14.9). Now that the handler is looking for the object to manipulate, it says None (Object).

5. Expand the button game object in the Hierarchy view so you can see the Text child object. Drag the Text object onto the Object property of the event handler.

6. In the function drop-down (which says No Function), specify what you want the button to do to the chosen object. To do this, click the drop-down (see #1 in Figure 14.10) and then select **Text** (#2) **> string text** (#3).

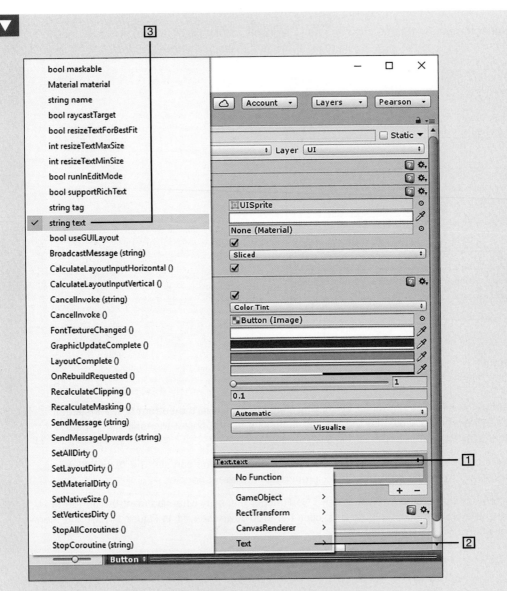

FIGURE 14.10
Setting the click event to change the button text.

7. In the value box that appears, type **Released**.

8. Play the game and try hovering over the button, pressing and holding, and then releasing the button. Notice that the color changes and the text changes when you click.

TIP

Sorting Elements

Now that you are familiar with various elements, it is a good time to mention how they are drawn. You may have noticed that the Canvas component you looked at earlier in this hour has a Sorting Layer property (like the ones you've seen with 2D images in other hours). This property is only used to sort between multiple canvases within the same scene. To sort UI elements on the same canvas, you use the order of the objects in the Hierarchy view. Therefore, if you want an object drawn on top of another object, you move it lower in the Hierarchy view so it is drawn later.

TIP

Presets

Unity 2018.1 added the concept of component presets. *Presets* are the saved properties of a component (such as the UI Text component) that can be applied to quickly set up new components. The presets menu is in the upper-right corner of a component, next to the settings cog in the Inspector view. While presets can work for any type of component, they are specifically mentioned here, instead of earlier, because of how well they work with the UI. A very common use case is wanting all the text in your game to match. You don't necessarily want to make all your text a prefab, but you can quickly apply a text preset.

Canvas Render Modes

Unity offers three powerful options for the way your UI is rendered to the screen. You can choose the mode in the Inspector by selecting **Canvas** and choosing **Render Mode**. You then see the modes shown in Figure 14.11. The use of each canvas mode is very complex, so you shouldn't try to master them right now. Instead, the aim here is to describe the three modes (Screen Space–Overlay, Screen Space–Camera, and World Space) so that you can choose what is best for your games.

FIGURE 14.11
The three different canvas render modes.

Screen Space–Overlay

Screen Space–Overlay, which is the default mode, is the easiest-to-use and also least powerful version of the canvas modes. A UI in Screen Space–Overlay mode draws over the top of everything on the screen, regardless of the camera settings or the position of the camera in the world. In fact, where this UI appears in the Scene view bears no relationship to the objects in the world because it isn't actually rendered by a camera.

The UI appears in the Scene view at a fixed position, with the bottom-left at (0, 0, 0) in the world. The scale of the UI is different from the world scale, and what you see on the canvas is at a scale of 1 world unit for every pixel in your Game view. If you are using this type of UI in your game and find its place in the world to be inconvenient while you're working, you can hide it to get it out of the way. To do so, you can click the **Layers** drop-down in the editor and hide the eye icon next to the UI layer (see Figure 14.12). The UI is then hidden in the Scene view only (through it will still be there when you run your game). Just be sure not to forget to turn it back on, or you might get confused about why your UI won't show up!

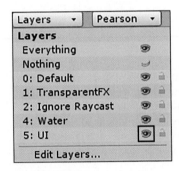

FIGURE 14.12
Hiding your UI.

Screen Space–Camera

Screen Space–Camera mode is similar to Screen Space–Overlay, but the UI is rendered by the camera of your choice. You can rotate and scale UI elements to create much more dynamic 3D interfaces.

Unlike Screen Space–Overlay mode, this mode uses the camera to render the UI. This means effects such as lighting affect the UI, and objects can even pass between the camera and the UI. This can take some extra work, but the payoff is that your interface can feel much more part of the world.

Note that in this mode, the UI stays in a fixed position relative to the camera you chose to render it. Moving the camera also moves the canvas. It can be a good idea to use a second camera solely for rendering your canvas (so it isn't in the way of the rest of your scene).

World Space

The final UI mode to consider is the World Space mode. Imagine a virtual museum, where every object you look at has detailed information about the object right next to it. Furthermore, this pop-up information could include buttons to allow you to read more or go to other sections of the museum. If you can imagine that, then you are only scratching the surface of what you can do with a World Space mode canvas.

Notice that the Rect transform of the canvas in World Space mode is no longer grayed out, and the Canvas component itself can be edited and resized (see Figure 14.13). Because in this mode the canvas is actually a game object in the world, it is no longer drawn over the rest of your game, like a HUD. Instead, it is fixed in the world and can be a part of or blended with the rest of your scene objects.

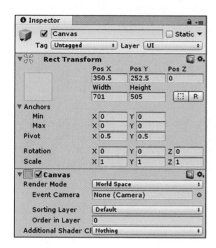

FIGURE 14.13
The Rect transform, available with the World Space mode.

TRY IT YOURSELF ▼

Exploring the Render Modes

Follow these steps to look at the three different UI render modes:

1. Create a new 3D scene or project.

2. Add a UI canvas to the scene (by selecting **GameObject > UI > Canvas**).

3. Note that the Rect transform is disabled. Also try zooming in to the Scene view to see where the canvas sits.

4. Switch the render mode to Screen Space–Camera. For Render Camera choose **Main Camera**. Notice that the canvas changes size and position when you do this.

5. Notice what happens when you move the camera. Also notice what happens when you change the camera's Projection property from Perspective to **Orthographic** and back.

6. Switch to the World Space mode. Note that you can now change the Rect transform for the canvas, move it, rotate it, and scale it.

Summary

You started this lesson by looking at the building blocks of any UI: the canvas and event system. You then learned about the Rect transform and how anchor points help you make versatile UIs that can work on many devices. From there, you explored various UI elements available for use. You then briefly looked at the fundamentally different UI modes: Screen Space–Overlay, Screen Space–Camera, and World Space.

Q&A

Q. Does every game need a user interface?

A. Usually a game benefits from having a well-thought-out UI. It is rare for a game to have no UI whatsoever. That said, it is always a good idea to be a minimalist with a UI, giving the players just the information they need—when they need it.

Q. Can I mix canvas render modes in a scene?

A. Yes, you can. You might want to have more than one canvas in a scene and give them different render modes.

Workshop

Take some time to work through the questions here to ensure that you have a firm grasp of the material.

Quiz

1. What does UI stand for?

2. What two game objects always come along with a UI in Unity?

3. What UI render mode would you use to put a question mark above a player's head in a 3D game?

4. What render mode is most likely to be best for a simple HUD?

Answers

1. User interface (This was an easy warm-up question!)

2. Canvas and EventSystem components

3. You would use World Space mode because the interface element is positioned within world space, not relative to the player's eyes.

4. Screen Space–Overlay

Exercise

In this exercise, you will build a simple but complete menu system that you can adapt for use in all your games. You will make use of a splash screen, a fade-in, some background music, and more.

1. Create a new 2D project. Add a UI panel (by selecting **GameObject > UI > Panel**). Note that Unity also adds the required Canvas and EventSystem components to the Hierarchy view for you.

2. Import the Hour14Package.unitypackage file provided in the book files. Click **clouds.jpg** in your Assets folder, and ensure that Texture Type is set to **Sprite (2D and UI)**.

3. Set this image as the source image in the Panel's Inspector. Note that the image is a little transparent by default, letting the Main Camera's background color show through. Feel free to adjust the transparency by bringing up the color dialog and adjusting the A slider (where A stands for alpha).

4. Add a title and a subtitle (by selecting **GameObject > UI > Text**). Move them so they sit nicely on the panel (see Figure 14.14).

FIGURE 14.14
The complete UI.

5. Add a button (by selecting **GameObject > UI > Button**). Name the button **Start** and set its Text child object to say **Start Game**. Position the button where you wish, remembering to select the button (not the Text child object) before you drag.

6. Save your scene as **Menu** (by selecting **File > Save Scene**). Now create a new scene to act as a placeholder for your game and save it as **Game**. Finally, add both scenes to the build order by opening the build settings (by selecting **File > Build Settings**) and dragging both scenes into the Scenes in Build section. Ensure that the Menu scene is on top.

7. Switch back to your menu scene. Drag the LevelManager prefab that you imported from your Assets folder into the Hierarchy view.

8. Find the Start button and set its On Click () property to the level manager's LoadGame () method (see Figure 14.15).

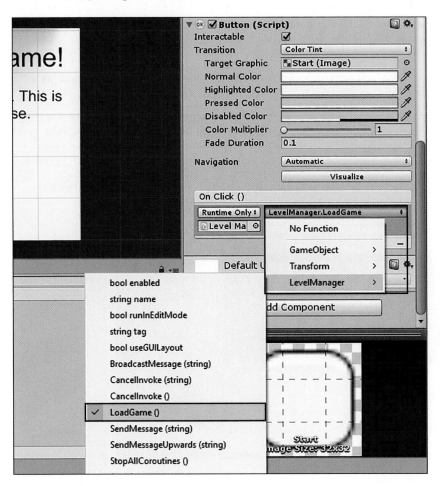

FIGURE 14.15
Setting the Start Game button's On Click () handler.

9. Play your scene. Click the Start Game button, and the game should switch to the empty Game scene. Congratulations! You have a menu system to use in future games!

Game 3: *Captain Blaster*

What You'll Learn in This Hour:

▶ How to design the game *Captain Blaster*

▶ How to build the *Captain Blaster* world

▶ How to build the *Captain Blaster* entities

▶ How to build the *Captain Blaster* controls

▶ How to further improve *Captain Blaster*

Let's make a game! In this hour, you'll make a 2D scrolling shooter game titled *Captain Blaster*. You'll start by designing the various elements of the game. From there, you'll begin building the scrolling background. Once the idea of motion is established, you'll begin building the various game entities. When the entities are done, you'll construct the controls and gamify the project. You'll finish this hour by analyzing the game and identifying ways to improve it.

TIP

The Completed Project

Be sure to follow along in this hour to build the complete game project. In case you get stuck, you can find a completed copy of the game in the book assets for Hour 15. Take a look at it if you need help or inspiration.

Design

You learned about design elements in Hour 6, "Game 1: *Amazing Racer*." This hour, you'll dive right into them.

The Concept

As mentioned earlier, *Captain Blaster* is a 2D scrolling shooter-style game. The premise is that the player will be flying around a level, destroying meteors, and trying to stay alive. The neat thing about 2D scrolling games is that the players themselves don't actually have to move at all. The scrolling background simulates the idea that the player is going forward. This reduces the required player skill and allows you to create more challenges in the form of enemies.

The Rules

The rules of this game state how to play and allude to some of the properties of the objects. The rules for *Captain Blaster* are as follows:

▶ The player plays until being hit by a meteor. There is no win condition.

▶ The player can fire bullets to destroy the meteors. The player earns 1 point per meteor destroyed.

▶ The player can fire two bullets per second.

▶ The player is bounded by the sides of the screen.

▶ Meteors come continuously until the player loses.

The Requirements

The requirements for this game are simple:

▶ A background sprite to be outer space.

▶ A ship sprite.

▶ A meteor sprite.

▶ A game manager. This will be created in Unity.

▶ Interactive scripts. These will be written in MonoDevelop or Visual Studio as usual.

The World

Because this game takes place in space, the world will be fairly simple to implement. The game will be 2D, and the background will move vertically behind the player to make it seem like the player is moving forward. In actuality, the player will be stationary. Before you get the scrolling in place, though, you need to set up your project. Start with these steps:

1. Create a new 2D project named Captain Blaster.

2. Create a folder named Scenes and save your scene as Main.

3. In the Game view, change the aspect ratio to **5:4** (see Figure 15.1).

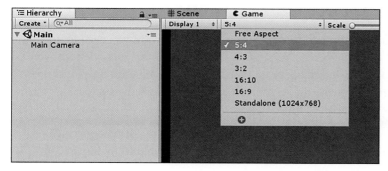

FIGURE 15.1
Setting the game's aspect ratio.

The Camera

Now that the scene is set up properly, it is time to work on the camera. Because this is a 2D project, you have an orthographic camera, which lacks depth perspective and is great for making 2D games. To set up the Main Camera, simply set the Size property to 6. (See Figure 15.2 for a list of the camera's properties.)

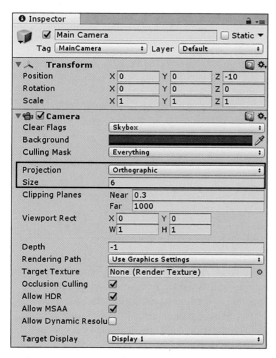

FIGURE 15.2
The Main Camera properties.

The Background

The scrolling background can be a little tricky to set up correctly. Basically, you need to have two background objects moving down the screen. As soon as the bottom object goes offscreen, you place it above the screen. You keep flipping back and forth between them, and the player doesn't know this is what's happening. To create the scrolling background, follow these steps:

1. Create a new folder named Background. Locate the Star_Sky.png image from the book files and import it into Unity by dragging it into the Background folder you just created. Remember that because you made a 2D project, this image automatically imports as a sprite.

2. Select the newly imported sprite in the Project view and change its Pixels per Unit property in the Inspector view to **50**. Drag the Star_Sky sprite into the scene and ensure that it is positioned at (0, 0, 0).

3. Create a new script in your Background folder named ScrollBackground and drag it onto the background sprite in the scene. Put the following code in the script:

```
public float speed = -2f;
public float lowerYValue = -20f;
public float upperYValue = 40;

void Update()
{
    transform.Translate(0f, speed * Time.deltaTime, 0f);
    if (transform.position.y <= lowerYValue)
    {
        transform.Translate(0f, upperYValue, 0f);
    }
}
```

4. Duplicate the background sprite and place it at (0, 20, 0). Run the scene. You should see the background seamlessly stream by.

NOTE

Alternate Organization

Up until now, you have used a fairly straightforward system for organization. Assets went into corresponding folders: sprites in a sprites folder, scripts in a scripts folder, and so on. In this hour, however, you are going to do something new. This time, you are going to group assets based on their "entity": all background files together, ship assets together, and so on. This system works well for finding all related assets quickly. Don't worry if you like the other system, though. You can still search and sort asset names and types by using the search bar and filter properties located at the top of the Project view. As Ben Tristem (Howdy, Ben!) recently told me, "There's more than one way to do things!"

NOTE

Seamless Scrolling

You might notice a small line in the scrolling background you just created. This is due to the fact that the image used for the background wasn't made specifically to tile together. Generally, it isn't very noticeable, and the actions of the game will more than cover it up. If you want a more seamless background in the future, however, you should use an image made to tile together.

Game Entities

In this game, you need to make three primary entities: the player, the meteor, and the bullet. The interaction between these items is very simple. The player fires bullets. Bullets destroy meteors. Meteors destroy the player. Because the player can technically fire a large number of bullets, and because a large number of meteors can spawn, you need a way to clean them up. Therefore, you also need to make triggers that destroy bullets and meteors that enter them.

The Player

Your player will be a spaceship. The sprites for both the spaceship and the meteors can be found in the book assets for Hour 15. (Thanks to Krasi Wasilev, at http://freegameassets.blogspot.com.) To create the player, follow these steps:

1. Create a new folder in your Project view called Spaceship and import spaceship.png from the book files into this folder. Note that the spaceship sprite is currently facing downward. This is okay.

2. Select the spaceship sprite and in the Inspector set Sprite Mode to **Multiple** and click **Apply**. Then click **Sprite Editor** to start slicing your sprite sheet. (If you've forgotten about slicing, look back at Hour 12, "2D Game Tools.")

3. Click **Slice** in the upper left of the Sprite Editor window and set Type to **Grid By Cell Size**. Set x to **116** and y to **140** (see Figure 15.3). Click **Slice** and notice the outlines around the ships. Click **Apply** and close the Sprite Editor window.

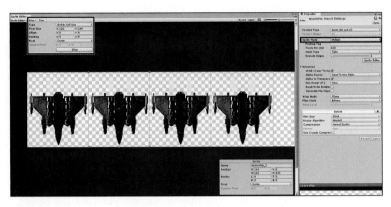

FIGURE 15.3
Slicing the spaceship sprite sheet.

4. Open the tray of the spaceship and select all the frames. You can do this by clicking the first frame, holding down **Shift**, and then clicking the last frame.

5. Drag the sprite frames to the Hierarchy view or Scene view. This causes a Create New Animation dialog to appear, which will save your new animation as an .anim file. Name this animation **Ship**. When you are done, an animated sprite will be added to the scene, and an animator controller and animation clip asset will be added to the Project view as in Figure 15.4. (You will learn more about animation in Hour 17, "Animations," and Hour 18, "Animators.")

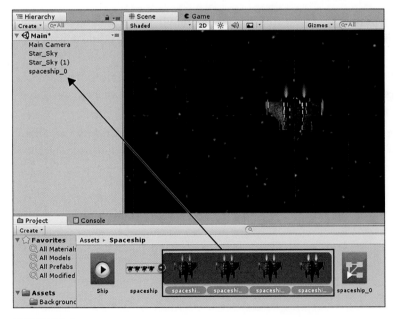

FIGURE 15.4
The finished spaceship sprite.

6. Set the ship's position to (0, -5, 0) and scale it to (1, -1, 1). Note that scaling to -1 in the y axis turns the ship to face upward.

7. On the ship's Sprite Renderer component, set the Order in Layer property to 1. This ensures that the ship always appears in front of the background.

8. Add a Polygon Collider component to the ship (by selecting **Add Component > Physics2D > Polygon Collider**). This collider will automatically surround your ship for very decent collision detection accuracy. Be sure to check the **Is Trigger** property in the Inspector to ensure that it is a trigger collider.

9. Play the game and notice the subtle animation of the ship's engines.

You should now have a nice, animated upward-facing spaceship ready to destroy some meteors.

The Meteors

The steps for creating the meteors are similar to those for creating the spaceship. The only difference is that the meteors will end up in a prefab for later use. Follow these steps:

1. Create a new folder called Meteor and import meteor.png into it. This is a sprite sheet that contains 19 frames of animation.

2. Set Sprite Mode to **Multiple** and then enter the Sprite Editor as before.

3. Set Slice Type to **Automatic** and leave the rest of the settings at their defaults. Click **Apply** to apply your changes and close the Sprite Editor window.

4. Expand the tray of the meteor sprite and select all 19 frames of the meteor sprite sheet. Drag these frames into the Hierarchy view and, when prompted, name the animation **Meteor**. Unity creates another animated sprite with the necessary animation components for you. Handy!

5. Select the meteor_0 game object in the Hierarchy view and add a Circle Collider 2D component (by selecting **Add Component > Physics2D > Circle Collider 2D**). Note that the green outline roughly fits the outline of the sprite. This is good enough to work in the *Captain Blaster* game. A polygon collider would be less efficient and would not give you a noticeable improvement in accuracy.

6. On the meteor's Sprite Renderer component, set the Order in Layer property to 1 to ensure that the meteor always appears in front of the background.

7. Add a Rigidbody2D component to the meteor (by selecting **Add Component > Physics2D > Rigidbody2D**). Set the Gravity Scale property to 0.

8. Rename the meteor_0 game object **Meteor** and then drag it from your Hierarchy view into your Meteor folder in the Project view (see Figure 15.5). Unity creates a prefab of the meteor that you will use later.

9. Now that you have captured the meteor setup in a prefab, delete the instance in your Hierarchy view. You now have a reusable meteor just waiting to cause havoc.

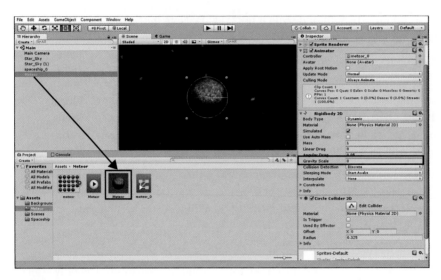

FIGURE 15.5
Creating the meteor prefab.

The Bullets

Setting up bullets in this game is simple. Because they will be moving very quickly, they don't need any detail. To create the bullet, follow these steps:

1. Create a folder named Bullet and import bullet.png into it. With the new bullet sprite selected in the Project view, set the Pixels per Unit property in the Inspector to **400**.

2. Drag a bullet sprite into your scene. Using the Color property of the Sprite Renderer component, give the bullet a strong green color.

3. On the Sprite Renderer component of the bullets, set the Order in Layer property to **1** to ensure that the bullet always appears in front of the background.

4. Add a Circle Collider 2D component to the bullet. Also add a Rigidbody2D component to the bullet (by selecting **Add Component > Physics2D > Rigidbody2D**) and set the Gravity Scale property to **0**.

5. To keep with convention, rename the bullet game object **Bullet**. Drag the bullet from the Hierarchy view into your Bullet folder to turn it into a prefab. Delete the Bullet object from your scene.

That's the last of the primary entities. The only thing left to make is the triggers that will prevent the bullets and meteor from traveling forever.

The Triggers

The triggers (which in this game will be called "shredders") are simply two colliders, one of which will sit above the screen and the other below it. Their job is to catch any errant bullets and meteors and "shred" them. Follow these steps to create the shredders:

1. Add an empty game object to the scene (by selecting **GameObject > Create Empty**) and name it **Shredder**. Position it at (0, -10, 0).

2. Add a Box Collider 2D component to the shredder object (by selecting **Add Component > Physics2D > Box Collider 2D**). In the Inspector view, be sure to put a check next to the **Is Trigger** property of the Box Collider 2D component and set its size to (16, 1).

3. Duplicate the shredder and place the new one at (0, 10, 0).

Later these triggers will be used to destroy any objects that hit them, such as stray meteors or bullets.

The UI

Finally, you need to add a simple user interface to display the player's current score and to say "Game Over" when the player dies. Follow these steps:

1. Add a UI Text element to the scene (by selecting **GameObject > UI > Text**) and rename it **Score**.

2. Position the score text's anchor in the upper-left corner of the canvas and set its position to (100, -30, 0) (see Figure 15.6).

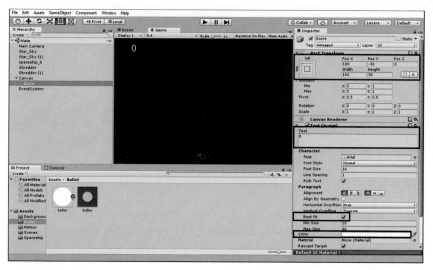

FIGURE 15.6
The player score settings.

3. Set the Text property of the Score object to **0** (which is the initial score), check **Best Fit**, and set Color to white.

Now you can add the Game Over text that will appear when the player loses:

1. Add another UI Text element to the scene and rename it **Game Over**. Leave the anchor in the center and set its position to (0, 0, 0).

2. Set the width of the Game Over text object to **200** and set the height to **100**.

3. Change the Text to **Game Over!**, check the **Best Fit** property, set the paragraph alignment to centered, and change the color to red.

4. Finally, uncheck the box next to the Text (Script) component's name to disable the text until it is needed (see Figure 15.7). Note that Figure 15.7 illustrates the text before being disabled so you can see what it looks like.

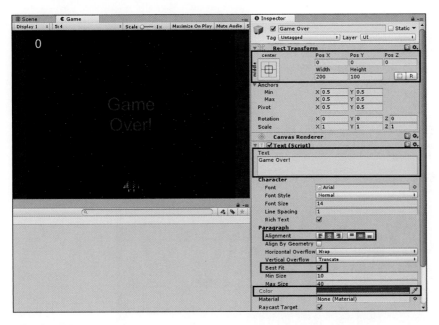

FIGURE 15.7
The Game Over! sign settings.

Later you will connect this score display to your GameManager script so that it can be updated. Now all your entities are in place, and it is time to begin turning this scene into a game.

Controls

Various script components need to be assembled to make this game work. The player needs to be able to move the ship and shoot bullets. The bullets and meteors need to be able to move automatically. A meteor spawn object must keep the meteors flowing. The shredders need to be able to clean up objects, and a manager needs to keep track of all the action.

The Game Manager

The game manager is basic in this game, and you can add it first. To create the game manager, follow these steps:

1. Create an empty game object and name it **GameManager**.

2. Because the only asset you have for the game manager is a script, create a new folder called Scripts so that you have a place for any simple scripts you create.

3. Create a new script named **GameManager** in the Scripts folder and attach it to the GameManager game object. Overwrite the contents of the script with the following code:

```
using UnityEngine;
using UnityEngine.UI; // Note this new line is needed for UI

public class GameManager : MonoBehaviour
{
    public Text scoreText;
    public Text gameOverText;

    int playerScore = 0;

    public void AddScore()
    {
        playerScore++;
        // This converts the score (a number) into a string
        scoreText.text = playerScore.ToString();
    }

    public void PlayerDied()
    {
        gameOverText.enabled = true;
        // This freezes the game
        Time.timeScale = 0;
    }
}
```

In this code, you can see that the manager is responsible for keeping the score and knowing when the game is running. The manager has two public methods: `PlayerDied()` and `AddScore()`. `PlayerDied()` is called by the player when a meteor hits it. `AddScore()` is called by a bullet when it kills a meteor.

Remember to drag the Score and Game Over elements onto the GameManager script (see Figure 15.8).

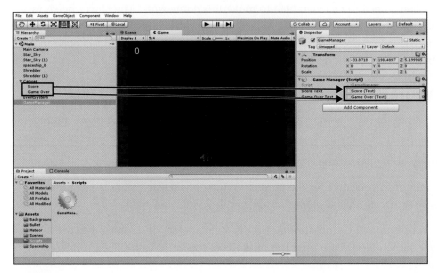

FIGURE 15.8
Attaching the text elements to the game manager.

The Meteor Script

Meteors are basically going to fall from the top of the screen and get in the player's way. To create the meteor script:

1. Create a new script in your Meteor folder and call it **MeteorMover**.

2. Select your meteor prefab. In the Inspector view, locate the Add Component button (see Figure 15.9) and select **Add Component > Scripts > MeteorMover**.

3. Overwrite the code in the MeteorMover script with the following:

```
using UnityEngine;

public class MeteorMover : MonoBehaviour
{
    public float speed = -2f;

    Rigidbody2D rigidBody;

    void Start()
    {
        rigidBody = GetComponent<Rigidbody2D>();
        // Give meteor an initial downward velocity
        rigidBody.velocity = new Vector2(0, speed);
    }
}
```

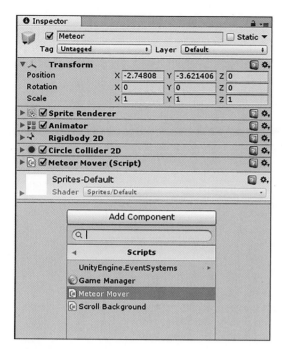

FIGURE 15.9
Adding the Meteor script to the meteor prefab.

The meteor is very basic and contains only a single public variable to represent its downward velocity. In the `Start()` method, you get a reference to the Rigidbody 2D component on the meteor. You then use that rigidbody to set the velocity of the meteor; it moves downward because the speed has a negative value. Notice that the meteor is not responsible for determining collision.

Feel free to drag the meteor prefab into the Hierarchy view and click **Play** so you can see the effect of the code you just wrote. The meteor should slide down and spin slightly. If you do this, be sure to delete the Meteor instance from the Hierarchy view when you're done.

The Meteor Spawn

So far, the meteors are just prefabs with no way of getting into the scene. You need an object to be responsible for spawning the meteors at an interval. Create a new empty game object, rename it **Meteor Spawn**, and place it at (0, 8, 0). Create a new script named MeteorSpawn in your Meteor folder and place it on the Meteor Spawn object. Overwrite the code in the script with the following:

```
using UnityEngine;

public class MeteorSpawn : MonoBehaviour
{
    public GameObject meteorPrefab;
    public float minSpawnDelay = 1f;
    public float maxSpawnDelay = 3f;
    public float spawnXLimit = 6f;

    void Start()
    {
        Spawn();
    }

    void Spawn()
    {
        // Create a meteor at a random x position
        float random = Random.Range(-spawnXLimit, spawnXLimit);
        Vector3 spawnPos = transform.position + new Vector3(random, 0f, 0f);
        Instantiate(meteorPrefab, spawnPos, Quaternion.identity);

        Invoke("Spawn", Random.Range(minSpawnDelay, maxSpawnDelay));
    }
}
```

This script is doing a few interesting things. First, it creates two variables to manage the meteor timing. It also declares a GameObject variable, which will be the meteor prefab. In the Start() method you call the function Spawn(). This function is responsible for creating and placing the meteors.

You can see that the meteor is spawned at the same y and z coordinate as the spawn point, but the x coordinate is offset by a number between -6 and 6. This allows the meteors to spawn across the screen and not always in the same spot. When the position for the new meteor is determined, the Spawn() function instantiates (creates) a meteor at that position with default rotation (Quaternion.identity). The last line invokes a call to the spawn function again. This method, Invoke(), calls the named function (in this case Spawn()) after a random amount of time. That random amount is controlled by the two timing variables.

In the Unity editor, click and drag your meteor prefab from the Project view onto the Meteor Prefab property of the Meteor Spawn Script component of the Meteor Spawn object. (Try saying that fast!) Run the scene, and you should see meteors spawning across the screen. (Attack, my minions!)

The DestroyOnTrigger Script

Now that you have meteors spawning everywhere, it is a good idea to begin cleaning them up. Create a new script called DestroyOnTrigger in your Scripts folder (since it is a single unrelated asset) and attach it to both the upper and the lower shredder objects you created previously. Add the following code to the script, ensuring that this code is outside a method but inside the class:

```
void OnTriggerEnter2D(Collider2D other)
{
    Destroy(other.gameObject);
}
```

This basic script simply destroys any object that enters it. Because the players cannot move vertically, you don't need to worry about them getting destroyed. Only bullets and meteors can enter the triggers.

The ShipControl Script

Right now, meteors are falling down, and the player can't get out of the way. You need to create a script to control the player next. Create a new script called ShipControl in your Spaceship folder and attach it to the spaceship object in your scene. Replace the code in the script with the following:

```
using UnityEngine;

public class ShipControl : MonoBehaviour
{
    public GameManager gameManager;
    public GameObject bulletPrefab;
    public float speed = 10f;
    public float xLimit = 7f;
    public float reloadTime = 0.5f;

    float elapsedTime = 0f;

    void Update()
    {
        // Keeping track of time for bullet firing
        elapsedTime += Time.deltaTime;

        // Move the player left and right
        float xInput = Input.GetAxis("Horizontal");
        transform.Translate(xInput * speed * Time.deltaTime, 0f, 0f);

        // Clamp the ship's x position
        Vector3 position = transform.position;
        position.x = Mathf.Clamp(position.x, -xLimit, xLimit);
        transform.position = position;

        // Spacebar fires. The default InputManager settings call this "Jump"
        // Only happens if enough time has elapsed since last firing.
```

```
        if (Input.GetButtonDown("Jump") && elapsedTime > reloadTime)
        {
            // Instantiate the bullet 1.2 units in front of the player
            Vector3 spawnPos = transform.position;
            spawnPos += new Vector3(0, 1.2f, 0);
            Instantiate(bulletPrefab, spawnPos, Quaternion.identity);

            elapsedTime = 0f; // Reset bullet firing timer
        }
    }

    // If a meteor hits the player
    void OnTriggerEnter2D(Collider2D other)
    {
        gameManager.PlayerDied();
    }
}
```

This script does a lot of work. It starts by creating variables for the game manager, the bullet prefab, speed, movement limitations, and bullet timing.

In the Update() method, the script starts by getting the elapsed time. This is used to determine whether enough time has passed to fire a bullet. Remember that according to the rules, the player can fire a bullet only every half a second. The player is then moved along the x axis based on input. The player's x axis position is *clamped* (that is, limited) so that the player cannot go off the screen to the left or right. After that, the script determines whether the player is pressing the spacebar. Normally in Unity, the spacebar is used for a jump action. (This could be renamed in the input manager, but it was left as it is to avoid any confusion.) If it is determined that the player is pressing the spacebar, the script checks the elapsed time against the reloadTime (currently half a second). If the time is greater, the script creates a bullet. Notice that the script creates the bullet just a little above the ship. This prevents the bullet from colliding with the ship. Finally, the elapsed time is reset to 0 so the count for the next bullet firing can start.

The last part of the script contains the OnTriggerEnter2D() method. This method is called whenever a meteor hits the player. When that happens, the GameManager script is informed that the player died.

Back in the Unity editor, click and drag the bullet prefab onto the Bullet property of the Ship Control component on the spaceship. Likewise, click and drag the Game Manager object onto the Ship Control component to give it access to the GameManager script (see Figure 15.10). Run the scene and notice that you can now move the player. The player should be able to fire bullets (although they don't move). Also notice that the player can now die and end the game.

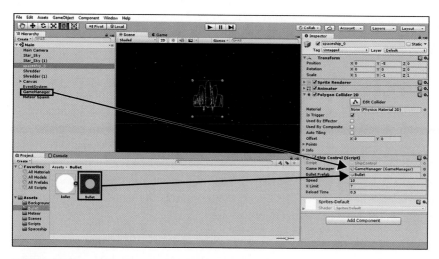

FIGURE 15.10
Connecting the ShipControl script.

The Bullet Script

The last bit of interactivity you need is to make the bullets move and collide. Create a new script called Bullet in your Bullet folder and add it to the bullet prefab. Replace the code in the script with the following:

```
using UnityEngine;

public class Bullet : MonoBehaviour
{
    public float speed = 10f;

    GameManager gameManager; // Note this is private this time

    void Start()
    {
        // Because the bullet doesn't exist until the game is running
        // we must find the Game Manager a different way.
        gameManager = GameObject.FindObjectOfType<GameManager>();

        Rigidbody2D rigidBody = GetComponent<Rigidbody2D>();
        rigidBody.velocity = new Vector2(0f, speed);
    }

    void OnCollisionEnter2D(Collision2D other)
    {
        Destroy(other.gameObject); // Destroy the meteor
```

```
        gameManager.AddScore(); // Increment the score
        Destroy(gameObject); // Destroy the bullet
    }
}
```

The major difference between this script and the meteor script is that this script needs to account for collision and the player scoring. The Bullet script declares a variable to hold a reference to the GameManager script, just as the ShipControl script does. Because the bullet isn't actually in the Scene view, however, it needs to locate the GameManager script a little differently. In the `Start()` method, the script searches for the GameControl object by type using the `GameObject.FindObjectOfType<Type>()` method. The reference to the GameManager script is then stored in the variable `gameManager`. It is worth noting that Unity's `Find()` methods (such as the one used here) are very slow and should be used sparingly.

Because neither the bullet nor the meteor has a trigger collider on it, the use of the `OnTriggerEnter2D()` method will not work. Instead, the script uses the method `OnCollisionEnter2D()`. This method does not read in a `Collider2D` variable. Instead, it reads in a `Collision2D` variable. The differences between these two methods are irrelevant in this case. The only work being done is destroying both objects and telling the GameManager script that the player scored.

Go ahead and run the game. You should find that the game is now fully playable. Although you cannot win (that is intentional), you certainly can lose. Keep playing and see what kind of score you can get!

As a fun challenge, consider trying to make the values of `minSpawnDelay` and `maxSpawnDelay` get smaller over time, causing the meteors to spawn more quickly as the game is played.

Improvements

It is time to improve the game. As with the games you have created in earlier hours, several parts of *Captain Blaster* are left intentionally basic. Be sure to play through the game several times and see what you notice. What things are fun? What things are not fun? Are there any obvious ways to break the game? Note that a very easy cheat has been left in the game to allow players to get a high score. Can you find it?

Here are some things you could consider changing:

▶ Try modifying the bullet speeds, firing delay, or bullet flight path.

▶ Try allowing the player to fire two bullets side by side.

▶ Make the meteors spawn faster as time goes on.

▶ Try adding a different type of meteor.

▶ Give the player extra health—and maybe even a shield.

▶ Allow the player to move vertically as well as horizontally.

This is a common genre, and there are many ways you can make it unique. Try to see just how custom you can make the game. It is also worth noting that you will learn about particle systems in Hour 16, "Particle Systems," and this game is a prime candidate for trying them out.

Summary

In this hour, you made the game *Captain Blaster*. You started by designing the game elements. Next, you built the game world. You constructed and animated a vertically scrolling background. From there, you built the various game entities. You added interactivity through scripting and controls. Finally, you examined the game and looked for improvements.

Q&A

Q. Did *Captain Blaster* really achieve the military rank of captain, or is it just a name?

A. It's hard to say, as it is all mostly speculation. One thing is for certain: They don't give spaceships to mere lieutenants!

Q. Why delay bullet firing by half a second?

A. Mostly it is a balance issue. If the player can fire too fast, the game has no challenge.

Q. Why use a polygon collider on the ship?

A. Because the ship has an odd size, a standard shaped collider wouldn't be very accurate. Luckily, you can use the polygon collider to map closely to the geometry of the ship.

Workshop

Take some time to work through the questions here to ensure that you have a firm grasp of the material.

Quiz

1. What is the win condition for the game?

2. How does the scrolling background work?

3. Which objects have rigidbodies? Which objects have colliders?

4. True or False: The meteor is responsible for detecting collision with the player.

Answers

1. This is a trick question. The player cannot win the game. The highest score, however, allows the player to "win" outside the game.

2. Two identical sprites are positioned, one above the other, on the y axis. They then leapfrog across the camera to seem endless.

3. The bullets and meteors have rigidbodies. The bullets, meteors, ship, and triggers have colliders.

4. False. The ShipControl script detects the collision.

Exercise

This exercise is a little different from the ones you have done so far. A common part of the game refinement process is to have a game playtested by people who aren't involved with the development process. This allows people who are completely unfamiliar with the game to give honest, first-experience feedback, which is incredibly useful. For this exercise, have other people play the game. Try to get a diverse group of people—some avid gamers and some people who don't play games, some people who are fans of this genre and some people who aren't. Compile their feedback into groupings of good features, bad features, and things that can be improved. In addition, try to see whether there are any commonly requested features that currently aren't in the game. Finally, see if you can implement or improve your game based on the feedback received.

HOUR 16
Particle Systems

What You'll Learn in This Hour:

▶ The basics of particle systems
▶ How to work with modules
▶ How to use the Curves Editor

In this hour, you'll learn how to use Unity's particle system. You'll start by learning about particle systems in general and how they work. You'll experiment with the many different particle system modules. You'll wrap up the hour by experimenting with the Unity Curves Editor.

Particle Systems

A particle system is basically an object or component that emits other objects, commonly referred to as *particles*. These particles can be fast, slow, flat, shaped, small, large, and so on. The definition is very generic because these systems can achieve a great variety of effects with the proper settings. They can make jets of fire, plumes of billowing smoke, fireflies, rain, fog, or anything else you can think of. These effects are commonly referred to as *particle effects*.

Particles

A *particle* is a single entity that is emitted by a particle system. Because many particles are generally emitted quickly, it is important for particles to be as efficient as possible. This is the reason that most particles are 2D billboards. A *billboard* is a flat image that always faces the camera. This gives the illusion that billboards are 3D, while still giving great performance.

Unity Particle Systems

To create a particle system in a scene, you can either create a particle system object or add a particle system component to an existing object. To create a particle system object, select **GameObject > Effects > Particle System**. To add a particle system component to an existing object, select the object and click **Add Component > Effects > Particle System**.

▼ TRY IT YOURSELF

Creating a Particle System

Follow these steps to create a particle system object in a scene:

1. Create a new project or scene.

2. Add a particle system by selecting **GameObject > Effects > Particle System**.

3. Notice how the particle system emits white particles in the Scene view (see Figure 16.1). This is the basic particle system. Try rotating and scaling the particle system to see how it reacts.

FIGURE 16.1
The basic particle system.

NOTE

Custom Particles

By default, the particles in Unity are small white spheres that fade into transparency. This is a really useful generic particle, but it can only take you so far. Sometimes you want something more specific (to make fire, for example). If you want, you can make your own particles out of any 2D image to create effects that exactly suit your needs.

Particle System Controls

You might have noticed that when you added a particle system to your scene, it began emitting particles in the Scene view. You may also have noticed that particle effect controls appeared (see Figure 16.2). These controls allow you to pause, stop, and restart the particle animation in a scene. This can be very helpful when tweaking the behavioral components of a particle system.

FIGURE 16.2
The particle effect control.

These controls also allow you to speed up the playback and tell you how long an effect has been playing. This can be very useful when testing duration effects. Note that the controls show the playback speed and playback time only when the game is stopped.

NOTE

Particle Effects

To create complex and visually appealing effects, you can have several particle systems work together (a smoke and a fire system, for example). Multiple particle systems working together creates a *particle effect*. In Unity, creating a particle effect is achieved by nesting particle systems together. One particle system can be the child of another, or they can both be children of a different object. The result of a particle effect in Unity is that the effects are treated as one system, and you can use the particle effect controls to control the entire particle effect as one unit.

Particle System Modules

At its root, a particle system is just a point in space that emits particle objects. How particles look and behave and the effects they cause are all determined by modules. *Modules* are various properties that define some form of behavior. In Unity's particle system, modules are an integrated and essential component. This section lists the modules and explains briefly what each one does.

Note that with the exception of the default module (covered first), all modules can be turned on and off. To turn modules on or off, put a check mark by the module's name. To hide or show modules, click the plus sign (+) next to Particle System (see Figure 16.3). You can also click the name of a particle system in the list to toggle its visibility. By default, all modules are visible, and only the Emission, Shape, and Renderer modules are enabled. To expand a module, simply click its title.

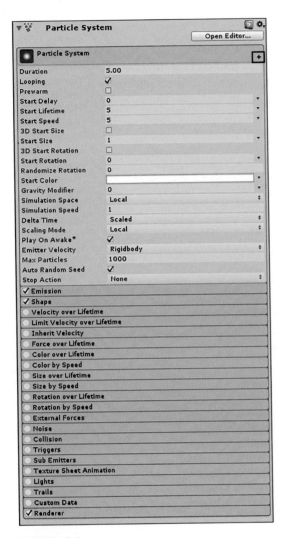

FIGURE 16.3
Showing all modules.

Properties Overview, Briefly

Several modules have properties that are either self-explanatory (like the length and width property of a rectangle) or have been covered previously. For the sake of simplicity (and to prevent this hour from being 50 pages), these properties are not described in this section. So if you see more properties on your screen than are covered in this text, don't worry; that is intentional.

Constant, Curve, Random

A value curve allows you to change the value of a property over the lifetime of a particle system or an individual particle. You can tell that a property can use curves because there is a downward-facing arrow next to the value. The options you see are Constant, Curve, Random Between Two Constants, and Random Between Two Curves. In this section, the value is always Constant. Later in this hour, you'll get a chance to explore the Curves Editor in detail.

Default Module

The default module is simply labeled Particle System. This module contains all the specific information that every particle system requires. Table 16.1 describes the properties of the default module.

TABLE 16.1   Default Module Properties

Property	Description
Duration	Specifies how long, in seconds, the particle system runs.
Looping	Determines whether the particle system starts over when the Duration value has been reached.
Prewarm	Specifies whether the particle system should start as if it had already emitted particles from a previous cycle.
Start Delay	Specifies how long, in seconds, the system waits before emitting particles.
Start Lifetime	Specifies how long, in seconds, each particle lives.
Start Speed	Determines the initial speed of particles.
Start Size	Specifies the initial size of a particle. If you check the property 3D Start Size, you can provide different size values along the three axes. Otherwise, it is one size fits all.
Start Rotation	Specifies the initial rotation of particles. If you check the property 3D Start Rotation, you can specify a rotation value about the three axes. Otherwise, only one value is used.
Randomize Rotation	Causes some particles to rotate in the opposite direction.
Start Color	Specifies the color of emitted particles.
Gravity Modifier	Specifies how much of the world's gravity is applied to the particles.
Simulation Space	Determines whether the coordinate and axes values are based on the world coordinate system or the local coordinate system of a parent game object.

Property	Description
Simulation Speed	Allows fine-tuning of the speed for an entire particle system.
Delta Time	Determines whether the timing of a particle system is based on scaled time or unscaled time.
Scaling Mode	Determines whether the scale is based on the game object, the object's parent, or the shape of the emitter.
Play on Wake	Determines whether the particle system begins emitting particles immediately when created.
Emitter Velocity	Allows you to choose whether velocity is calculated from the object's transform or its rigidbody (if it has one).
Max Particles	Specifies the total number of particles that can exist for a system at a time. If this number is reached, the system ceases emitting until some particles die.
Auto Random Seed	Determines whether the particle system will look different each time it is played.
Stop Action	Allows you to specify what happens when the particle system finishes. For instance, you could disable or destroy the game object or request a script callback to occur.

Emission Module

The Emission module is used to determine the rate at which particles are emitted. Using this module, you can dictate whether particles stream at a constant rate, in bursts, or somewhere in between. Table 16.2 describes the Emission module properties.

TABLE 16.2 Emission Module Properties

Property	Description
Rate over Time	Specifies the number of particles emitted over time.
Rate over Distance	Specifies the number of particles emitted over distance.
Bursts	Specifies bursts of particles at specific time intervals. You can create a burst by clicking the plus sign (+) and remove a burst by clicking the minus sign (−) (see Figure 16.4).

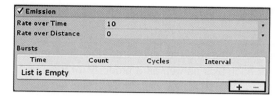

FIGURE 16.4
The Emission module.

Shape Module

Just as its name implies, the Shape module determines the shape formed by the emitted particles. The shape options are Sphere, Hemisphere, Cone, Donut, Box, Mesh, Mesh Renderer, Skinned Mesh Renderer, Circle, and Edge (whew!). In addition, each shape has a set of properties used to define it, such as radius for cones and spheres. These properties are fairly self-explanatory, so they are not covered here.

Velocity over Lifetime Module

The Velocity over Lifetime module directly animates each particle by applying an x, y, and z axis velocity to it. Note that this is a velocity change of each particle over the lifetime of the particle, not over the lifetime of the particle system. Table 16.3 describes the properties of the Velocity over Lifetime module.

TABLE 16.3 Velocity over Lifetime Module Properties

Property	Description
XYZ	Specifies the velocity applied to each particle. This can be a constant, curve, or random number between a constant or curve.
Space	Dictates whether the velocity is added based on local or world space.
Speed Modifier	Allows you to scale the individual velocities all at once.

Limit Velocity over Lifetime Module

This long-named module can be used to dampen or clamp the velocity of a particle. Basically, it prevents, or slows down, particles that exceed a threshold speed on one or all of the axes. Table 16.4 describes the properties for the Limit Velocity over Lifetime module.

TABLE 16.4 Limit Velocity over Lifetime Module Properties

Property	Description
Separate Axis	If unchecked, uses the same value for each axis. If checked, uses speed properties for each axis as well as a property for local or world space.
Speed	Specifies the threshold speed for each or all axes.
Dampen	Specifies the value, between 0 and 1, by which a particle will be slowed if it exceeds the threshold, as determined by the Speed property. A value of 0 does not slow a particle at all, but a value of 1 slows the particle 100%.
Drag	Specifies the amount of linear drag to apply to particles.
Multiply by Size	Determines whether larger particles will be slowed more.
Multiply by Velocity	Determines whether faster particles will be slowed more.

Inherit Velocity Module

The Inherit Velocity Module is very simple and determines how much, if any, of the velocity of the emitter should be applied to the particle. The first property, Mode, specifies if only the initial velocity is applied or if the particle should continue receiving the velocity of the emitter. Finally, the Multiplier property determines the proportion of velocity to apply.

Force over Lifetime Module

The Force over Lifetime module is similar to the Velocity over Lifetime module. The difference is that this module applies a force, not a velocity, to each particle. This means the particle will continue to accelerate in the specified direction. This module also allows you to randomize the force each frame, as opposed to all up front.

Color over Lifetime Module

The Color over Lifetime module allows you to change the color of a particle as time passes. This is useful for creating effects like sparks, which start out bright orange and end a dark red before disappearing. To use this module, you must specify a gradient of color. You can also specify two gradients and have Unity randomly pick a color between them. Gradients can be edited using Unity's Gradient Editor (see Figure 16.5).

FIGURE 16.5
The Gradient Editor.

Note that the color of the gradient is multiplied by the Start Color property of the default module. Therefore, if your start color is black, the Color over Lifetime module will have no effect.

Color by Speed Module

The Color by Speed module allows you to change the color of a particle based on its speed. Table 16.5 describes the properties of the Color by Speed module.

TABLE 16.5   Color by Speed Module Properties

Property	Description
Color	Specifies a gradient (or two gradients for random colors) that is used to dictate the color of the particle.
Speed Range	Specifies the minimum and maximum speed values that are mapped to the color gradient. Particles going the minimum speed are mapped to the left side of the gradient, and colors at the maximum speed (or beyond) are mapped to the right side of the gradient.

Size over Lifetime Module

The Size over Lifetime module allows you to specify a change in the size of a particle. The size value must be a curve, and it dictates whether the particle grows or shrinks as time elapses.

Size by Speed Module

Much like the Color by Speed module, the Size by Speed module changes the size of a particle based on its speed between minimum and maximum values.

Rotation over Lifetime Module

The Rotation over Lifetime module allows you to specify a rotation over the life of a particle. Note that the rotation is of the particle itself, not a curve in the world coordinate system. This means that if your particle is a plain circle, you will not be able to see the rotation. If the particle has some detail, however, you will notice it spin. The values for the rotation can be given as a constant, curve, or random number.

Rotation by Speed Module

The Rotation by Speed module is the same as the Rotation over Lifetime module except that it changes values based on the speed of the particle. Rotation changes based on minimum and maximum speed values.

External Forces Module

The External Forces module allows you to apply a multiplier to any forces that exist outside the particle system. A good example of this is any wind forces that exist in a scene. The Multiplier property scales the forces either up or down, depending on its value.

Noise Module

The Noise module is a relatively new module for Unity's particle system. This module allows you to apply some randomization to the movement of a particle (think lightning bolts, for example). It accomplishes this by generating a *Perlin noise* image to use as a lookup table. You can see the noise being used in the Preview window of the module. Table 16.6 lists the properties of the Noise module.

TABLE 16.6 Noise Module Properties

Property	Description
Separate Axes	Dictates whether the noise will be applied equally to all axes or whether different values will be derived for each.
Strength	Defines how strong the noise effect is on a particle over its lifetime. Higher values make particles move faster and farther.
Frequency	Specifies how often particles change their direction of travel. Low values create soft, smooth noise, and high values create rapidly changing noise.

Property	Description
Scroll Speed	Causes the noise field to move over time to cause more unpredictable and erratic particle movement.
Damping	Determines whether strength is proportional to frequency.
Octaves	Determines how many overlapping layers of noise are applied. Higher numbers give more rich and interesting noise but at the cost of performance.
Octave Multiplier	Reduces the strength of each additional noise layer.
Octave Scale	Adjusts the frequency for each additional noise layer.
Quality	Allows you to adjust the quality of the noise to regain some performance.
Remap and Remap Curve	Allows you to remap the final value of the noise into something else. You can use a curve to specify which noise values should be translated into other values.
Position, Rotation, and Size Amount	Control how much the noise affects position, rotation, and scale of a particle.

Collision Module

The Collision module allows you to set up collisions for particles. This is useful for all sorts of collision effects, like fire rolling off a wall or rain hitting the ground. You can set the collision to work with predetermined planes (Planes mode is the most efficient) or with objects in the scene (World mode slows performance). The Collision module has some common properties and some unique properties, depending on the collision type chosen. Table 16.7 describes the common properties of the Collision module. Tables 16.8 and 16.9 describe the properties of Planes mode and World mode, respectively.

TABLE 16.7 Common Collision Module Properties

Property	Description
Planes and World	Dictates the type of collision used. Planes collide off predetermined planes. World mode collides off any object in a scene.
Dampen	Determines the amount a particle is slowed when it collides. Values range from 0 to 1.
Bounce	Determines what fraction of the component of velocity is kept. Unlike Dampen, this only affects the axes the particle bounces on. Values range between 0 and 1.
Lifetime Loss	Determines how much life of a particle is lost on collision. Values range from 0 to 1.

Property	Description
Min Kill Speed	Specifies the minimum speed of a particle before it is killed by collision.
Max Kill Speed	Specifies the speed above which particles that collide will be removed from the system.
Radius Scale	Adjusts the radius of the particle collision spheres so it more closely fits the visual edges of the particle graphic.
Send Collision Messages	Determines whether collision messages are sent to objects that collide with particles.
Visualize Bounds	Renders the collision bounds of each particle as a wireframe shape in the Scene view.

TABLE 16.8 Planes Mode Properties

Property	Description
Planes	Determines where the particles can collide. The y axis of the transforms provided determines the rotation of the plane.
Visualization	Determines how the planes are drawn in the Scene view. They can either be solid or grid.
Scale Plane	Resizes the visualization of the planes.

TABLE 16.9 World Mode Properties

Property	Description
Collision Mode	Specifies whether to use 2D or 3D.
Collision Quality	Indicates the quality of the world collision. The values are High, Medium, and Low. Obviously, High is the most CPU intensive and most accurate, and Low is the least.
Collides With	Determines which layers the particles collide with. This is set to Everything by default.
Max Collision Shapes	Specifies the number of shapes that can be considered for collision. Excess shapes are ignored, and terrains take priority.
Enabled Dynamic Colliders	Determines whether particles can collide with non-static (non-kinematic) colliders.
Collider Force and Multiply Options	Allow particles to apply force to objects they collide with. This allows particles to push objects. Additional check boxes allow more force to be applied based on angle of collision, speed of particle, and size of particle.

Making Particles Collide

In this exercise, you'll set up collision with a particle system. This exercise uses both Planes and World collision modes. Follow these steps:

1. Create a new project or scene. Add a sphere to the scene and place it at (0, 5, 0) with a scale of (3, 3, 3). Give the sphere a Rigidbody component.

2. Add a particle system to the scene and place it at (0, 0, 0). Under the Emission module in the Inspector, set Rate over Time to 100.

3. Enable the Collision module by clicking the circle next to its name. Set Type to World and set Collider Force to 20 (see Figure 16.6). Notice how the particles are already bouncing off the sphere.

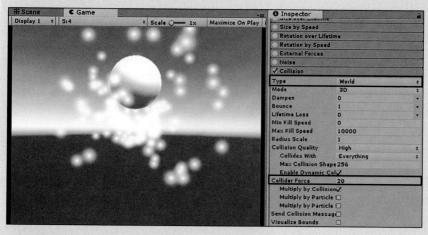

FIGURE 16.6
Adding a plane transform.

4. Enter Play mode and notice how the sphere is buoyed by the particles.

5. Experiment with the various emission, shape, and collision settings. See how long you can keep the sphere in the air.

TIP

Emitter Versus Particle Settings

Some modules modify the emitter, while others modify the particles. You may wonder why there is a Color property and also a Color over Lifetime property. One controls the color over the life of the emitter, while the other makes particles change color over their life.

Triggers Module

The Triggers module "triggers" a response to a particle entering a collider volume. You can respond to the event of a particle being inside a volume, outside a volume, entering a volume, and exiting a volume. When any of these happens, you can ignore the event, destroy the particle, or call a method in some code and define custom behavior.

Sub Emitter Module

The Sub Emitter module is an incredibly powerful module that enables you to spawn a new particle system at certain events for each particle of the current system. You can create a new particle system every time a particle is created, dies, or collides. In doing this, you can generate complex and intricate effects, such as fireworks. This module has three properties: Birth, Death, and Collision. Each of these properties holds zero or more particle systems to be created on the respective events.

Texture Sheet Module

The Texture Sheet module allows you to change the texture coordinates used for a particle over the life of the particle. In essence, this means you can put several textures for a particle in a single image and then switch between them during the life of a particle (as you did with the sprite animation in Hour 15, "Game 3: *Captain Blaster*"). Table 16.10 describes the properties of the Texture Sheet module.

TABLE 16.10   Texture Sheet Module Properties

Property	Description
Mode	Determines whether you will use the tradition texture sheet method or provide individual sprite to cycle through.
Tiles	Specifies the number of tiles the texture is divided into in the x (horizontal) and y (vertical) directions.
Animation	Determines whether the whole image contains textures for the particle or whether only a single row does.
Cycles	Specifies the speed of the animation.
Flip U and Flip V	Determine whether some of the particles will be flipped horizontally or vertically.

Lights Module

The Lights module allows a portion of the particles to also contain a point light. This allows the particle systems to add illumination to a scene (think of a torch effect, for example). Most of the properties for this module are self-explanatory, but a very important one is the Ratio property.

A value of 0 means that no particles will have a light, and a value of 1 means that all will have a light. It is important to note that adding lights to too many particles will greatly slow down your scene, so use this module sparingly.

Trails Module

The Trails module allows particles to leave a trail behind them. Using the module is a great way to create streaked effects, such as fireworks or lightning bolts. Almost all properties of this module have been covered in other modules or are self-explanatory. The only property that needs to be covered here is the Minimum Vertex Distance property. This property determines how far a particle needs to travel before its trail gets a new vertex. Lower numbers make for smoother trails but are also less efficient.

Custom Data Module

The Custom Data module is really beyond the scope of this book because it performs a very technical and very powerful function. Essentially, this module allows you to pass data from the particle system into a custom shader you've written to utilize that data.

Renderer Module

The Renderer module dictates how the particles are actually drawn. It is here that you can specify the texture used for the particles and their other drawing properties. Table 16.11 describes some of the properties of the Renderer module.

TABLE 16.11 Renderer Module Properties

Property	Description
Render Mode	Determines how the particles are actually drawn. The modes are Billboard, Stretched Billboard, Horizontal Billboard, Vertical Billboard, and Mesh. All the billboard modes cause the particles to align with either the camera or two out of three axes. The Mesh mode causes the particles to be drawn in 3D, as determined by a mesh.
Normal Direction	Dictates how much the particles face the camera. A value of 1 causes the particles to look directly at the camera.
Material and Trail Material	Specify the material used to draw the particle and the particle's trail, respectively.
Sort Mode	Specifies the order in which particles are drawn. Can be None, By Distance, Youngest First, or Oldest First.

Property	Description
Sorting Fudge	Determines the order in which the particle system is drawn. The lower the value, the more likely the system is to be drawn on top of other particles.
Min Particle Size and Max Particle Size	Specify the smallest or largest particle size (regardless of other settings), expressed as a fraction of the viewport size. Note that this setting is only applied when Rendering Mode is set to Billboard.
Render Alignment	Determines whether particles are aligned with the camera, the world, their own transform, or the direct position of the camera (useful for VR).
Pivot	Defines a custom pivot point for particles.
Masking	Determines whether particles interact with a 2D mask.
Custom Vertex Stream	In conjunction with the Custom Data module, determines which particle system properties are passed into custom vertex shaders.
Cast Shadows	Determines whether particles cast shadows.
Receive Shadows	Determines whether particles receive shadows.
Motion Vectors	Determines whether particles use motion vectors for rendering. Leave the default setting for now.
Sorting Layer and Order in Layer	Allow particles to be sorted using the sprite sorting layer system.
Light and Reflection Probes	Allow particles to work with light and reflection probes (if they exist).

The Curves Editor

Several values in the various modules listed previously can be set as Constant or Curve. The Constant option is fairly self-explanatory: You give it a value, and it is that value. What if you want that value to change over a period of time, though? That is where the curve system comes in very handy. This feature gives you a very fine level of control over how a value behaves. You can see the Curves Editor at the bottom of the Inspector view (see Figure 16.7). You may need to drag it up by the horizontal handle.

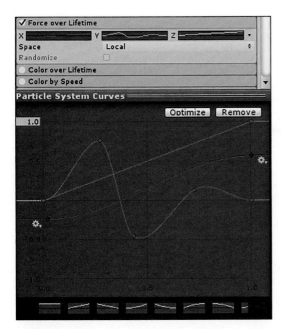

FIGURE 16.7
The Curves Editor in the Inspector.

The title of the curve is whatever value you are determining. In Figure 16.7, the value is for the force applied along the x axis in the Force over Lifetime module. The range dictates the minimum and maximum values available. This can be changed to allow for a greater or lesser range. The curve is the values themselves over a given course of time, and the presets are generic shapes that you can give to the curve.

The curve is movable at any of the key points. These key points are show as visible points along the curve. By default, there are only two key points: one at the beginning and one at the end. You can add a new key point anywhere on the curve by right-clicking it and choosing **Add Key Point** or by double-clicking the curve.

You can get an even larger Curves Editor by clicking the **Open Editor** button at the top right of the Particle System component or by right-clicking the title bar of the Curves Editor.

▼ TRY IT YOURSELF

Using the Curves Editor

To get familiar with the Curves Editor, in this exercise, you'll change the size of the particles emitted over the duration of one cycle of the particle system. Follow these steps:

1. Create a new project or scene. Add a particle system and position it at (0, 0, 0).

2. Click the drop-down arrow next to the Start Size property and choose **Curve**.

3. Change the range of the curve from 1.0 to 2.0 by changing the value in the top left of the Curves Editor.

4. Right-click the curve at about the midpoint and add a key. Now drag the start and end points of the curve down to 0 (see Figure 16.8). Notice how the particles emitted change in size over the 5-second cycle of the particle system.

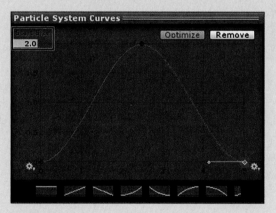

FIGURE 16.8
Start Size curve settings.

Summary

In this hour, you have learned the basics of particles and particle systems in Unity. You have also learned about the many modules that make up the Unity particle system. You wrapped up the hour by looking at the functionality of the Curves Editor.

Q&A

Q. Are particle systems inefficient?

A. They can be, depending on the settings you give them. A good rule of thumb is to use a particle system only if it provides some value to you. Particle systems can be great visually, but don't overdo it.

Workshop

Take some time to work through the questions here to ensure that you have a firm grasp of the material.

Quiz

1. What is the term for a 2D image that always faces the camera?

2. How do you open a larger particle effect editor window?

3. Which module controls how a particle is drawn?

4. True or False: The Curves Editor is used for creating curves that change values over time.

Answers

1. Billboard

2. Click the Open Editor button at the top of the Particle System component in the Inspector.

3. Renderer module

4. True

Exercise

In this exercise, you'll experiment with some exciting particle effects provided as standard packages with Unity. This exercise is a chance both to play around with existing effects and to create your own. There is no correct solution for you to look at. Just follow the steps here and use your imagination:

1. Import the particle effects package by selecting **Assets > Import Package > ParticleSystems**. Be sure to leave all assets checked and click **Import**.

2. Navigate to Assets\Standard Assets\ParticleSystems\Prefabs. Click and drag the FireComplex and Smoke prefabs into the Hierarchy view. Experiment with the positioning and settings of these effects. Click **Play** to see the effects.

3. Continue experimenting with the rest of the provided particle effects. (Be sure to check out the Explosion and Fireworks effects at least.)

4. Now that you have seen what is possible, see what you can create yourself. Try out the various modules and try to come up with your own custom effects.

What You'll Learn in This Hour:

▶ The requirements for animation

▶ The different types of animations

▶ How to create animations in Unity

In this hour, you'll learn about animations in Unity. You'll start by learning exactly what animations are and what is required for them to work. After that, you'll look at the different types of animations. From there, you'll learn how to create your own custom animations with Unity's animation tools.

Animation Basics

Animations are premade sets of visual motions. In a 2D game, an animation involves several sequential images that can be flipped through very quickly to give the appearance of movement (much like an old-fashioned flip book). Animation in a 3D world is much different. In 3D games, you use models to represent game entities. You cannot simply switch between models to give the illusion of motion. Instead, you have to actually move the parts of the model. Doing so requires both a rig and an animation. Furthermore, animations can also be thought of as "automations"; that is, you can use animations to automate object changes such as the size of colliders, the value of script variables, or even the color of materials.

The Rig

Achieving complex animated actions, such as walking, without a rig is impossible (or impossibly difficult). Without a rig, the computer has no way of knowing which parts of a model are supposed to move and how they are supposed to move. So, what exactly is a rig? Much like a human skeleton (see Figure 17.1), a rig dictates the parts of a model that are rigid, which are often called *bones*. It also dictates which parts can bend; these bendable parts are called *joints*.

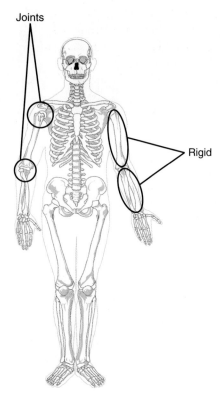

Joints

Rigid

FIGURE 17.1
The skeleton as a rig.

The bones and joints work together to define a physical structure for a model. It is this structure that is used to actually animate the model. It is worth noting that 2D animations, simple animations, and animations on simple objects do not require any particular or complex rig.

The Animation

Once a model has a rig (or not, in the case of simple animations), it can be given an animation. On a technical level, an animation is just a series of instructions for a property or a rig. These instructions can be played just like a movie. They can even be paused, stepped through, or reversed. Furthermore, with a proper rig, changing the action of a model is as simple as changing the animation. The best part of all is that if you have two completely different models that have the same rigging (or different but similar rigging, as you will discover in Hour 18, "Animators"), you can apply the same animations to each of them identically. Thus, an orc, a human, a giant, and a werewolf can all perform exactly the same dance.

NOTE

3D Artists Wanted

The truth about animation is that most of the work is done outside programs like Unity. Generally speaking, modeling, texturing, rigging, and animations are all created by professionals, known as 3D artists, in programs such as Blender, Maya, and 3ds Max. Creating these assets requires a significant amount of skill and practice. Therefore, their creation is not covered in this text. Instead, this book shows you how to build interactive experiences in Unity by putting together already made assets. Remember that there is more to making a game than simply putting together pieces. You may make a game, but artists make a game look good!

Animation Types

So far you've read about things like animations, rigs, and automations. These terms may seem a bit nonsensical at this point, and you may be wondering how they relate and what exactly you need in order to use animations in a game. This section looks at the various types of animation and helps you understand how they work so that you can begin making them.

2D Animations

In a sense, 2D animations are the simplest type of animations. As explained earlier in this hour, a 2D animation functions very much like a flip book (or an animated cartoon or even a film-based movies). The idea behind a 2D animation is that images are presented in sequential order at a very fast pace, tricking the eye into seeing motion.

Setting up 2D animations within Unity is very easy, but modifying them is more difficult. The reason is that 2D animations required art assets (the images being shown) in order to work. Any changes to an animation require you (or an artist) to make changes to the images themselves in other software, such as Photoshop or Gimp. It isn't possible to make changes to the images themselves within Unity.

▼ TRY IT YOURSELF

Slicing a Sprite Sheet for Animation

In this exercise, you will prepare a sprite sheet for animation. The project created in this exercise will be used later, so be sure to save it. Follow these steps:

1. Create a new 2D project.

2. Import the RobotBoyRunSprite.png image from the 2D assets package. (While this image has already been prepared for animation—it is an animated character in the 2D assets package—you examine it in this exercise as a review.) You can do this by selecting **Assets > Import Package > 2D** and importing *only* the RobotBoyRunSprite.png asset (see Figure 17.2). Alternatively, you can find the RobotBoyRunSprite.png asset in the book files for Hour 17.

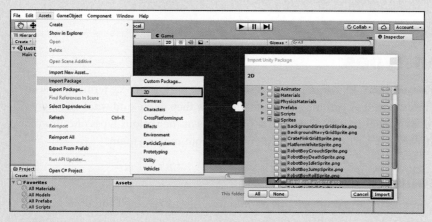

FIGURE 17.2
Importing a sprite sheet.

3. Select the newly imported RobotBoyRunSprite.png file in the Project view.

4. In the Inspector view, ensure that Sprite Mode is set to Multiple and then click **Sprite Editor**. In the upper-left corner, click **Slice** and then choose **Grid by Cell Size** as the type. Notice the grid sizes and the resulting sprite slices (see Figure 17.3).

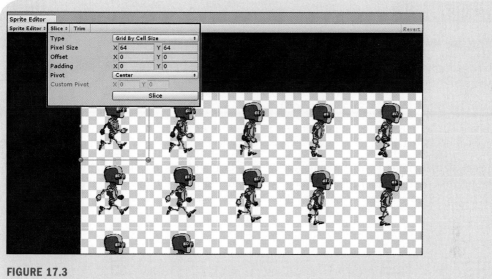

FIGURE 17.3
Slicing the sprite sheet.

   5. Close the Sprite Editor window.

Now that you have a series of sprites, you can turn them into an animation.

NOTE

Reinventing the Wheel

This hour you are using assets from Unity's 2D asset package. You may have noticed that these assets are already animated, which means you are doing work that has already been done. This way, you can see the work that originally went into animating these characters. Better yet, you can explore the completed assets in the 2D assets package to figure out how they are put together and to see how more complex examples are achieved.

Creating an Animation

You've prepared your assets, so you are now ready to turn them into an animation. There is a simple way to do this, and there is also a complicated way to accomplish this. The complicated way involves creating an animation asset, specifying sprite renderer properties, adding key frames, and providing values. Because you haven't learned how to do all that yet (although you will in the next section), let's go with the simple route. Unity has a strong automated workflow, and you will tap into that to create your animation.

▼ TRY IT YOURSELF

Creating an Animation

Use the project you created in the Try It Yourself "Slicing a Sprite Sheet for Animation" and follow these steps to make an animation:

1. Open the project you created in the Try It Yourself "Slicing a Sprite Sheet for Animation."

2. Locate the RobotBoyRunSprite asset in the Project view. Expand the sprite drawer (by clicking the small arrow on the right side of the sprite) to see all the subsprites.

3. Select all the sprites from that sprite sheet by selecting the first sprite and then selecting the last sprite while holding the **Shift** key. Then drag all the frames into the Scene view (or Hierarchy view; either works) and let go (see Figure 17.4).

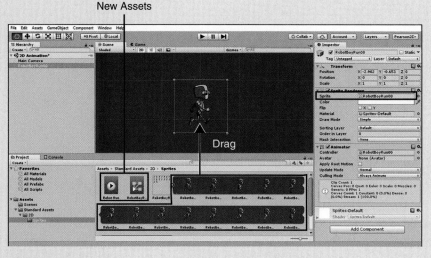

FIGURE 17.4
Creating the animation.

4. If you are prompted with a Save As dialog, choose a name and location for your new animation. If you aren't prompted, two new assets are created in the same folder as the sprite sheet. Either way, Unity has now automated the process of creating an animated sprite character in your scene. The two assets created (the animation asset and another asset called an animator controller) are covered in greater detail in Hour 18.

5. Run your scene, and you see the animated robot boy playing its running sequence. In the Inspector view, you can see the Sprite property of the Sprite Renderer component cycling through the various frames of the animation.

That's it! 2D animations really are very easy to create.

NOTE

More Animations

You now know how to make a single 2D animation, but what if you want a series of animations (such as walk, run, idle, jump, and so on) that all work together? Luckily, the concepts you've just learned continue to work in more complex scenarios. Getting the animations to work together, however, requires greater understanding of Unity's animation system. You will learn that system in great detail in Hour 18, where you will be using imported 3D animations. Just remember that anywhere you can use a 3D animation, you can also use any other type of animation. Thus, the concepts you'll learn in Hour 18 are equally applicable to 2D and custom animations.

Animation Tools

Unity has a set of animation tools built in that you can use to create and modify animations without leaving the editor. You already used them unknowingly when you made a 2D animation, and now it is time to dig in and see just what you can do.

Animation Window

To begin using Unity's animation tools, you need to open the Animation window. You can do this by clicking **Window > Animation** (not Animator). This opens a new view that you can resize and dock like any other Unity window. Generally, it is a good idea to dock this window so you can use it and other parts of the editor without their overlapping. Figure 17.5 shows the Animation window and its various elements.

Note that for the purpose of this figure, the 2D animated sprite from the previous exercise is selected. See if you can identify how Unity used the sprites you dragged into the scene to make the animation you saw when you ran your project. Table 17.1 runs through some of the most important parts of the Animation window.

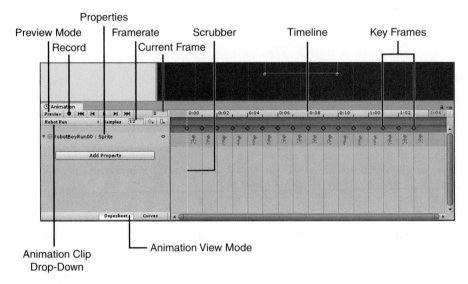

FIGURE 17.5
The Animation window.

TABLE 17.1   Important Parts of the Animation Window

Component	Description
Properties	The list of the component properties modified by this animation. Expanding a property allows you to see the value of that property based on the value of the scrubber on the timeline.
Samples	The number of animation frames available in one second of animation. This is otherwise known as the *framerate*.
Timeline	The visual representation of changes to properties over time. The timeline allows you to specify when values change.
Key frames	Special points on the timeline. A key frame allows you to specify the desired property value at a particular point of time. Regular frames (not shown) also contain values, but you cannot directly control them.
Add key frame	A button that allows you to add a key frame to the timeline for the selected property at the position of the scrubber.
Scrubber	The red line, which allows you to choose the point on the timeline that you would like to edit. (*Note:* If you aren't in Record mode, the scrubber line is white.)
Current frame	An indicator of what frame the scrubber is currently on.

Component	Description
Preview	A toggle that allows you to preview the animation. This is enabled automatically if you play the animation using the play controls in the Animation view.
Record Mode	A toggle that puts you into and out of Record mode. In Record mode, any changes you make to the selected object are recorded into the animation. Use with caution!
Animation clip drop-down	A menu that allows you to change between the various animations associated with the selected object as well as create new animation clips.

Hopefully, looking at this window gives you more insight into how your 2D animation works. Figure 17.5 shows that an animation called Robot Run was created. This animation has a sample rate of 12 frames per second. Each frame of the animation contains a key frame, which sets the Sprite property of the object's Sprite Renderer to a different image, thus causing your character to appear to change. All this (and more) was done automatically.

Creating a New Animation

Now that you're familiar with the animation tools, you're ready to put them to use. Creating animations involves placing key frames and then choosing values for them. The values of the frames in between all the key frames are calculated for you to smoothly transition between them—for example, to make an object move up and down. You could easily achieve this by choosing to modify the position of the object's transform and adding three key frames. The first would have a "low" y axis value, the second would be higher, and the third would be the same as the first. As a result, the object would bounce up and down. This is all fairly conceptual, so work through the following example to get a better feel for the process.

TRY IT YOURSELF ▼

Making an Object Spin

In this exercise you are going to make an object spin. You will be doing this to a simple cube, but in reality you could apply this animation to any object you wanted, and the result would be the same. Be sure to save the project you create here for later use:

1. Create a new 3D project.

2. Add a cube to the scene and ensure that it is positioned at (0, 0, 0).

3. Open the Animation window (by selecting **Window > Animation**) and dock it in your editor.

4. With the cube selected, you should see a Create button right in the middle of the Animation view. Click it, and when you are prompted to save your animation, do so and name it **ObjectSpinAnim**.

5. Click the **Add Property** button in the Animation view and then click the **+** icon next to Transform > Rotation (see Figure 17.6).

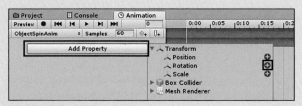

FIGURE 17.6
Adding the Rotation property.

You should now have two key frames added to your animation: one at frame 0 and another at frame 60 (or "1 second"; see the following tip for more info about the timing). If you expand the Rotation property, you can see the properties of the individual axes. Furthermore, selecting a key frame allows you to see and adjust the values of that key frame.

6. Move the scrubber bar over the ending key frame (by clicking and dragging on the timeline) and then set the value of the Rotation.y property to **360** (see Figure 17.7). Even though the starting value of 0 and ending value of 360 are technically the same, doing this causes the cube to rotate. Play your scene to see the animation.

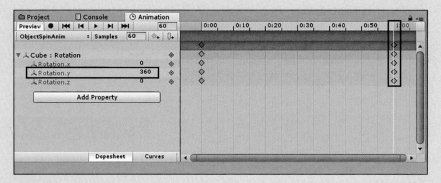

FIGURE 17.7
Adding the Rotation.y value.

7. Save your scene because you will be using it later.

TIP

Animation Timing

The values on the timeline might seem a bit odd at first glance. In fact, reading the timeline helps you understand the sample rate of the given animation clip. Based on a default sample rate of 60 frames per second, the timeline would count frames 0 to 59 and then, instead of frame 60, it has 1:00 (for 1 second). Therefore, a time of 1:30 would mean 1 second and 30 frames. This is easy when you have a 60-frames-per-second animation, but what happens with a 12-frames-per-second animation? Then the counting would be "1, 2, 3,...11, 12, one second." To put it another way, you could see "0:10, 0:11, 1:00, 1:01, 1:02,...1:10, 1:11, 2:00,..." The most important thing to take away from this is that the number preceding the colon is the seconds, and the number following it is the frames.

TIP

Moving the Timeline

If you would like to zoom out or pan into the timeline to see more frames or look at different frames, you can do so easily. The window uses the same navigation style as a Scene view in 2D mode. That is, scrolling the mouse wheel zooms the timeline in and out, while holding **Alt** (**Option** on Mac) and dragging pans around.

Record Mode

Although the tools you have used so far have been very easy to use, there are even easier ways to work with animations. An important element in the animations tool is *Record mode* (refer to Figure 17.5 for its location). In Record mode, any changes you make to an object are recorded into the animation. This can be a very powerful way to make quick and accurate additions to an animation. It can also be very dangerous. Consider what would happen if you forgot you were in Record mode and made a bunch of changes to an object. Those changes would be recorded into the animation and repeated over and over whenever it was played. It is therefore generally advisable to always ensure that you are not in Record mode when you don't want to use it.

This is quite a scary warning for a tool you haven't even used yet, but don't worry. It really isn't that bad (and it is super powerful to boot). With a little discipline, it is a fantastic tool. In the worst-case scenario, if Unity records something for you that you don't want, you can manually delete it from the animation yourself.

▼ TRY IT YOURSELF

Using Record Mode

Follow these steps to make the cube you created in the Try It Yourself "Making an Object Spin" change color while it spins:

1. Open the scene with the spinning cube from the Try It Yourself "Making an Object Spin." Create a new material called CubeColor and apply it to the cube (so you can change the color).

2. Ensure that the cube is selected, and then open the Animation window. You should see the rotation animation you previously created; if you don't, make sure the cube is selected.

3. Enter Record mode by clicking the Record Mode button in the Animation window. The Rotation property in the Inspector view turns red, signifying that the rotation values are driven by the animation. Click and drag along the timeline to move the scrubber and position the scrubber at frame 0:00 (see Figure 17.8).

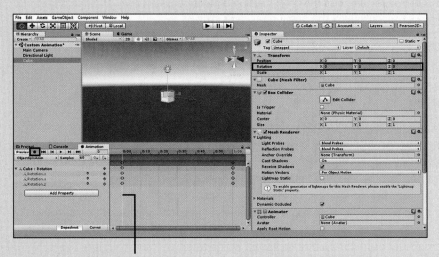

Place Scrubber Here

FIGURE 17.8
Getting ready to record.

4. In the Inspector view, locate the CubeColor material on the cube and change its Albedo setting to red. Notice that a new property and key frame have been added to the Animation window. If you expand the new property, you see the r, g, b, and a values of the color at that key frame (1, 0, 0, 1).

5. Move the scrubber further down the timeline and change the color in the Inspector again. Repeat this step as many times as you'd like. If you'd like the animation to loop smoothly, be sure that the last key frame (at position 1:00, so it synchronized with the rotation as well) is the same color as the first key frame (see Figure 17.9).

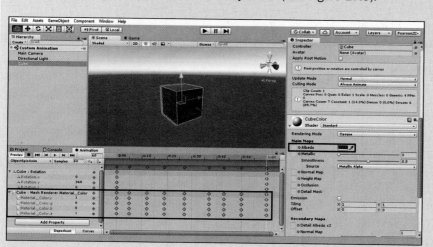

FIGURE 17.9
Recording the color values.

6. Play your scene to see your animation run in the Game view. Note that playing a scene brings you out of Record mode (which is handy because you are done using it). You should now have a spinning multicolored cube in your scene.

The Curves Editor

The last tool you are going to look at in this hour is the Curves Editor. So far, you have been in the Dopesheet view, which is the view with the key frames listed and itemized in a flat fashion. You may have noticed that while you drive the values of the key frames, you don't control the values in between. If you wondered how the values are determined, wonder no more. Unity blends the values (in a process called *interpolation*) between key frames to create smooth transition. In the Curves Editor, you can see what that looks like. To enter the Curves Editor, simply click the button labeled **Curves** at the bottom of the Animation view (see Figure 17.10).

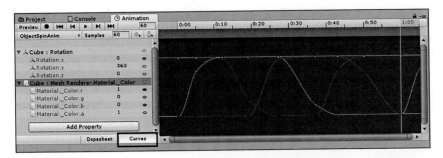

FIGURE 17.10
The Curves Editor.

In this mode, you can toggle which values you want to see by clicking their properties on the left. In the Curves Editor, you can see exactly how values are being transitioned between the key frames. You can drag a key frame to change its value or even double-click the curve to create a new key frame at the point where you clicked. If you don't like how Unity is generating the value in between the key frames, you can right-click a key frame and choose **Free Smooth**. Unity then gives you two handles that you can move to change how values are smoothed. Feel free to play around and see what sort of craziness you can create with the curves.

▼ TRY IT YOURSELF

Using the Curves Editor

You may have noticed that the cube from the Try It Yourself "Using Record Mode" doesn't spin smoothly and instead has a slow start-and-stop motion. In this exercise you will modify the animation to give the cube a smooth spinning motion. Follow these steps:

1. Open the scene with your spinning cube from the Try It Yourself "Using Record Mode." In the Animation view, click the **Curves** button to switch to the Curves Editor (refer to Figure 17.10).

2. Click the **Rotation.y** property to show its curve in the timeline. If the curve is small or doesn't fit in the window, simply move your mouse cursor over the timeline and press the **F** key.

3. Straightening out the rotation curve will give your cube a nice smooth animation (see Figure 17.11), so right-click the first keyframe (at time 0:00) and select **Auto**. Do the same for the last keyframe.

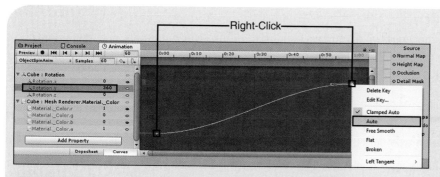

FIGURE 17.11
Modifying the rotation curve.

4. Now that the curve is straightened out, enter Play mode to see the modified cube animation.

Summary

In this hour you were introduced to animations in Unity. You started by looking at the basics of animations, including rigging. From there, you learned about the various types of animations in Unity. After that, you began creating animations, starting with 2D animations. Then you created custom animations both manually and in Record mode.

Q&A

Q. Can animations be blended?

A. Yes, they can. You can blend animations with the Unity Mecanim system, as discussed in Hour 18.

Q. Can any animation be applied to any model?

A. Only if they are rigged exactly the same or if the animation is a simple one that doesn't require a rig. Otherwise, the animations may behave very strangely or just may not work at all.

Q. Can a model be rerigged in Unity?

A. Sort of, as you will see in Hour 18.

Workshop

Take some time to work through the questions here to ensure that you have a firm grasp of the material.

Quiz

1. The "skeleton" of a model is known as what?

2. Which animation type flips through images quickly?

3. What is the name for a frame of animation that has an explicit value?

Answers

1. Rig or rigging

2. 2D animation

3. Key frame

Exercise

This exercise is a sandbox type of exercise. Feel free to take some time and get used to creating animations. Unity has a very powerful toolset, and it certainly pays to be familiar with it. Try completing the following:

▶ Make an object fly around a scene in a large arc.

▶ Make an object flicker by cycling its renderer on and off.

▶ Change the properties of an object's scale and material to make it appear to morph.

HOUR 18
Animators

What You'll Learn in This Hour:

▶ The basics of animators
▶ How to use an animator's state machines
▶ How to control animations from script via parameters
▶ An introduction to blend trees

In this hour, you'll take what you've already learned about animations and put it to use with Unity's Mecanim animation system and animators. You'll start by learning about animators and how they work. From there, you'll look at how to rig or change the rigging of models in Unity. After that, you'll create an animator and configure it. Finally, you will see how animations are blended to produce amazingly realistic results.

NOTE

Warning: Get Your Hands Dirty!

This section is like one big Try It Yourself. Make sure you save your project in between the practical exercises, as each builds on the one before. You will certainly want to be in front of your computer while you read this section. The topic is best learned by doing!

Animator Basics

All animation in Unity starts with an Animator component. In Hour 17, while you were creating and learning about animations, you were using animators without really knowing it. At its heart, Unity's animation system (Mecanim) comprises three pieces: the animation clip, the Animator controller, and the Animator component. These three pieces all exist to make your characters come to life.

Figure 18.1, which is taken from Unity's online documentation about the Animator component (https://docs.unity3d.com/Manual/class-Animator.html), shows how these parts relate to one another.

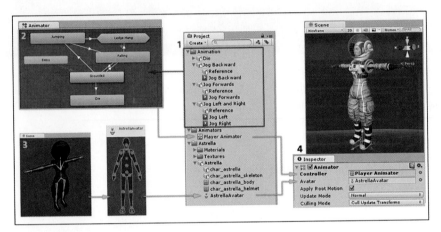

FIGURE 18.1
How the parts of a humanoid animation relate to each other.

The animation clips (see #1 in Figure 18.1) are the various motions that you either import or create in Unity. The Animator controller (#2) contains your animations and determines which clips should play at any given moment. Models have something called an avatar (#3) that acts as the "translator" between the Animator controller and the rigging of the model. You can generally ignore the avatar because it is set up and used automatically. Finally, both the Animator controller (which you can just call the "controller") and the avatar are put together on the model using an Animator component (#4). Does it seem like a lot to remember? Don't worry. Most of this stuff is either intuitive or automatic.

One of the best things about Unity's animation system is that you can use it to "retarget" an animation onto other game objects. If you animate a cube, you can also apply that animation to a sphere. If you animate a character, you can apply the animation to another character with the same rigging (or different rigging, as you will soon see). This means you can, for example, have an orc and a man doing the same happy dance together.

NOTE

Analyzing a Specific Use Case

In order to get the most out of this hour, you will work with a very specific use case: 3D animations on a humanoid model (a very common use case to be sure). This will allow you to learn about 3D animations, importing models and animations, working with rigs, and using Unity's awesome humanoid retargeting system. Just remember that, with the exception of humanoid retargeting, everything covered in this hour applies completely to any other type of animation. So, if you are building a multipart 2D animation system, all the knowledge learned here still matters.

Rigging Revisited

In order to begin building a complex animation system, you first need to ensure that your model's rigging is prepared. Recall from Hour 17, "Animations," that models and animations have to be rigged exactly the same way in order to function. This means that it can be very difficult to get animations made for one model to work on a different model. Therefore, animations and models are generally made specifically to work together.

If you are using a humanoid model, though (two arms, two legs, head, and torso), you have the ability to tap into Mecanim's animation retargeting tools. With the Mecanim system, humanoids can have their rigging remapped in the editor without using any 3D modeling tools. The result is that any animation made for a humanoid model can work with any other humanoid you have. This means animators (the people, not the Unity asset) can produce large libraries of animations that can be applied to a large range of models using many different rigs.

Importing a Model

For this hour, you will use Ethan, a model from the Characters standard asset pack. This model comes with a lot of different items, and you will go through each piece to ensure that it is configured properly. To import the model, select **Assets > Import Package > Characters**. Leave everything checked and click **Import**.

Now go ahead and find Ethan in your Project tab under Assets\Standard Assets\Characters \ThirdPersonCharacter\Models (see Figure 18.2).

If you click the little arrow to the right of the Ethan file, you can expand the model to see all the constituent parts (see Figure 18.2). How these parts are structured depends on how the model was exported from the 3D application used to make it.

These components are, from left to right, Ethan's body with texture, the textured glasses, the definition of the skeleton, the raw EthanBody mesh, the raw EthanGlasses mesh, and finally a definition of Ethan's avatar (which is used for rigging).

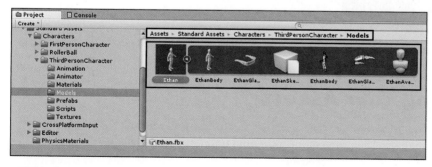

FIGURE 18.2
Finding the Ethan model.

NOTE

Previewing Meshes

If you click either the Ethan or the Glasses model in the tray, you should notice a small preview window at the bottom of the Inspector. (If not, drag it up to show it.) Here you can rotate that submodel around to take a look at it from all angles (see the bottom of Figure 18.3).

When you're done looking at the components, collapse the Ethan.fbx tray by clicking the arrow to the right of the asset.

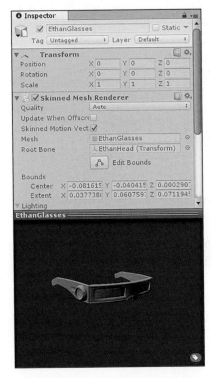

FIGURE 18.3
The model's Inspector view.

Configuring Your Assets

Now that you have imported a model and animations (which came with the rest of the assets), you need to configure them. The process for configuring animations is fairly identical to configuring models.

With a model selected, you can see the import settings listed in the Inspector view. The Model tab is home to all the settings that dictate how the model is imported into Unity. These items can be safely ignored for the purposes of this hour. The tab you are concerned with for now is the Rig tab. (The Animations tab is covered a little later in this hour.)

Rig Preparation

You configure a model's rig in the import settings, under the Rig tab in the Inspector view. The property you are most concerned with here is Animation Type (see Figure 18.4). There are currently four types available in the drop-down: None, Legacy, Generic, and Humanoid. Setting this property to None causes Unity to ignore this model's rig. Legacy is for Unity's old animation system and shouldn't be used. Generic is for all nonhumanoid models (simple models, vehicles, building, animals, and so on), and all models imported into Unity default to this animation type. Finally, Humanoid (which is the one you will be using) is for all humanoid characters. This setting allows Unity to retarget animations for you.

As you can see, Ethan is already set up properly as a humanoid. When you set a model as humanoid, Unity automatically goes through the process of mapping the rig for you. If you'd like to see how easy this is, you can simply change Animation Type to Generic, click Apply, and then change it back (which is exactly how this model was set up for you originally; no extra work was hidden). To see the work that Unity does for you, you can enter the rigging tool by clicking the Configure button (see Figure 18.4).

FIGURE 18.4
The rig settings.

▼ TRY IT YOURSELF

Exploring How Ethan Is Rigged

In this exercise, you'll take a look at how Ethan is rigged. This will give you a much more practical idea of how a rigged model is assembled. Follow these steps:

1. If you haven't already done so, create a new project and import the character assets from Standard Assets. Locate the Ethan.fbx asset and select it to display its import settings in the Inspector view, as described earlier in this hour.

2. Click **Configure** on the Rig tab. Doing so launches you into a new scene, so save your old one if prompted.

3. Rearrange your interface so that you can see mainly the Hierarchy and Inspector views. (Hour 1, "Introduction to Unity," covers how to close and move tabs.) You may want to save this layout. You can always go back to Default later.

4. With the Mapping tab selected, click on various green circles (see Figure 18.5). Notice how this highlights the corresponding child of EthanSkeleton in the Hierarchy view and puts a blue circle around the corresponding skeleton point below the outline. Notice all the extra points of the rig in the Hierarchy view. Those pieces aren't important for humanoids and thus aren't retargeted. Don't worry, though: They still play a part in ensuring that the model looks correct when moving.

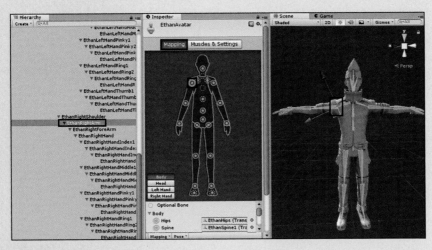

FIGURE 18.5
The Rigging view with the right arm selected.

5. Continue to explore other body parts by clicking **Body, Head, Left Hand**, and so on. These are all joints, which can be completely retargeted for any humanoid.

6. Click **Done** when you are finished. Notice that the temporary Ethan(Clone) disappears from the Hierarchy view.

At this point, you have previewed Ethan and seen how his skeleton is arranged. He is now ready to go!

Animation Preparation

For this hour, you could use the animations that came with Ethan, but that would be boring and wouldn't illustrate the flexibility of the Mecanim system. Instead, you are going to use some other animations provided in the book files for Hour 18. Each animation has options that control how the animation behaves that must be specifically configured the way you want them. For example, you need to ensure that the walking animation loops appropriately so that transitions don't have any obvious seams. This section walks you through preparing each animation.

Start by dragging the Animations folder from the book assets into the Unity editor. You will be working with four animations: Idle, WalkForwardStraight, WalkForwardTurnRight, and WalkForwardTurnLeft (though the Animations folder only contains three files; more on that soon). Each of these animations needs to be set up uniquely. If you look in the Animations folder, you will see that the animations are actually .fbx files. This is because the animations themselves are located inside their default models. Don't worry, though: You will be able to modify and extract them inside Unity.

Idle Animation

To set up the Idle animation, follow these steps (see Table 18.1 for an explanation of the settings):

1. Select the **Idles.fbx** file in the Animations folder. In the Inspector, select the **Rig** tab. Change the animation type to **Humanoid** and click **Apply**. This tells Unity that the animation is for a humanoid.

2. When the rig is configured, click the **Animations** tab in the Inspector. Set the starting frame to 128 and check the boxes next to **Loop Time** and **Loop Pose**. In addition, check the box **Bake into Pose** for all the Root Transform properties. Ensure that your settings match the ones in Figure 18.6 and then click **Apply**.

3. To ensure that the animation is now properly configured, expand the **Idles.fbx** file (see Figure 18.7). Be sure to remember how to access that animation. (The model is irrelevant. It's the animation you want.)

TABLE 18.1   Important Animation Settings

Setting	Description
Loop Time	Indicates whether the animation loops.
Root Transform	Controls whether the animation is allowed to change an object's rotation, vertical position (y axis), and horizontal position (x/z plane).
Bake into Pose	Indicates whether the animation is allowed to actually move an object. If you check this box, the animation will not actually change the object but will just appear to.
Offset	Specifies some amount by which to modify the original position of the animation. For instance, by modifying the offset under Root Transform Rotation, you make small rotation changes to the model along the y axis. This is useful for correcting any motion error in the animation.

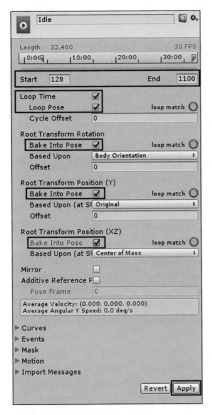

FIGURE 18.6
The Idle animation.

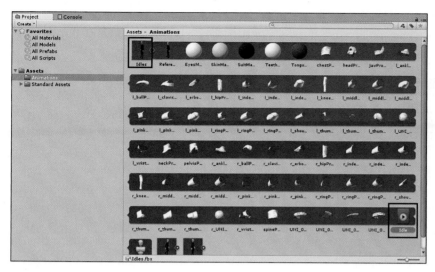

FIGURE 18.7
Finding the animation clip.

NOTE

Red Light, Green Light

You might have noticed the green circles present in the animation settings (refer to Figure 18.6). Those are nifty little tools you can use to designate whether your animations are lined up. The fact that the circles are green means that they will loop seamlessly. A circle that is yellow indicates that the animation comes close to looping seamlessly, but there is a minor difference that will create a bit of a seam. A red circle indicates that the beginning and end of the animation don't line up at all, and a seam will be very apparent. If you have an animation that doesn't line up, you can change the Start and End properties to find a segment of the animation that does.

WalkForwardStraight Animation

To set up the WalkForwardStraight animation, follow these steps:

1. Select the **WalkForward.fbx** file in the Animations folder and complete the rigging the same way you did for the Idle animation.

2. Change the clip's currently very generic name (Take 001) to **WalkForwardStraight** by clicking the name and changing it (see Figure 18.8).

3. On the Animations tab, ensure that your settings are the same as the ones shown in Figure 18.8. You should note two things. First, Root Transform Position (XZ) has a red circle next to it. This is good; it means that at the end of the animation, the model is in a different x and z axis position. Because this is a walking animation, that is the behavior you want. The other thing you should notice is the Average Velocity indicator. You should

notice a nonzero velocity in the x axis and z axis. The z axis velocity is good because you want the model moving forward, but the x axis velocity is a problem because it will cause the model to drift sideways while walking. You will adjust this setting in step 4.

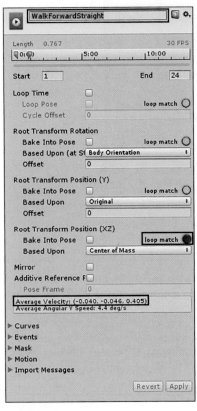

FIGURE 18.8
The WalkForwardStraight animation settings.

4. To adjust the x axis velocity, check the **Bake into Pose** check box for both the Root Transform Rotation and the Root Transform Position (Y) properties. Also change Root Transform Rotation Offset so that the x axis value of Average Velocity becomes **0**.

5. Set the End frame to 244.9 and the Start frame to 215.2 (in that order) so the animation only contains the walking frames.

6. Finally, check the **Loop Time** and **Loop Pose** check boxes.

7. Ensure that your settings match the final settings shown in Figure 18.9 and click the **Apply** button.

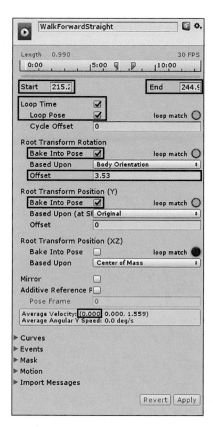

FIGURE 18.9
The fixed WalkForwardStraight animation settings.

WalkForwardTurnRight Animation

The WalkForwardTurnRight animation allows the model to smoothly change direction while walking forward. This one differs a little from the two you have already created in that you need to make two animations out of a single animation recording. This sounds trickier than it really is. Follow these steps:

1. Select the **WalkForwardTurns.fbx** file in the Animations folder and complete the rigging the same way you did for the Idle animation.

2. By default, there will be a long animation with the name _7_a_U1_M_P_ WalkForwardTurnRight. Rename it by typing **WalkForwardTurnRight** into the Clip Name text field and pressing the **Enter** key.

3. With the WalkForwardTurnRight clip selected, set the properties to match those shown in Figure 18.10. The shorter Start and End times will cut the clip down and ensure that it only contains the model moving in a rightward circle. (Be sure to preview it to see what it looks like.) After you have done this, click **Apply**.

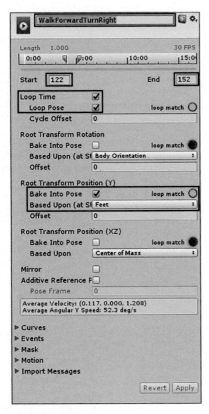

FIGURE 18.10
The WalkForwardTurnRight settings.

4. Create a WalkForwardTurnLeft animation clip by clicking the +icon in the Clips list (see Figure 18.11). The properties for the WalkForwardTurnLeft clip will be exactly the same as the WalkForwardTurnRight clip except that you need to put a check in the **Mirror** property (see Figure 18.11). Remember to click **Apply** when you're done with the settings.

At this point, all the animations are set up and ready to go. Now all that's left to do is build the animator.

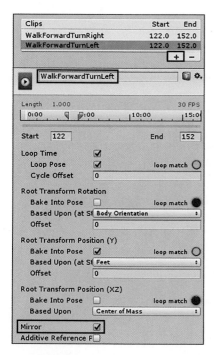

FIGURE 18.11
Mirroring the animation.

Creating an Animator

Animators in Unity are assets. This means they are a part of a project and exist outside any one scene. This is nice because it allows for easy reuse over and over again. To add an animator to your project, in Project view you simply right-click a folder and select **Create > Animator Controller** (but don't do that just yet).

▼ TRY IT YOURSELF

Setting Up the Scene

In this exercise, you'll set up a scene and prepare for the rest of this hour. Be sure to save the scene created here because you'll need it later. Follow these steps:

1. If you have not done so already, create a new project and complete the model and animation preparation steps in the previous section.

2. Drag the Ethan model into your scene (from Assets\Standard Assets\Characters \ThirdPersonCharacter\Models) and give it the position (0, 0, -5).

3. Nest the Main Camera under Ethan (by dragging the Main Camera onto the Ethan game object in the Hierarchy view) and position the camera at (0, 1.5, -1.5) with a rotation of (20, 0, 0).

4. In your Project view, create a new folder named Animators. Right-click the new folder and select **Create > Animator Controller**. Name the animator **PlayerAnimator**. With Ethan selected in the scene, drag the animator onto the Controller property of the Animator component in the Inspector (see Figure 18.12).

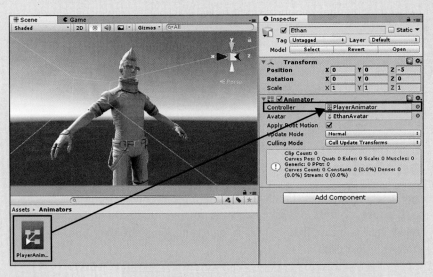

FIGURE 18.12
Adding the animator to the model.

5. Add a plane to your scene. Position the plane at (0, 0, -5) with a scale of (10, 1, 10).

6. Locate the file Checker.tga in the book assets for Hour 18 and import it into your project. Create a new material named Checker and set **Checker.tga** as the albedo for the material (see Figure 18.13).

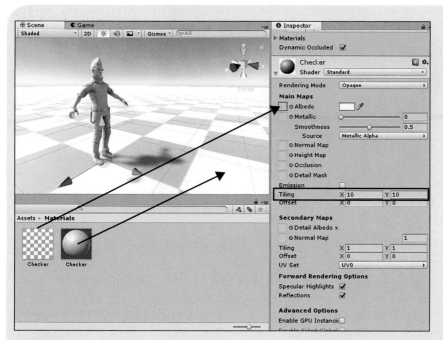

FIGURE 18.13
Setting the tiling of the checker texture.

7. Set both the X and the Y Tiling properties to **10** and apply the material to the plane. (The plane isn't super useful right now, but it will become important later in this hour.)

The Animator View

Double-clicking an animator brings up the Animator view (which you can also open by selecting **Window > Animator**). This view functions like a flow graph, allowing you to visually create animation paths and blending. This is the real power of the Mecanim system.

Figure 18.14 shows the basic Animator view. You can move around the Animator view by dragging with the middle mouse button held down, and you can zoom with the scroll wheel. This new animator is very plain: It has only a base layer, no parameters, Entry and Exit nodes, and an Any State node. (These components are discussed in more detail later in this hour.)

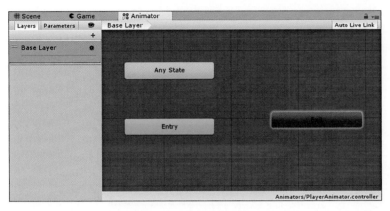

FIGURE 18.14
The Animator view.

The Idle Animation

The first animation you want to apply to Ethan is the Idle animation. You completed the long setup process earlier, and now, adding this animation is simple. You need to locate the Idle animation clip, which is stored inside the Idles.fbx file (refer to Figure 18.7, earlier in the hour), and drag it onto the animator in the Animator view (see Figure 18.15).

FIGURE 18.15
Applying the Idle animation.

You should now be able to run your scene and see the Ethan model looping through the Idle animation.

Slip and Slide

When you run the scene to see the Ethan model playing the idle animation, you may notice the model's feet sliding on the ground. This is due to how this particular animation was authored. In this animation, the character is determining its motion based on its hips as opposed to its feet (causing it to rotate a little bit like a pinwheel). You can fix this in the Animator view. Simply select the **Idle** animation state, and in the Inspector view, select the **Foot IK** check box (see Figure 18.16). The model now attempts to track its feet to the ground. This causes the character to animate correctly, with its feet firmly planted. By the way, IK stands for Inverse Kinematics; the details of such are mostly out of the scope of this text.

FIGURE 18.16
Selecting **Foot IK**.

Parameters

Parameters are like variables for an animator. You set them up in the Animator view and then manipulate them with scripts. These parameters control when animations are transitioned and blended. To create a parameter, simply click the + in the Parameters tab in the Animator view.

Adding Parameters

In this exercise, you'll add two parameters. This exercise builds on the project and scene you have been working on thus far this hour. Follow these steps:

1. Make sure you've completed all the steps up to this point.

2. In the Animator view, click the **Parameters** tab on the left and then click the **+** to create a new parameter. Choose a Float parameter and name it **Speed** (see Figure 18.17).

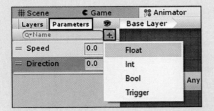

FIGURE 18.17
Adding parameters.

3. Repeat step 2 to create a float parameter named Direction.

States and Blend Trees

Your next step is to create a new state. A state is essentially a status that the model is currently in that defines what animation is playing. You created a state earlier, when you added the Idle animation to the Animator controller. The model Ethan will have two states: Idle and Walking. Idle is already in place. Because the Walking state can be any of three animations, you want to create a state that uses a *blend tree*, which seamlessly blends one or more animations, based on some parameter. To create a new state, follow these steps:

1. Right-click a blank spot in the Animator view and select **Create State > From New Blend Tree**. In the Inspector view, name the new state **Walking** (see Figure 18.18).

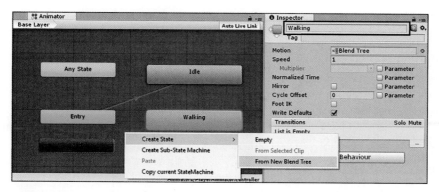

FIGURE 18.18
Creating and naming a new state.

2. Double-click the new state to expand it and select the new **Blend Tree** state. In the Inspector, click the Parameter property drop-down and change it to **Direction**. Then add three motions by clicking the + under the motions and selecting **Add Motion Field**. Under the graph, set the minimum value to **-1** and the maximum value to **1** (see Figure 18.19).

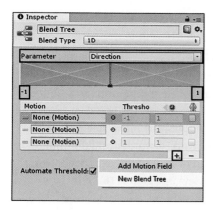

FIGURE 18.19
Adding motion fields.

3. Drag each of the three walking animations into one of the three motion fields, in this order: WalkForwardTurnLeft, WalkForwardStraight, WalkForwardTurnRight (see Figure 18.20). Remember that the turning animation clips are located under WalkForwardTurns.fbx, and the straight walking animation is under WalkForward.fbx.

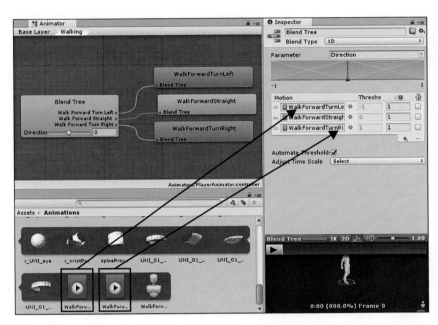

FIGURE 18.20
Changing minimum values and adding animations to a blend tree.

Your walking animation is now ready to blend, based on the Direction parameter. Basically, you told the blend state to evaluate the parameter Direction. Based on the value of that parameter, the blend tree will choose some percentage amount of each animation to blend to give you the final unique animation. For instance, if Direction equals -1, the blend tree plays 100% of the WalkForwardTurnLeft animation. If Direction equals .5, the blend tree plays 50% of the WalkForwardStraight animation blended with 50% of the WalkForwardTurnRight animation. You can easily see how powerful blend trees can be! In order to get out of the expanded view, click the **Base Layer** breadcrumb at the top of the Animator view (see Figure 18.21).

FIGURE 18.21
Navigating the Animator view.

Transitions

The last thing you need to do to ensure that your animator is finished is to tell the animator how to transition between the Idle and Walking animations. You need to set up two transitions.

One of them transitions the animator from idle to walking, and the other transitions back. To create a transition, follow these steps:

1. Right-click the Idle state and select **Make Transition** to create a white line that follows your mouse. Click the **Walking** state to connect it to the Idle state.

2. Repeat step 1, except this time connect the Walking state to the Idle state.

3. Edit the Idle to Walking transition by clicking the white arrow on it. Add a condition and set it to be **Speed Greater** than the value **.1** (see Figure 18.22). Do the same for the Walking to Idle transition, except set the condition to **Speed Less Than** the value **.1**.

4. Uncheck the **Has Exit Time** box to allow the Idle animation to be interrupted when the walk key is pressed.

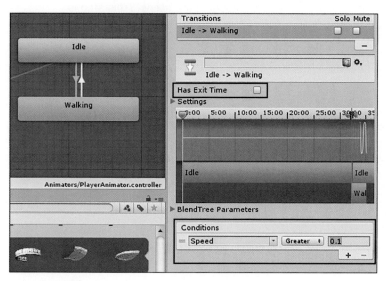

FIGURE 18.22
Modifying transitions.

The animator is finished. You might notice that when you run the scene, there aren't any working movement animations. This is because the speed and direction parameters are never changed. In the next section, you'll learn how to change these through scripting.

Scripting Animators

Now that everything has been set up with the model, the rigging, the animations, the animator, the transitions, and the blend tree, it is finally time to make the whole thing interactive.

Luckily, the actual scripting components are simple. Most of the hard work was already done in the editor. At this point, all you need to do is manipulate the parameters you created in the animator to get Ethan up and running. Because the parameters you set up were of type `float`, you need to call the animator method:

```
SetFloat (<name> , <value>);
```

▼ TRY IT YOURSELF

Adding the Final Touches

In the following steps, you will add a scripted component to the project you have been working on during this hour to make it all work:

1. Create a new folder called Scripts and add a new script to it. Name the script **AnimationControl**. Attach the script to the Ethan model in the scene. (This step is important!)

2. Add the following code to the AnimationControl script:

```
Animator anim;
void Start ()
{
    // Get a reference to the animator
    anim = GetComponent<Animator> ();
}
void Update ()
{
    anim.SetFloat ("Speed", Input.GetAxis ("Vertical"));
    anim.SetFloat ("Direction", Input.GetAxis("Horizontal"));
}
```

3. Run the scene and notice that the animations are controlled with the vertical and horizontal input axes. (If you've forgotten, the horizontal and vertical input axes are the WASD keys and the arrow keys.)

That's it! If you run your scene after adding this script, you might notice something strange. Not only does Ethan animate through idle, walking, and turning, but the model also moves. This is due to two factors.

The first factor is that the animations chosen have built-in movement to them. This was done by the animators outside Unity. If this hadn't been done, you would have to program the movement yourself.

The second factor is that by default, the animator allows the animation to move the model. This can be changed by selecting the Apply Root Motion property of the Animator component (see Figure 18.23), but in this case it will cause some strange effects!

The final project file is included in the book files in case you want to compare notes.

FIGURE 18.23
Root motion animator property.

Summary

You started this hour by building a very simple animation from scratch. You started with a cube and added an Animator component. You then created an Animator controller and linked it to the animator. Next, you created animation states and corresponding motion clips. Finally, you learned how to make the states blend.

Q&A

Q. Can you do key frame animations on humanoids in Unity?

A. Unity doesn't allow key frame animation on humanoids, and although you may find work-arounds on the Internet, you are better off creating humanoid animations in a dedicated 3D package and importing them into Unity.

Q. Can an object be moved by both the animator and the physics engine?

A. Although this is possible with some care, generally you want to avoid trying to mix the two. At least at any one time, you want to be clear on whether the animator or the physics engine is controlling a game object.

Workshop

Take some time to work through the questions here to ensure that you have a firm grasp of the material.

Quiz

1. To what must an Animator component have a reference in order to work?

2. What color is the default animation state in the Animator tab?

3. How many motion clips (motions) can an animation state have?

4. What do you use to trigger animation transitions from script?

Answers

1. An Animator controller must be created and connected to the Animator component. In the case of humanoid characters, an avatar is also required.

2. Orange

3. It depends; an animation state can be a single clip, a blend tree, or another state machine.

4. Animator parameters

Exercise

A lot of information is required to produce a robust and high-quality animation system. In this hour, you got to see one way and one group of settings to achieve this. Plenty of other assets are available, however, and learning is paramount to success.

Your exercise for this hour is to continue studying the Mecanim system. Be sure to start by browsing Unity's documentation on the system. You can find it on Unity's website at https://docs.unity3d.com/Manual/AnimationSection.html.

You can also explore the fully animated Ethan prefab, found at Assets\Standard Assets \Characters\ThirdPersonCharacter\Prefabs\ThirdPersonController.prefab. This prefab has a much more complex animator than the Ethan you worked with in this hour, with three blend trees for Airborne, Grounded, and Crouching states.

What You'll Learn in This Hour:

▶ An introduction to Timeline system
▶ How to add and sequence clips
▶ More complex Timeline use cases

In this hour, you'll take a look at a very powerful sequencing tool in Unity: the Timeline. You'll begin by looking at the structure and concept of a timeline and a director. From there you'll explore the concept of clips and how they can be sequenced on a timeline. Finally, you'll finish this hour by looking at more ways you can use the Timeline to bring sophistication and complexity to your projects.

NOTE

Its Mystery Is Exceeded Only by Its Power

Throughout this hour, you are going to be looking at the various parts of the Timeline system in Unity. One of the things to note about the Timeline is that it is a very capable and very complex tool. In truth, this hour only scratches the surface of what is possible with this sequencer. The whole system is built out of simple but modular pieces, which allows it to be used in many custom and interesting ways (much like a certain interlocking plastic construction toy that shall not be named). The point of this note is to tell you that if you are ever wondering, "Hmm, I wonder if I can do this with the Timeline," the answer is probably yes. It may not always be easy, but it's probably possible!

Timeline Basics

At its heart, the Timeline is a sequencing tool. This means it can be used to cause things to happen at specific times in relation to each other. What those things are is really up to you. In a way, a timeline is very similar to an Animator controller (see Hour 18, "Animators," for a refresher). An Animator controller is used to sequence and control which animations are played on an object. The limitation, though, is that an Animator controller can only control itself or child objects. It can't be used, for example, to create a cinematic where two guards talk to each other while a thief sneaks behind them in the shadows. This is exactly the type of work that the Timeline was intended to do. You can use it to sequence many different objects doing many different things at many different times.

Anatomy of a Timeline

The core element of a sequenced item is called a *clip*. While this would indicate that the Timeline is used for animations, the truth is that a clip can be anything from an audio clip, to a control track, to a custom data event, or even enabling and disabling game objects. You can even program your own clips and make them do whatever you want.

You place clips on one or more *tracks* (see Figure 19.1). The tracks determine what types of clips can be placed on them and what objects they control. In order to animate two characters in sequence, for example, you need two animation tracks (one for each character), with one or more animations on each.

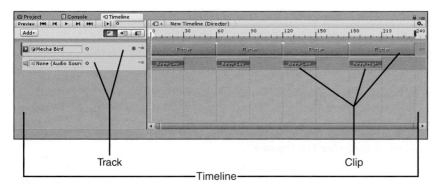

FIGURE 19.1
The anatomy of a timeline.

Both the clips and the tracks rest on a timeline asset (pictured in Figure 19.1). This asset can be reusable between scenes or can even have multiple instances in a single scene. The timeline keeps track of the objects it controls through *bindings*. These bindings can be set up through code, but usually you just drag the objects you want to control onto the timeline.

Finally, the Timeline system uses a *Playable Director* component to control the timeline. This component is added to a game object in a scene and determines when the timeline plays, when it stops, and what happens when it finishes.

Creating a Timeline

As mentioned earlier in this hour, a timeline asset is the piece that all the other parts fit into. Thus, the first step in working with the Timeline is to create a timeline asset. To do this, right-click in the Project view and select **Create > Timeline** (see Figure 19.2).

FIGURE 19.2
Creating a timeline.

Once a timeline is created, it needs to be controlled by a Playable Director component, which is added to a game object in the scene. In order to add a Playable Director component to a game object, you can simply select it and then click **Add Component > Playables > Playable Director**. Then you need to set the timeline asset as the Playable property of the Playable Director component. An easier way to complete both of these steps at once is to drag the timeline asset from the Project view onto the game object in the Hierarchy view that you want to control the timeline (see Figure 19.3).

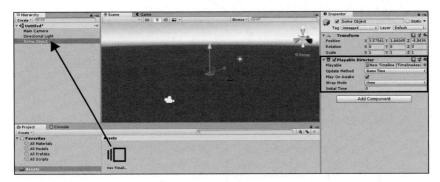

FIGURE 19.3
Adding a Playable Director component to a game object.

▼ TRY IT YOURSELF

Creating a Timeline Asset

Take a moment to create a timeline asset and add a Playable Director component to a game object. Be sure to save the project and scene you create in this exercise so that you can use it later in this hour. Follow these steps:

1. Create a new project or scene. Add a new folder named Timelines to your project.

2. In the Timelines folder, create a new timeline by right-clicking and selecting **Create > Timeline**.

3. Add a new game object to your scene (by selecting **GameObject > Create > Create Empty**). Name the new object **Director**.

4. Drag your new timeline asset from the Project view onto the Director game object in the Hierarchy view. (It won't work if you try to drag it onto the Scene view or Inspector view.)

5. Select the **Director** game object and ensure that a Playable Director component appears in the Inspector view.

Working with Timelines

Creating a timeline is a simple enough process, but a timeline doesn't really achieve anything on its own. To use a timeline, you need to create tracks and clips that control and sequence objects in your scene. All this work is done through the Timeline window, which is very similar to the Animation window explored in Hour 17, "Animations."

The Timeline Window

In order to see and work with a timeline, you need to open the Timeline window. You can do this by clicking **Window > Timeline** or simply double-clicking a timeline asset in the Project view. This window features controls for previewing and playback, mode controls, and a large area for working with tracks and clips (see Figure 19.4).

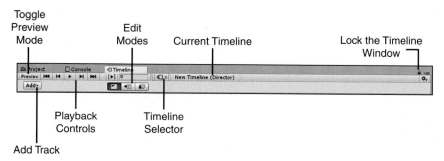

FIGURE 19.4
The Timeline window.

There would be little point to examining the Timeline window now, as it is rather empty. Instead, let's move on, and you can learn more about the Timeline window as it becomes applicable.

TIP

Locking the Timeline Window

When working within the Timeline window, you will often be clicking on other objects in the Scene or Project window. Doing so, however, deselects your Director game object and causes the Timeline window to go blank. This can get very frustrating. A better way to work with the Timeline window is to lock it (refer to Figure 19.4). This prevents your current select from changing what the Timeline window is focused on. Then you can choose which timeline you want to modify by using the timeline selector in the Timeline window. Much easier!

CAUTION

Preview Mode

The Timeline window has a Preview mode (refer to Figure 19.4). When this mode is enabled, you can see how the timeline will affect objects in your scene. This is of paramount importance for sequencing and ensuring that everything lines up. Luckily, working in the Timeline window automatically puts you in Preview mode. While in Preview mode, however, some functionality is disabled. One example is that you can't apply any prefab changes. If you notice that something just doesn't look correct, try leaving Preview mode to ensure that the Timeline window isn't playing tricks on you.

Timeline Tracks

The tracks on a timeline determine what things can be done, what object does those things, and what things the object does. In essence, a timeline track does a lot of work for you. To add a track to a timeline, click the **Add** button in the Timeline window (refer to Figure 19.4). Table 19.1 lists the built-in track types and describes what they do.

TABLE 19.1 Timeline Track Types

Type	Description
Track Group	This track type doesn't contain any functionality on its own. Instead, it allows you to group tracks under it for easier organization.
Activation Track	This track type allows you to activate and deactivate game objects.
Animation Track	This track type allows you to play animations on a game object. Note that this track type takes priority over any animations being played on the object by an animator.
Audio Track	This track type allows you to play and stop audio clips.
Control Track	This track type allows you to control other playables. A *playable* is any asset created with Unity's playable system. The most common use case for this track type is to allow one timeline to play another timeline. Thus, you could use a timeline to sequence and control several child timelines.
Playable Track	This is a specialized track type for controlling custom playables (that is, playables that are custom built to extend the Timeline system).

NOTE

Even More Tracks

Table 19.1 lists the tracks that existed in Unity at the time this book was published (obviously). The Timeline is a fairly new feature, and a lot of things are constantly in the works to expand its capabilities. This list will continue to grow as new track types get added in future releases. Furthermore, the Timeline is extendable. If there is currently some missing functionality you want, you can create your own custom tracks. Even now, many developers are creating their own custom tracks. Many of them can be found in Unity's Asset Store. If you are interested, a great place to start would be Unity's own Default Playables Library (see https://www.assetstore.unity3d.com/en/#!/content/95266).

Adding Tracks

In this exercise you'll add tracks to the timeline asset you created earlier in this hour. Be sure to save this scene because you will continue using it later in this hour. Follow these steps:

1. Open the scene you created in the Try It Yourself "Creating a Timeline Asset." Add a cube to the scene and position it at (0, 0, 0).

2. Open the Timeline window (by selecting **Window > Timeline**). Select the **Director** game object in the scene. You should see your timeline appear in the Timeline window (though it doesn't have any tracks yet).

3. Lock the Timeline window by clicking the lock icon in the upper-right corner (refer to Figure 19.4).

4. Add an animation track by clicking the **Add** button and selecting **Animation Track**.

5. Bind the Cube game object to this animation track by dragging the Cube object from the Hierarchy view onto the Track Binding property in the Timeline window (see Figure 19.5).

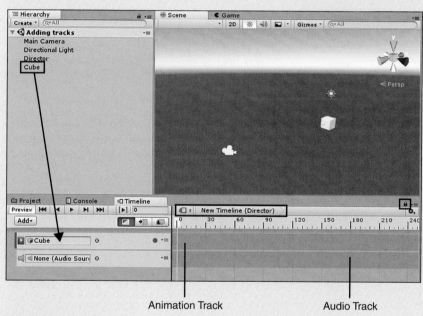

        Animation Track   Audio Track

FIGURE 19.5
Binding a track.

6. When prompted, click **Create Animator on Cube**.

7. Add an audio track by clicking the **Add** button and selecting **Audio Track**. The audio track doesn't need to be bound to a game object in order to function.

Timeline Clips

Once you have tracks on your timeline, you need to add clips. The way clips behave varies slightly depending on the type of track you have, but the general functionality of all clips is the same. To add a clip to a track, simply right-click a track and select **Add From** *<type of clip>*. So, for example, if you were adding a clip to an audio track, the menu would say Add from Audio Clip (see Figure 19.6). A menu pops up, allowing you to pick the clip to add to the track. Alternatively, you can add a clip to a track by dragging a relevant asset from the Project view onto the track in the Timeline window.

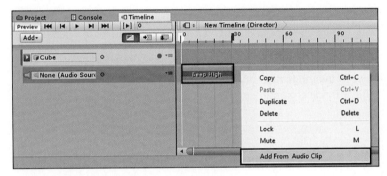

FIGURE 19.6
Adding the clip called Beep High to an audio track.

Once there is a clip on the track, you can move it around to control when it plays. You can also resize the clip to change how long it plays. You can even use a clip's duration to crop or loop an animation over a period of time. Note that the exact behavior of a clip's duration depends on the track type.

Besides dragging clips around on a track to adjust their play settings, you can also select a clip and then modify the settings in the Inspector view. This gives you a finer level of control and tuning when working with clips (though it isn't as fast as simply clicking and dragging).

Sequencing Clips

It's finally time to actually get some stuff happening in your timeline! You will be adding clips to the timeline tracks you created in the Try It Yourself "Adding Tracks." Be sure to save this scene again because you will continue using it later in this hour. Follow these steps:

1. Open the scene you created in the Try It Yourself "Adding Tracks." Locate the book assets for Hour 19 and import two folders: **Animations** and **Audio**.

2. In the Timeline window, right-click the animation track bound to the Cube game object and select **Add from Animation Clip**.

3. In the Select AnimationClip dialog that pops up, choose the newly imported **Red** animation clip.

4. Repeat step 3, adding clips for **Orange**, **Yellow**, **Green**, **Blue**, **Indigo**, and **Violet** (see Figure 19.7).

5. Right-click the audio track and select **Add from Audio Clip**. Select the **Beep High** audio clip.

6. Duplicate the Beep High clip on the audio track six times by selecting the clip and pressing **Ctrl+D** on a PC or **Command+D** on a Mac.

7. Move the audio clips so that the timing lines up with the changing of the cube's color.

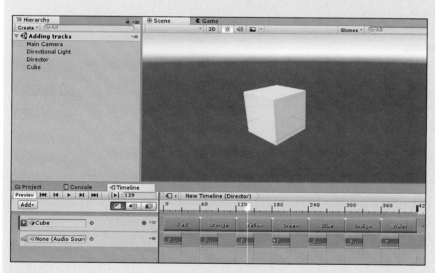

FIGURE 19.7
The final timeline setup.

8. Preview the timeline by moving the scrubber or clicking the Play button in the Timeline window. Notice that the audio isn't also previewed. (This will be added in a later version of Unity.) Save your scene and then play it. Notice the cube's color changing sequenced with the audio clips.

TIP
_____

Fast Animations

Animation tracks work great with both imported animations and animations created in Unity using the Animation window. If you want to quickly animate an object for use with a timeline, however, there is an even easier way. With a game object bound to an animation track, you can click the Record button directly on the track itself (see Figure 19.8). This functions identically to the Record mode of the Animation window (seen in Hour 17). The only difference is that in this case, instead of making a new separate animation clip, the animation data is stored directly in the timeline asset. Using this method, you can quickly produce simple animations that add a lot of depth to your cinematics.

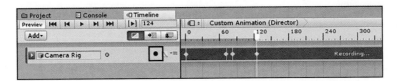

FIGURE 19.8
Recording within the Timeline window.

_____

TIP
_____

Muting and Locking

Each track in the Timeline window can be locked to prevent accidental changes. Simply select a track and press **L** or right-click and select **Lock**. In addition, a track can be muted so that it doesn't play when the timeline does. To mute a track, select it and press **M** or right-click and select **Mute**.

_____

Going Beyond Simple Control

You have only just begun to scratch the surface of what you can do with the Timeline system. Obviously, this system is very good for cinematics, but it can also be used to create many types of rich behaviors. A few examples are controlling guard movements, making a crowd look more lifelike, or deploying a complex set of screen effects when a character takes damage.

Blending Clips on a Track

So far in this hour, you've looked at working with clips as individual items on a track. That doesn't necessarily have to be the case, though. You can actually use a timeline to blend two different clips to get a new, combined result. Doing so simply requires that you drag one clip onto another one. Figure 19.9 shows the result of blending the Red and Orange clips from the Try It Yourself "Sequencing Clips."

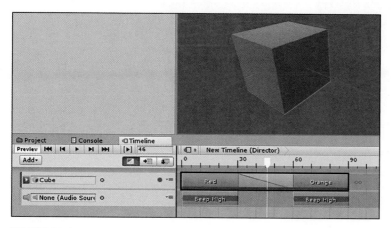

FIGURE 19.9
Blending clips in the Timeline window.

Blending works for more than just animation clips. You can also blend audio tracks and many of the custom tracks being created by the Unity community. Being able to blend clips allows for unprecedented levels of control and smooth action "tweening" between key frames.

TRY IT YOURSELF ▼

Blending Clips

The following steps show you how to blend the clips you added in the Try It Yourself "Sequencing Clips" to create a smooth color transition across the rainbow. Be sure to save this scene again because you will continue using it later in this hour. Follow these steps:

1. Open the scene you created in the Try It Yourself "Sequencing Clips." Ensure that the Timeline window is open and that the **Director** game object is selected.

2. In the Timeline window, drag the **Orange** clip so that it halfway covers the **Red** clip. In the Inspector view, the Orange clip should start on frame 30 and end on frame 90.

3. Continue blending the color clips leftward until the timeline consists of an almost continuous blend (see Figure 19.10).

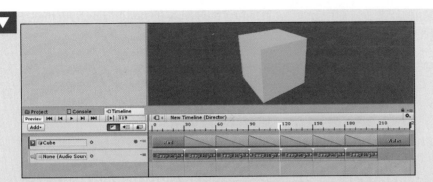

FIGURE 19.10
Blending all color clips.

4. Shift the audio clips so that each one matches up with the beginning of a color animation. These sound cues will help identify each color as it is applied.

Scripting with the Timeline

For the most part, the code required to build custom playable tracks and clips is fairly complex and beyond the scope of this text. Something simple you can do, however, is to tell a timeline when to run instead of letting it run automatically when the scene first begins. This enables you to trigger cinematics or in-game events.

In order to write code that works with the Timeline system, you need to tell Unity to use the `Playables` library:

```
using UnityEngine.Playables;
```

Then you can create a variable of type `PlayableDirector` and use it to control the timeline. The two primary methods to use are `Play()` and `Stop()`:

```
PlayableDirector director = GetComponent<PlayableDirector>();

director.Play(); // Start a timeline
director.Stop(); // Stop a timeline
```

Another thing you can do is tell a director what playable to play at runtime. One potential use case for this is to have a collection of timelines that get chosen randomly or to determine what timeline to play depending on the results of gameplay:

```
public PlayableAsset newTimeline;

void SomeMethod()
{
    director.Play(newTimeline);
}
```

Using these simple method calls, you can provide most of the functionality you need from the
Timeline system at runtime.

Playing Timelines with Code

In this exercise you'll finish the example for this hour by controlling your timeline with a script:

1. Open the scene you created in the Try It Yourself "Blending Clips." Add a folder named
Scripts and add to the folder a script named InputControl.

2. Select the **Director** game object and uncheck **Play on Awake** on the Playable Director component. Attach the InputControl script to the Director game object and then modify the code
to contain so that it looks as follows:

```
using UnityEngine;
using UnityEngine.Playables;

public class InputControl : MonoBehaviour
{
    PlayableDirector director;

    void Start()
    {
        director = GetComponent<PlayableDirector>();
    }

    void Update()
    {
        if (Input.GetButtonDown("Jump"))
        {
            if (director.state == PlayState.Paused)
                director.Play();
            else
                director.Stop();
        }
    }
}
```

3. Run the scene. Now whenever you press the spacebar, you toggle the timeline on and off.

Summary

You started this hour by exploring the Timeline system in Unity. You examined how to create
timeline assets and fill them with tracks and clips. From there, you learned to mix and blend
clips, and you finished the hour with some scripting to control timelines.

Q&A

Q. **What is the difference between a timeline and a playable?**

A. A timeline is a playable. It just happens to be a playable that plays playables (which also contain playables). Get it?

Q. **How many timelines can be playing in a scene?**

A. You can have—and play—as many timelines as you want in a scene. Be aware, though, that if two timelines are trying to control the same object, one of them will take priority over the other.

Workshop

Take some time to work through the questions here to ensure that you have a firm grasp of the material.

Quiz

1. What component plays a timeline in a scene?

2. How many track types are built into Unity?

3. What is the term for telling a timeline track which game object it controls?

4. How do you blend two clips?

Answers

1. Playable Director component

2. Five (six if you count the group track)

3. This is called *binding* the object to the track.

4. Simply drag one clip onto the other on a track.

Exercise

This exercise is a bit of an open-ended invitation to play with the Timeline system. Besides practicing more with the Timeline, you are encouraged to check out some of Unity's video training on the topic (see https://unity3d.com/learn/tutorials/s/animation). Here are some things to try in this hour:

▶ Create a dynamic UI using animations.

▶ Create a guard patrolling pattern.

▶ Set up a series of complex camera animations.

▶ Use an activation track to cause several lights to behave like strobes or a marquee.

Game 4: *Gauntlet Runner*

What You'll Learn in This Hour:

▶ How to design the game *Gauntlet Runner*

▶ How to build the *Gauntlet Runner* world

▶ How to build the *Gauntlet Runner* entities

▶ How to build the *Gauntlet Runner* controls

▶ How to further improve *Gauntlet Runner*

Let's make a game! In this hour, you'll make a 3D gauntlet-running game appropriately titled *Gauntlet Runner*. You'll start the hour with the design of the game. From there, you'll focus on building the world. Next, you'll build the entities and controls. You'll wrap up the hour by playing the game and seeing where improvements can be made.

TIP

Completed Project

Be sure to follow along in this hour to build the complete game project. If you get stuck, you can find a complete copy of the game in the book assets for Hour 20. Take a look at it if you need help or inspiration.

Design

You learned about design elements in Hour 6, "Game 1: *Amazing Racer.*" In this hour, you'll dive right into them.

The Concept

In this game, you will be playing as a cyborg running as far as possible through a gauntlet tunnel, attempting to grab power-ups to extend your game time. You need to avoid obstacles that will slow you down. The game ends when you run out of time.

The Rules

The rules of this game state how to play and allude to some of the properties of the objects. The rules for *Gauntlet Runner* are as follows:

▶ The player can move left or right and "phase out" (become ghost-like). The player cannot move in any other manner.

▶ A player who hits an obstacle is slowed by 50% for 1 second.

▶ If a player grabs a power-up, the player's time is extended by 1.5 seconds.

▶ The player is bounded by the sides of the tunnel.

▶ The loss condition for the game is running out of time.

▶ There is no win condition, but the player aims to travel as far as possible.

The Requirements

The requirements for this game are simple:

▶ A gauntlet texture.

▶ A wall texture.

▶ A player model.

▶ A custom shader for when the player is phased out (as discussed later in this hour).

▶ A power-up and an obstacle. These will be created in Unity.

▶ A game manager. This will be created in Unity.

▶ A power-up particle effect. This will be created in Unity.

▶ Interactive scripts. These will be written in Visual Studio.

In an effort to make this game more visually appealing, you will be using more assets built by the great game development community. In this case, you will be using textures and a player model from the *Adventure* sample game released by Unity Technologies (https:// www.assetstore.unity3d.com/en/#!/content/76216). You will also be using a custom shader that was graciously provided for free by Andy Duboc (https://github.com/andydbc/HologramShader).

The World

The world for this game will simply be three cubes configured to look like a gauntlet. The entire setup is fairly basic; it's the other components of the game that add challenge and fun.

The Scene

Before setting up the ground and its functionality, get your scene set up and ready to go. To prepare the scene, do the following:

1. Create a new 3D project called **Gauntlet Runner**. Create a new folder called Scenes and save your scene as Main in that folder.

2. Position the Main Camera at (0, 3, -10.7) with a rotation of (33, 0, 0).

3. In the book assets for Hour 20, locate two folders: **Textures** and **Materials**. Drag those folders into the Project view to import them.

4. In the Materials folder, locate the material Dark Sky. This material represents a skybox; notice that its shader type is Skybox/Procedural (see Figure 20.1). Drag the **Dark Sky** material from the Project view into the Scene view to change the sky.

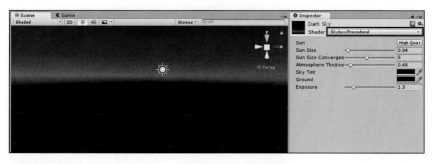

FIGURE 20.1
The new Dark Sky material.

The camera for this game will be in a fixed position, hovering over the gameplay. The rest of the world will pass underneath it.

NOTE

Meta Madness

In this section you imported three folders from the book assets. If you looked inside those folders, you might have noticed that for each asset, there was another file with the same name and the .meta extension. These .meta files store information that allows assets to link to each other. If the .meta files weren't included in the book files, the materials would still have their settings, but they wouldn't know which textures to use. Likewise, the player model wouldn't know about its material.

The Gauntlet

The ground in this game will be scrolling gauntlet in nature; however, unlike with the scrolling background used in *Captain Blaster* (see Hour 15, "Game 3: *Captain Blaster*"), you will not actually be scrolling anything. This is explained in more detail in the next section, but for now just understand that you need to create only one ground object to make the scrolling work. The ground itself will consist of a basic cube and two quads. To create the ground, follow these steps:

1. Add a cube to the scene. Name it **Ground** and position it at (0, 0, 15.5) with a rotation of (0, 180, 0) and a scale of (10, .5, 50).

2. Add to the scene a quad named Wall and position it at (-5.25, 1.2, 15.5) with a rotation of (0, -90, 0) and a scale of (50, 2, 1). Duplicate the Wall object and position the new object at (5.25, 1.2, 15.5).

3. In the Materials folder you imported previously, examine the Ground and Wall materials. The Ground material is slightly metallic with some texture tiling. One of the built-in particle shaders gives the Wall material a glowing effect (see Figure 20.2).

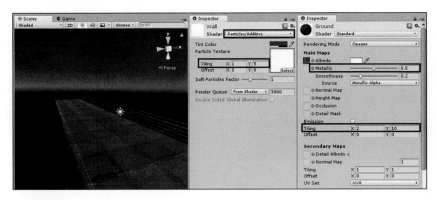

FIGURE 20.2
The gauntlet materials.

4. Drag the **Ground** material onto the Ground game object. Drag the **Wall** material onto both Wall game objects.

That's it! The gauntlet is fairly basic.

Scrolling the Ground

You saw in Hour 15 that you can scroll a background by creating two instances of that background and moving them in a "leapfrog" manner. In the *Gauntlet Runner* game, you are going to use an even more clever solution. Each material has a set of texture offsets. These can be seen in the Inspector when a material is selected (right below tiling). You need to modify those offsets at runtime via a script. If the texture is set to repeat (which it is by default), the texture will loop around seamlessly. The result, if done correctly, is an object that seems to scroll—without any actual movement. To create this effect, follow the steps on the next page.

1. Create a new folder named **Scripts**. Create a new script called **TextureScroller**. Attach the script to the ground.

2. Add the following code to the script (replacing the `Start()` and `Update()` methods that are already there):

```
public float speed = .5f;

Renderer renderer;
float offset;

void Start()
{
    renderer = GetComponent<Renderer>();
}

void Update()
{
    // Increase offset based on time
    offset += Time.deltaTime * speed;
    // Keep offset between 0 and 1
    if (offset > 1)
        offset -= 1;
    // Apply the offset to the material
    renderer.material.mainTextureOffset = new Vector2(0, offset);
}
```

3. Run the scene and notice your gauntlet scrolling. This is an easy and efficient way to create a scrolling 3D object.

The Entities

Now that you have a scrolling world, it is time to set up the entities: the player, the power-ups, the obstacles, and a trigger zone. The trigger zone will be used to clean up any items that make it past the player. You do not need to create a spawn point for this game. Instead, you are going to explore a different way of handling it: by letting the game control create the power-ups and obstacles.

The Power-ups

The power-ups in this game are going to be simple spheres with some effects added to them. You will be creating a sphere, positioning it, and then making a prefab out of it. To create the power-up, follow these steps:

1. Add a sphere to the scene. Position the sphere at (0, 1.5, 42) with a scale of (.5, .5, .5). Add a rigidbody to the sphere and uncheck **Use Gravity**.

2. Create a new material named **Powerup** and give it a yellow color. Set Metallic to **0** and Smoothness to **1**. Apply the material to the sphere.

3. Add a point light to the sphere (by selecting **Add Component > Rendering > Light**). Give the light a yellow color.

4. Add a particle system to the sphere (by selecting **Component > Effects > Particle System**). If the particles have an odd purplish coloring, don't worry. Just see the following caution for the fix.

5. In the main particle module, set Start Lifetime to **.5**, set Start Speed to **–5**, set Start Size to **.3**, and set Start Color to a light-yellow color.

6. In the Emission module, set Rate over Time to **30**. In the Shape module, set Shape to **Sphere** and set Radius to **1**.

7. In the Renderer module, set Render Mode to **Stretched Billboard** and Length Scale to **5**.

8. Create a new folder called **Prefabs**. Rename the sphere **Powerup** and click and drag it from the Hierarchy view into the **Prefabs** folder. Then delete the power-up from the scene.

CAUTION

Particle Problems

Depending on your version of Unity, you may see strange colored squares instead of particles when you add a particle system to a power-up. If you do, you need to manually apply the Default Particle material to the Renderer module of the Particle System component. To do that, simply click the circle selector next to the Material property of the Renderer module and select **Default-Particle** from the list (see Figure 20.3)

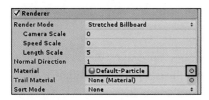

FIGURE 20.3
Assigning the Default-Particle material.

By setting the position of the object before putting it into the prefab, you can simply instantiate the prefab, and it will appear at that spot. As a result, you do not need a spawn point. Figure 20.4 illustrates the finished power-up (though the image doesn't really do it justice).

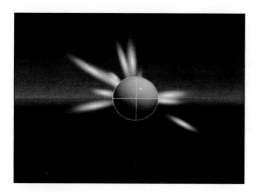

FIGURE 20.4
The power-up.

The Obstacles

For this game, the obstacles are represented by small glowing red cubes. The player has the option of either avoiding them or phasing through them. To create the obstacles, follow these steps:

1. Add a cube to the scene and name it **Obstacle**. Position it at (0, .4, 42) with a scale of (1, .2, 1). Add a rigidbody to the cube and uncheck **Use Gravity**.

2. Add a Light component to the obstacle and give it a red color.

3. Create a new material called **Obstacle** and apply it to the Obstacle game object. Make the color of the material red, check the **Emission** check box, and give it a dark red emissive color (see Figure 20.5).

4. Drag the **Obstacle** game object into the Prefabs folder to turn it into a prefab. Delete the Obstacle game object.

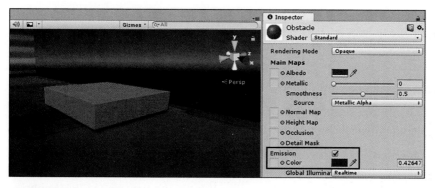

FIGURE 20.5
The obstacle and material.

The Trigger Zone

Just as in games you've created in earlier hours, the trigger zone in *Gauntlet Runner* exists to clean up any game objects that make it past the player. To create the trigger zone, follow these steps:

1. Add a cube to the scene. Rename the cube **TriggerZone** and position it at (0, 1, -20) with a scale of (10, 1, 1).

2. On the Box Collider component of the trigger zone, check the **Is Trigger** check box.

The Player

The player requires a large portion of the work for this game. The player will need to be animated and will also have a controller and use a custom shader. We have talked about shaders before, but we haven't yet used one that wasn't built in to Unity. Before we get ahead of ourselves though, let's get the player ready:

1. In the book files for this hour, locate the **Models** and **Animations** folders and drag them into the Project view to import them.

2. Inside the Models folder, select the **Player.fbx** model. As mentioned before, this asset is provided, free to use, in Unity's *Adventure* sample game.

3. Under the Rig tab, change the animation type to **Humanoid**. Click **Apply**. You should now see a check mark next to the Configure button. (If you need a refresher on Humanoid rigs, be sure to go back to Hour 18, "Animators.")

4. Drag the Player model into the scene and position it at (0, .25, -8.5). Give the Player game object the **Player** tag. (*Reminder:* An object's tag can be found in the top-left drop-down in the Inspector view.)

5. Add a capsule collider to the player (by selecting **Add Component > Physics > Capsule Collider**). Check the **Is Trigger** check box. Finally, set the Center Y value to .7, Radius to .3, and Height to **1.5**.

You now need to prepare and apply the Run animation, as follows:

1. From the Animations folder, select the **Runs.fbx** file. In the Inspector, click the **Rig** tab and change the animation type to **Humanoid**. Click **Apply**.

2. On the Animations tab, notice that there are three clips: RunRight, Run, and RunLeft. Select **Run** and ensure that the properties are set as shown in Figure 20.6. (To avoid drift, it is important that the x axis value for the Average Velocity property be 0.) Click **Apply**.

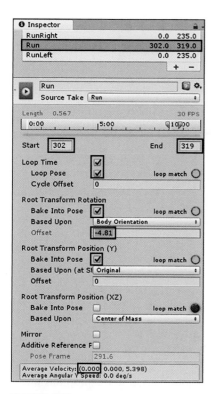

FIGURE 20.6
The Run animation properties.

3. Expand the asset tray on the Runs.fbx model by clicking the arrow on the right side of the asset in the Project view. Locate the Run animation clip and drag it onto the Player model in the scene. You'll know you did it correctly when an animator controller named Player appears in the folder next to Runs.fbx.

If you run the scene now, you will notice a couple animation issues. The first is that the player runs off into the distance. Recall that you only want to give the illusion that the player is moving—but not actually have the player move. The second issue is that the animation is too fast, and the player's feet slide on the ground as a result. Follow these steps to fix these issues:

1. In order to remove the root motion and get the player to run in place, select the **Player** game object in the scene. On the Animator component, uncheck **Apply Root Motion**.

2. In the Project view, double-click the **Player** animator controller (in the Animations folder) to open the Animator window.

3. In the Animator window, select the **Run** state. In the Inspector view, set Speed to **.7** and check **Foot IK** (see Figure 20.7). Run your scene and see how the player runs now.

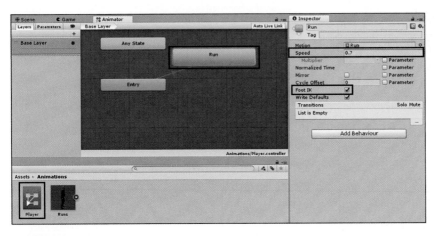

FIGURE 20.7
The Run state properties.

The player entity is ready (for now). In the following sections you will add code that provides some interesting functionality in the game.

The Controls

It's now time to add controls and interactivity to get this game going. Because the positions for the power-ups and obstacles are in the prefabs already, there is no need to create a spawn point. Therefore, almost all of the control will be placed on a game manager object.

Trigger Zone Script

The first script you need to make is the one for the trigger zone. Remember that the trigger zone simply destroys any objects that make their way past the player. To create this, simply create a new script named **TriggerZone** and attach it to the trigger zone game object. Place the following code in the script:

```
void OnTriggerEnter(Collider other)
{
    Destroy(other.gameObject);
}
```

The trigger script is very basic and just destroys any object that enters it.

The Game Manager Script

The game manager script is where a majority of the work takes place. To start, create an empty game object in the scene and name it **Game Manager**. This will simply be a placeholder for

your scripts. Create a new script named GameManager and attach it to the Game Manager
object you just created. In the following code for the game manager script, there is some
complexity, so be sure to read each line carefully to see what it is doing. Add the following
code to the script:

```
public TextureScroller ground;
public float gameTime = 10;

float totalTimeElapsed = 0;
bool isGameOver = false;

void Update()
{
    if (isGameOver)
        return;

    totalTimeElapsed += Time.deltaTime;
    gameTime -= Time.deltaTime;

    if (gameTime <= 0)
        isGameOver = true;
}

public void AdjustTime(float amount)
{
    gameTime += amount;
    if (amount < 0)
        SlowWorldDown();
}

void SlowWorldDown()
{
    // Cancel any invokes to speed the world up
    // Then slow the world down for 1 second
    CancelInvoke();
    Time.timeScale = 0.5f;
    Invoke("SpeedWorldUp", 1);
}

void SpeedWorldUp()
{
    Time.timeScale = 1f;
}

// Note this is using Unity's legacy GUI system
void OnGUI()
{
    if (!isGameOver)
```

```
    {
        Rect boxRect = new Rect(Screen.width / 2 - 50, Screen.height - 100, 100, 50);
        GUI.Box(boxRect, "Time Remaining");

        Rect labelRect = new Rect(Screen.width / 2 - 10, Screen.height - 80, 20, 40);
        GUI.Label(labelRect, ((int)gameTime).ToString());
    }
    else
    {
        Rect boxRect = new Rect(Screen.width / 2 - 60, Screen.height / 2 - 100, 120, 50);
        GUI.Box(boxRect, "Game Over");

        Rect labelRect = new Rect(Screen.width / 2 - 55, Screen.height / 2 - 80, 90, 40);
        GUI.Label(labelRect, "Total Time: " +(int)totalTimeElapsed);

        Time.timeScale = 0;
    }
}
```

NOTE

Old UI System

Note that, like *Amazing Racer* (which you created In Chapter 6, "Game 1: *Amazing Racer*"), the *Gauntlet Runner* game uses Unity's old GUI system. While you wouldn't typically use this GUI for an actual game, it is used here to save time and prevent this hour from being way too long. Don't worry, though: You'll get a chance to add the new UI yourself as part of the exercise at the end of this hour.

Remember that one of the premises of this game is that everything slows down when the player hits an obstacle. You make this happen by changing the `Time.timeScale` for the entire game. The remaining variables maintain the game timing and state.

The `Update()` method keeps track of time. It adds the time since the last frame (`Time.deltaTime`) to the `totalTimeElapsed` variable. It also checks whether the game is over, which happens when the time remaining reaches 0. If the game is over, it sets the `isGameOver` flag.

The `SlowWorldDown()` and `SpeedWorldUp()` methods work in conjunction with one another. Whenever a player hits an obstacle, the `SlowWorldDown()` method is called. This method basically slows down time. It then calls the `Invoke()` method, which basically says, "Call the method written here in *x* seconds," where the method called is the one named in the quotes and the number of seconds is the seconds value. You might have noticed the call to `CancelInvoke()` at the beginning of the `SlowWorldDown()` method. This basically cancels any `SpeedWorldUp()` methods waiting to be called because the player hit another obstacle. In the previous code, after 1 second, the `SpeedWorldUp()` method is called. This method speeds everything back up so that play can resume the game, as normal.

The `AdjustTime()` method is called whenever the player hits a power-up or an obstacle. This method adjusts the amount of time remaining. If that amount is negative (an obstacle), the method calls `SlowWorldDown()`.

Finally, the `OnGUI` method draws the remaining time to the scene while the game is running, and it shows the total time the game lasted after it ends.

The Player Script

The Player script has two responsibilities: Manage the player movement and collision controls, and manage the phase effect. Create a new script called **Player** and attach it to the Player object in the scene. Add the following code to the script:

```
[Header("References")]
public GameManager manager;
public Material normalMat;
public Material phasedMat;

[Header("Gameplay")]
public float bounds = 3f;
public float strafeSpeed = 4f;
public float phaseCooldown = 2f;

Renderer mesh;
Collider collision;
bool canPhase = true;

void Start()
{
    mesh = GetComponentInChildren<SkinnedMeshRenderer>();
    collision = GetComponent<Collider>();
}

void Update()
{
    float xMove = Input.GetAxis("Horizontal") * Time.deltaTime * strafeSpeed;

    Vector3 position = transform.position;
    position.x += xMove;
    position.x = Mathf.Clamp(position.x, -bounds, bounds);
    transform.position = position;

    if (Input.GetButtonDown("Jump") && canPhase)
    {
```

```
        canPhase = false;
        mesh.material = phasedMat;
        collision.enabled = false;

        Invoke("PhaseIn", phaseCooldown);
    }
}

void PhaseIn()
{
    canPhase = true;
    mesh.material = normalMat;
    collision.enabled = true;
}
```

To start things off, this script uses something called an *attribute*. Attributes are special tags that modify code. As you can see, this code uses the `Header` attribute, which causes Inspector view to display the header's string. (Check it out in the editor.)

The first three variables hold references to the game manager and two materials. When the player phases out, the materials are swapped. The rest of the variables handle gameplay preferences, such as the level bounds and the player's sideways speed.

The `Update()` method starts by moving the player based on input. It then checks to make sure the player isn't out of bounds. It does this by using the `Mathf.Clamp()` method. This keeps the player in the gauntlet. The `Update()` method then checks whether the player is currently pressing the spacebar (which the Input Manager calls `"Jump"`). If the user is pressing the spacebar, the player phases out and prepares to phase back in after a defined cooldown. A player who is phased out has a disabled collider so the player cannot hit obstacles or collect power-ups.

The Collidable Script

Both the power-ups and the obstacles need to move toward the player. They both also modify the game time when the player collides with them. Therefore, you can apply the same script to them to create this behavior. Create a script named **Collidable** and add it to both the power-up and obstacle prefabs. You can do this by selecting them both in the Inspector and clicking **Add Component > Scripts > Collidable**. Add the following code:

```
public GameManager manager;
public float moveSpeed = 20f;
public float timeAmount = 1.5f;

void Update()
{
    transform.Translate(0, 0, -moveSpeed * Time.deltaTime);
}
```

```
void OnTriggerEnter(Collider other)
{
    if (other.tag == "Player")
    {
        manager.AdjustTime(timeAmount);
        Destroy(gameObject);
    }
}
```

This script is simple. There are variables for the game manager script, the movement speed, and the time adjustment amount. Then, at each Update() method call, the object is moved. When the object collides with something, it checks to see if it collided with the player. If it did, it lets the game manager know and then it destroys itself.

The Spawner Script

The Spawner script is responsible for creating the objects in the scene. Because position data is in the prefabs, you won't need a dedicated spawner game object and can instead just place the script on the Game Manager object. Create a new script called **Spawner** and attach it to the Game Manager object. Add the following code to the script:

```
public GameObject powerupPrefab;
public GameObject obstaclePrefab;
public float spawnCycle = .5f;

GameManager manager;
float elapsedTime;
bool spawnPowerup = true;

void Start()
{
    manager = GetComponent<GameManager>();
}

void Update()
{
    elapsedTime += Time.deltaTime;
    if (elapsedTime > spawnCycle)
    {
        GameObject temp;
        if (spawnPowerup)
            temp = Instantiate(powerupPrefab) as GameObject;
        else
            temp = Instantiate(obstaclePrefab) as GameObject;

        Vector3 position = temp.transform.position;
        position.x = Random.Range(-3f, 3f);
        temp.transform.position = position;
```

```
        Collidable col = temp.GetComponent<Collidable>();
        col.manager = manager;

        elapsedTime = 0;
        spawnPowerup = !spawnPowerup;
    }
}
```

This script contains a reference to the power-up and obstacle game objects. The next variables control the timing and order of the object spawns. The power-ups and obstacles will take turns spawning; therefore, there is a flag to keep track of which one is going.

In the `Update()` method, the elapsed time is incremented and then checked to see if it is time to spawn a new object. If it is time, the script checks to see which object it should spawn. It then spawns either a power-up or an obstacle. The created object is then moved left or right randomly. The newly spawned object is given a reference to the game manager. Finally, the `Update()` method decreases the elapsed time and flips the power-up flag so that the opposite object will be spawned next time.

Putting It All Together

Now you're ready to work with the last part of the game. You need to link the scripts and objects. Start by selecting the **Game Manager** object in the Hierarchy view. Drag the **Ground** object to its corresponding property in the Game Manager Script component (see Figure 20.8). Drag the **Powerup** and **Obstacle** prefabs onto their corresponding properties in the Spawner (Script) component.

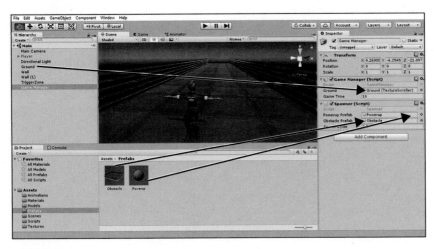

FIGURE 20.8
Dragging the objects to their properties.

Next, select the **Player** object in the Hierarchy view and drag the **Game Manager** object onto the Manager property of the Player (Script) component (see Figure 20.9). In addition, if you look in the Model folder in the Project view, you see the PhasedOut material. Right next to it is the Hologram custom shader. Feel free to take a look at them if you are curious, but keep in mind that understanding how to write your own shaders is very complex and beyond the scope of this book. Don't fret too much, though: Unity's very own visual shader creation tools are being released as an "experimental" feature in Unity 2018.1! When you are ready, drag the **Player** material and the **PhasedOut** material onto the corresponding properties on the player's Player (Script) component.

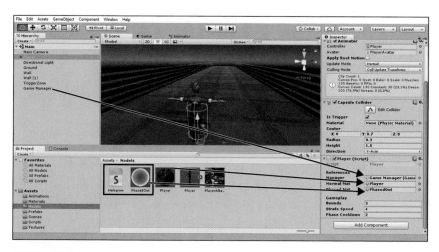

FIGURE 20.9
Adding the game control and materials to the player script.

Finally, select the **Obstacle** prefab and set the Time Amount property on the Collidable script to -.5. That's it! The game is now complete and playable.

Room for Improvement

As always, a game is not fully complete until it is tested and adjusted. Now it is time for you to play through the game and see what you like and what you don't like. Remember to keep track of the features that you think really enhance the gameplay experience. Also keep track of the items you feel detract from the experience. Be sure to make notes of any ideas you have for future iterations of the game. Try to have friends play the game as well and record their feedback about the game. All these things will help you make the game unique and more enjoyable.

Summary

In this hour, you have made the game *Gauntlet Runner*. You started by laying out the design elements of the game. From there, you built the gauntlet and got it to scroll using a texture trick. You then built the various entities for the game. After that, you built controls and scripts. Last but not least, you tested the game and recorded some feedback.

Q&A

Q. The movements of the objects and the ground aren't exactly lined up in *Gauntlet Runner*. Is that normal?

A. In this case, yes. A fine level of testing and tweaking would be required to get these to sync perfectly. This is one element you can focus on refining.

Q. Since the duration of "phasing out" is as long as the cooldown, couldn't the player always stay phased out?

A. Sure, I suppose. Though that would be able to happen for only about 10 seconds since players can't collect power-ups while phased out.

Workshop

Take some time to work through the questions here to ensure that you have a firm grasp of the material.

Quiz

1. How does the player lose the *Gauntlet Runner* game?

2. How does the scrolling background work?

3. How does the *Gauntlet Runner* game control the speed of all the objects in the scene?

Answers

1. The player loses the game when time runs out.

2. The gauntlet stays stationary, and the texture is scrolled along the object. The result is that the ground appears to move.

3. It changes the time scale of the entire game. However, notice that power-ups and obstacles still appear to move fast. Why could this be?

Exercise

It is time for you to attempt to implement some of the changes you noted when playtesting this game. You should attempt to make the game unique to you. Hopefully, you were able to identify some weaknesses of the game or some strengths that you would like to improve. Here are some things to consider changing:

▶ Try adding new/different power-ups and obstacles.

▶ Try changing the old GUI code to instead use Unity's new UI system.

▶ Try to increase or decrease the difficulty by changing how often power-ups and obstacles spawn. Also change how much time is added by power-ups or how long the world is slowed. You could even try to adjust how much the world is slowed or give different objects different slowed speeds.

▶ Give the power-ups and obstacles a new look. Play around with textures and particle effects to make them look awesome.

▶ Show the total distance traveled in place of a score, and perhaps even make the game speed continually increase to create a lose condition.

HOUR 21
Audio

What You'll Learn in This Hour:

▶ The basics of audio in Unity
▶ How to use audio sources
▶ How to work with audio via scripts
▶ How to use audio mixers

In this hour, you'll learn about audio in Unity. You'll start by learning about the basics of audio. From there, you'll explore the audio source components and how they work. You'll also take a look at individual audio clips and their role in the process. You'll then learn how to manipulate audio in code before wrapping up the hour with audio mixers.

Audio Basics

A large part of any experience involves the sounds of that experience. Imagine adding a laugh track to a scary movie. All of a sudden, what should be a tense experience would become a funny one. With video games, most of the time players don't realize it, but the sound is a very large part of the overall gameplay. Audio cues like chimes mark when a player unlocks a secret. Roaring battle cannons add a touch of realism to a war simulation game. Using Unity, implementing amazing audio effects is easy.

Parts of Audio

For sounds to work in a scene, you need three things: the audio listener, the audio source, and the audio clip. The *audio listener* is the most basic component of an audio system. The listener is a simple component whose sole responsibility is "hearing" the things that are happening in a scene. Listeners are like ears in a game world. By default, every scene starts with an audio listener attached to the Main Camera (see Figure 21.1). There are no properties available for the audio listener, and there is nothing you need to do to make it work.

It is a common practice to put the audio listener on whatever game object represents the player. If you put an audio listener on any other game object, you need to remove it from the Main Camera. Only a single audio listener is allowed per scene.

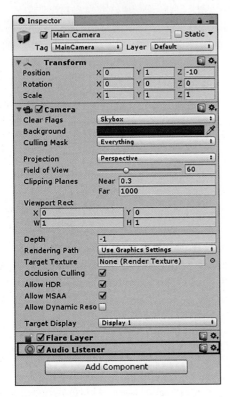

FIGURE 21.1
The audio listener.

The audio listener listens for sound, but it is the *audio source* that actually emits the sound. This source is a component that can be put on any object in a scene (even the object with the audio listener on it). There are many properties and settings involved with the audio source; they are covered in their own section later in this hour.

The last item required for functioning audio is the *audio clip*. Just as you would assume, the audio clip is the sound file that actually gets played by an audio source. Each clip has some properties that you can set to change the way Unity plays them. Unity supports the following audio formats: .aif, .aiff .wav, .mp3, .ogg, .mod, .it, .s3m, and .xm.

Together, these three items—audio listener, audio source, and audio clip—give your scene an audio experience.

2D and 3D Audio

One concept to be aware of with audio is the idea of 2D and 3D audio. 2D audio clips are the most basic types of audio. They play at the same volume regardless of the audio listener's proximity to the audio source in a scene. 2D sounds are best used for menus, warnings, soundtracks, or any audio that must always be heard exactly the same way. The greatest asset of 2D sounds is also their greatest weakness. Consider if every sound in your game played at exactly the same volume, regardless of where you were. It would be chaotic and unrealistic.

3D audio solves the problems of 2D audio. These audio clips feature something called *rolloff*, which dictates how sounds get quieter or louder depending on how close the audio listener gets to the audio source. In sophisticated audio systems, like Unity's, 3D sounds can even have a simulated Doppler effect (more on that later). If you are looking for realistic audio in a scene full of different audio sources, 3D audio is the way to go.

The dimensionality of each audio clip is managed on the audio source that plays the clip.

Audio Sources

As mentioned earlier in this hour, the audio sources are the components that actually play audio clips in a scene. The distance between these sources and the listeners determines how 3D audio clips sound. To add an audio source to a game object, select the desired object and click **Add Component > Audio > Audio Source**.

The Audio Source component has a series of properties that give you a fine level of control over how sound plays in a scene. Table 21.1 describes the various properties of the Audio Source component. In addition to these properties, the 3D Sound Settings section, covered later in this hour, has a number of settings you can apply to 3D audio clips.

TABLE 21.1   Audio Source Component Properties

Property	Description
Audio Clip	Specifies the actual sound file to play.
Output	(Optional) Makes it possible to output the sound clip to an audio mixer.
Mute	Determines whether the sound is muted.
Bypass Effects	Determines whether audio effects are applied to this source. Selecting this property turns off effects.
Bypass Listener Effects	Determines whether audio listener effects are applied to this source. Selecting this property turns off effects.

Property	Description
Bypass Reverb Zones	Determines whether reverb zone effects are applied to this source. Selecting this property turns off effects.
Play On Awake	Determines whether the audio source will begin playing the sound as soon as the scene launches.
Loop	Determines whether the audio source will restart the audio clip once it has finished playing.
Priority	Specifies the importance of the audio source. 0 is the most important, and 255 is the least important. Use 0 for music so it always plays.
Volume	Specifies the volume of the audio source, where 1 is the equivalent of 100% volume.
Pitch	Specifies the pitch of the audio source.
Stereo Pan	Sets the position in the stereo field of the 2D component of the sound.
Spatial Blend	Sets how much the 3D engine has an effect on the audio source. Use this to control if a sound is 2D or 3D.
Reverb Zone Mix	Sets the amount of the output signal that gets routed to the reverb zones.

NOTE

Audio Priorities

Every system has a finite number of audio channels. This number is not consistent and depends on many factors, such as the system's hardware and operating system. For this reason, most audio systems employ a priority system. In a priority system, sounds are played in the order in which they are received until the maximum number of channels are used. Once all the channels are in use, lower-priority sounds are swapped out for higher-priority sounds. Just be sure to remember that in Unity a lower-priority number means a higher actual priority!

Importing Audio Clips

Audio sources don't do anything unless they have audio to play. In Unity, importing audio is as easy as importing anything else. You just need to click and drag the files you want into the Project view to add them to your assets. The audio files used in this hour have been graciously provided by Jeremy Handel (http://handelabra.com).

Testing Audio

In this exercise, you'll test your audio in Unity and make sure everything works. Be sure to save this scene because you will use it again later in this hour. Follow these steps:

1. Create a new project or scene. Locate the **Sounds** folder in the book assets for Hour 21 and drag it into the Project view in Unity to import it.

2. Create a cube in your scene and position it at (0, 0, 0).

3. Add an audio source to the cube (by selecting **Add Component > Audio > Audio Source**).

4. Locate the file **looper.ogg** in the newly imported Sounds folder and drag it into the Audio Clip property of the audio source on the cube (see Figure 21.2).

5. Ensure that the **Play On Awake** property is checked, and run your scene. Notice the sound playing. The audio should stop after about 20 seconds (unless you set it to loop).

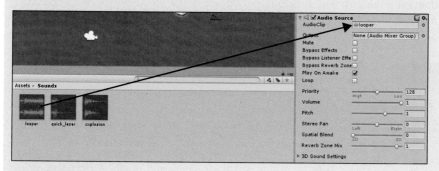

FIGURE 21.2
Adding a clip to a source.

NOTE

Mute Audio Button

At the top of the Game window is a button called Mute Audio (between Maximize on Play and Stats). If you don't hear anything when your game is playing, ensure that this button is not pressed in.

Testing Audio in the Scene View

It would get a bit taxing if you needed to run a scene every time you wanted to test your audio. Not only would you need to start up the scene, you would also need to navigate to the sound in the world. That is not always easy—or even possible. Instead, you can test your audio in the Scene view.

To test audio in the Scene view, you need to turn on scene audio. Do this by clicking the scene audio toggle (see Figure 21.3). When it is selected, an imaginary audio listener is used. This listener is positioned on your frame of reference in the Scene view (not on the position of the actual audio listener component).

FIGURE 21.3
The audio toggle.

▼ TRY IT YOURSELF

Adding Audio in the Scene View

This exercise shows you how to test your audio in the Scene view. It uses the scene created in the Try It Yourself "Testing Audio." If you have not completed that scene yet, do so before continuing. Follow these steps:

1. Open the scene you created in the Try It Yourself "Testing Audio."

2. Turn on the scene audio toggle (refer to Figure 21.3).

3. Move around the Scene view. Notice that the sound stays the same volume, regardless of your distance from the cube emitting the sound. By default, all sound sources default to 2D.

4. Drag the Spatial Blend slider over to 3D (see Figure 21.4). Now try moving around in Scene view again. Note that the sound now gets quieter as you get further away.

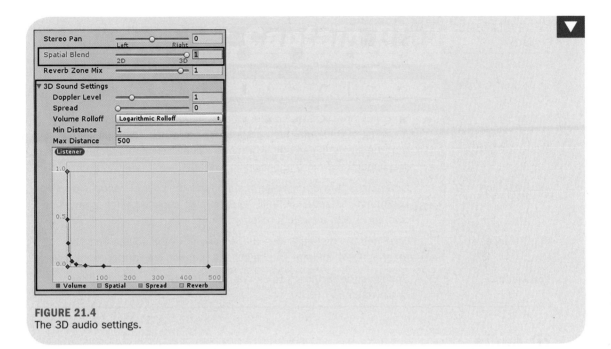

FIGURE 21.4
The 3D audio settings.

3D Audio

As mentioned earlier in this hour, all audio is set to be fully 2D by default. It is easy to change it to fully 3D by setting the Spatial Blend slider to **1**. This means all audio will be subject to the 3D audio effects that are distance and movement based. These effects are modified by the 3D properties of the audio component (refer to Figure 21.4).

Table 21.2 describes the various 3D audio properties.

TIP

Using the Graph

As you play with the options under 3D Sound Settings, look at the graph. It will tell you how loud the audio will be at various distances and is a great way of visualizing the effect of the controls. In this case, a picture really does say a thousand words!

TABLE 21.2   3D Audio Properties

Property	Description
Doppler Level	Determines how much Doppler effect (how sound is distorted while you are traveling toward or away from it) is applied to the audio. A setting of 0 means no effect will be applied.
Spread	Specifies how spread out the various speakers of a system are. A setting of 0 means that all speakers are at the same position and that the signal is essentially a mono signal. Leave this alone unless you understand more about audio systems.
Volume Rolloff	Determines how the change in sound volume over distance is applied. Logarithmic is set by default. You can also choose Linear or set your own curve with a custom rolloff.
Min Distance	Specifies the distance you can be away from the source and still receive 100% volume. The higher the number, the farther the distance.
Max Distance	Specifies the farthest you can be from the source and still hear some volume.

2D Audio

Sometimes you want some audio to play regardless of its position in the scene. The most common example of this is background music. To switch an audio source from 3D to 2D, drag the Spatial Blend slider over to 2D (this is the default; refer to Figure 21.4). Notice that you can also have a blend between 2D and 3D, meaning the audio will always be heard at least some amount, regardless of your distance from it.

The settings above the 3D Sound Settings section, such as Priority, Volume, Pitch, and so on, apply to both the 2D and the 3D portions of the sound. The settings in the 3D Sound Settings section obviously apply only to the 3D portion.

Audio Scripting

Playing audio from an audio source when it is created is nice, assuming that's the functionality that you want. If you want to wait and play a sound at a certain time, or if you want to play different sounds from the same source, however, you need to use scripting. Luckily, it isn't too difficult to manage your audio through code. Most of it works just like any audio player you're used to: Just pick a song and click **Play**. All audio scripting is done using variables and methods that are a part of the class `Audio`.

Starting and Stopping Audio

When dealing with audio in script, the first thing you need to do is get a reference to the Audio Source component. Use the following code to do this:

```
AudioSource audioSource;

void Start ()
{
    // Find the audio source component on the cube
    audioSource = GetComponent<AudioSource> ();
}
```

Now that you have a reference stored in the variable `audioSource`, you can start calling methods on it. The most basic functionality you could want is simply starting and stopping an audio clip. These actions are controlled by two methods simply named `Start()` and `Stop()`. Using these methods looks like this:

```
audioSource.Start(); // Starts a clip
audioSource.Stop();  // Stops a clip
```

This code will play the clip specified by the Audio Clip property of the Audio Source component. You also have the ability to start a clip after a delay. To do that, you use the method `PlayDelayed()`, which takes in a single parameter that is the time in seconds to wait before playing the clip and looks like this:

```
audioSource.PlayDelayed(<some time in seconds>);
```

You can tell whether a clip is currently playing by checking the `isPlaying` variable, which is part of the `audioSource` object. To access this variable, and thus see if the clip is playing, you could type the following:

```
if(audioSource.isPlaying)
{
    // The track is playing
}
```

As the name implies, this variable is true if the audio is currently playing and false if it is not.

▼ TRY IT YOURSELF

Starting and Stopping Audio

Follow these steps to see how to use scripts to start and stop an audio clip:

1. Open the scene you created in the Try It Yourself "Adding Audio in the Scene View."

2. On the Cube game object created previously, locate the Audio Source component. Uncheck the **Play On Wake** property and check the **Loop** property.

3. Create a new folder named **Scripts** and create a new script in it called **AudioScript**. Attach the script to the cube. Change the entire script code to the following:

```
using UnityEngine;

public class AudioScript : MonoBehaviour
{
    AudioSource audioSource;

    void Start()
    {
        audioSource = GetComponent<AudioSource>();
    }

    void Update()
    {
        if (Input.GetButtonDown("Jump"))
        {
            if (audioSource.isPlaying == true)
                audioSource.Stop();
            else
                audioSource.Play();
        }
    }
}
```

4. Play the scene. You can start and stop the audio by pressing the spacebar. Notice that the audio clip starts over every time you play the audio.

Unmentioned Properties

All the properties of the audio source that are listed in the Inspector are also available via scripting. For instance, the Loop property is accessed in code with the `audioSource.loop` variable. As mentioned earlier in this hour, all these variables are used in conjunction with the audio object. See how many you can find!

Changing Audio Clips

You can easily control which audio clips to play via scripts. The key is to change the Audio Clip property in the code before using the `Play()` method to play the clip. Always be sure to stop the current audio clip before switching to a new one; otherwise, the clip won't switch.

To change the audio clip of an audio source, assign a variable of type `AudioClip` to the `clip` variable of the `audioSource` object. For example, if you had an audio clip called `newClip`, you could assign it to an audio source and play it by using the following code:

```
audioSource.clip = newClip;
audioSoure.Play();
```

You can easily create a collection of audio clips and switch them out in this manner. You will do this in the exercise at the end of this hour.

Audio Mixers

So far you've seen how to play audio from a source and have it heard by a listener. That process has been very straightforward and easy to use, but you are using it "in a vacuum." That is, you are playing only a single audio clip—or a small number of them—at a time. Difficulties arise when you need to start balancing audio volumes and effects with each other. It could be quite a pain to constantly need to find and modify each audio source in a scene or prefab. This is where audio mixers come in. *Audio mixers* are assets that act as mixing boards, allowing a fine level of control when balancing audio.

Creating Audio Mixers

Audio mixer assets are very easy to create and use. To make one, simply right-click in the Project view and select **Create > Audio Mixer**. Once an audio mixer asset is created, you can double-click it to open the Audio Mixer view (see Figure 21.5). Alternatively, you can select **Window > Audio Mixer** to open the Audio Mixer view.

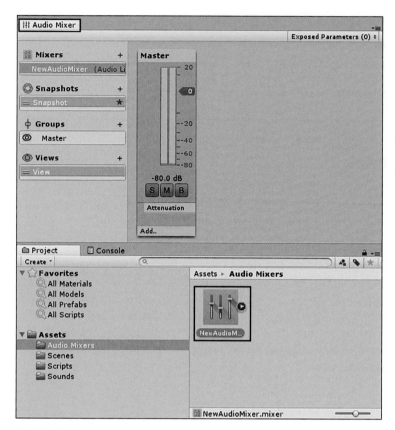

FIGURE 21.5
The Audio Mixer view.

Sending Audio to Mixers

Once you have an audio mixer, you need to route sounds through it. Routing audio through a mixer requires setting the output of an audio source to one of the audio mixer's groups. By default, an audio mixer has only a single group, called Master. You can add more groups to make organizing your audio easier (see Figure 21.6). Groups can even represent other audio mixers for a very modular approach to audio management.

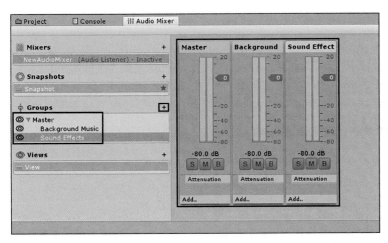

FIGURE 21.6
Adding groups.

Once you've created the desired audio groups, simply set the output property of an Audio Source component to your group (see Figure 21.7). Doing so allows the audio mixer to control the volume and effects of the audio clip. Furthermore, it overwrites the audio source's Spatial Blend property and treats the audio like a 2D audio source. By using the audio mixer, you can control the volume and effects for an entire collection of audio sources at once (see Figure 21.7).

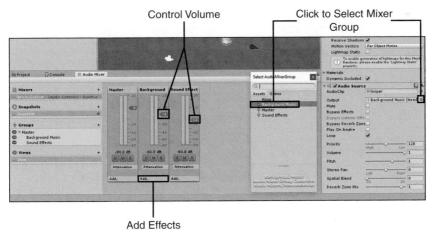

FIGURE 21.7
Routing audio.

Summary

In this hour, you've learned about using audio in Unity. You started by learning about the basics of audio and the components required to make it work. From there, you explored the Audio Source component. You learned how to test audio in the Scene view and how to use 2D and 3D audio clips. You finished the hour by learning to manipulate audio through scripts and exploring the use of audio mixers.

Q&A

Q. How many audio channels does a system have, on average?

A. It truly varies for every system. Most modern gaming platforms can simultaneously play dozens or hundreds of audio clips at the same time. The key is to know your target platform and use the priority system well.

Workshop

Take some time to work through the questions here to ensure that you have a firm grasp of the material.

Quiz

1. What items are needed for working audio?

2. True or False: 3D sounds play at the same volume, regardless of the listener's distance from the source?

3. What method allows you to play an audio clip after a delay?

Answers

1. Audio listener, audio source, and audio clip

2. False. 2D sounds play at the same volume, regardless of the listener's distance from the source.

3. `PlayDelayed()`

Exercise

In this exercise, you'll create a basic sound board. This sound board will allow you to play one of three sounds. You will also have the ability to start and stop the sounds and to turn looping on and off.

1. Create a new project or scene. Add a cube to the scene at position (0, 0, -10) and add an audio source to the cube. Be sure to uncheck the **Play On Awake** property. Locate the **Sounds** folder in the book assets for Hour 21 and drag it into the Assets folder.

2. Create a new folder called **Scripts** and create a new script named **AudioScript** in it. Attach the script to the cube. Replace the contents of the script with the following:

```
using UnityEngine;

public class AudioScript : MonoBehaviour
{
    public AudioClip clip1;
    public AudioClip clip2;
    public AudioClip clip3;

    AudioSource audioSource;

    void Start()
    {
        audioSource = GetComponent<AudioSource>();
        audioSource.clip = clip1;
    }

    void Update()
    {
        if (Input.GetButtonDown("Jump"))
        {
            if (audioSource.isPlaying == true)
                audioSource.Stop();
            else
            audioSource.Play();
        }

        if (Input.GetKeyDown(KeyCode.L))
        {
            audioSource.loop = !audioSource.loop; // toggles lopping
        }

        if (Input.GetKeyDown(KeyCode.Alpha1))
        {
            audioSource.Stop();
            audioSource.clip = clip1;
```

```
            audioSource.Play();
        }
        else if (Input.GetKeyDown(KeyCode.Alpha2))
        {
            audioSource.Stop();
            audioSource.clip = clip2;
            audioSource.Play();
        }
        else if (Input.GetKeyDown(KeyCode.Alpha3))
        {
            audioSource.Stop();
            audioSource.clip = clip3;
            audioSource.Play();
        }
    }
}
```

3. In the Unity editor, select the cube in your scene. Drag the audio files **looper.ogg**, **quick_laser.ogg**, and **xxplosion.ogg** from the Sounds folder onto the Clip1, Clip2, and Clip3 properties of the audio script.

4. Run your scene. Notice how you can change your audio clips with the keys **1**, **2**, and **3**. You can also start and stop the audio with the **spacebar**. Finally, you can toggle looping with the **L** key.

Mobile Development

What You'll Learn in This Hour:

▶ How to prepare for mobile development

▶ How to use a device's accelerometer

▶ How to use a device's touch display

Mobile devices such as phones and tablets are becoming common gaming devices. In this hour, you'll learn about mobile development with Unity for Android and iOS devices. You'll begin by looking at the requirements for mobile development. From there, you'll learn how to accept special inputs from a device's accelerometer. Finally, you'll learn about touch interface input.

NOTE

Requirements

This hour covers development for mobile devices specifically. So, if you do not have a mobile device (iOS or Android), you will not be able to follow along with any of the hands-on exercises in this hour. Don't worry, though: What you read here should still make sense, and you will still be able to make games for mobile devices but just won't be able to play them.

Preparing for Mobile

Unity makes developing games for mobile devices easy. You will also be happy to know that developing for mobile platforms is almost identical to developing for other platforms. The biggest difference to account for is that mobile platforms have different input (no keyboard or mouse, usually). If you approach your development with this in mind, however, you can build a game once and deploy it everywhere. There is no longer any reason you can't build your games for every major platform. This level of cross-platform capability is unprecedented. Before you can begin working with mobile devices in Unity, however, you need to get your computer set up and configured to do it.

NOTE

Multitudes of Devices

There are many different types of mobile devices. At the time this book was published, Apple had two classes of game-ready mobile devices: iPad and iPhone/iPod. Android had an untold number of phones and tablets, and many Windows mobile devices were available as well. Each of these types of devices has slightly different hardware and requires slightly different configuration steps. Therefore, this lesson simply attempts to guide you through the installation process. It would be impossible to write an exact guide that would work for everyone. In fact, several guides by Unity, Apple, and Android (Google) already exist that explain the process better than this text could. You are referred to them when needed.

Setting Up Your Environment

Before even opening Unity to make a game, you need to set up your development environment. The specifics of this differ depending on your target device and what you are trying to do, but the general steps are as follows:

1. Install the software development kit (SDK) of the device you are targeting.

2. Ensure that your computer recognizes and can work with that device (though this is important only if you want to test on the device).

3. For Android only, tell Unity where to find the SDK.

If these steps seem a bit cryptic to you, don't worry. Plenty of resources are available to assist you with these steps. The best place to start is with Unity's own documentation, which is available at http://docs.unity3d.com. This site contains living documentation about all facets of Unity.

As you can see in Figure 22.1, the Unity documentation has guides to assist you in setting up both the iOS and the Android environments. These documents are updated as the steps to set up the environments change. If you're not planning on following along with a device, continue on to the next section. If you are planning on following along with a device, complete the steps in the Unity documentation to configure your development environment before continuing on to the next section.

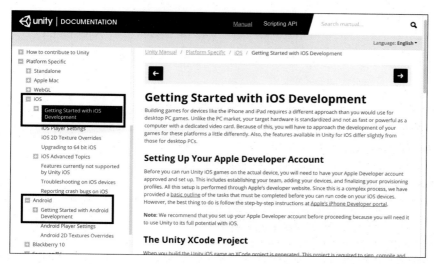

FIGURE 22.1
Platform-specific documentation.

Unity Remote

The most basic way to test your games on a device is to build your projects, put the resulting files on the device, and then run your game. This can be a cumbersome system and one you're sure to tire of quickly. Another way to test your games is to build a project and then run it through an iOS or Android emulator. Again, this requires quite a few steps and involves configuring and running an emulator. These systems can be useful if you are doing extensive testing on performance, rendering, and other advanced processes. For basic testing, though, there is a much better way: Use Unity Remote.

Unity Remote is an app you can obtain from your mobile device's application store that enables you to test your projects on your mobile device while it is running in the Unity editor. In a nutshell, this means you can experience your game running on a device in real time, alongside development, and use the device to send device inputs back to your game. You can find more information about Unity Remote at https://docs.unity3d.com/Manual/UnityRemote5.html.

To find the Unity Remote application, search for the term *Unity Remote* in your device's application store. From there, you can download and install it just as you would any other application (see Figure 22.2).

Once installed, Unity Remote acts as both a display for your game and a controller. You will be able to use it to send click information, accelerometer information, and multi-touch input back to Unity. It is especially effective because it gives you the ability to test your game (minimally) without installing any mobile SDKs or specialized developer accounts.

FIGURE 22.2
Unity Remote on the Google Play store.

▼ TRY IT YOURSELF

Testing Device Setup

This exercise gives you an opportunity to ensure that your mobile development environment is set up correctly. In this exercise, you'll use Unity Remote from your device to interact with a scene in Unity. If you don't have a device set up, you won't be able to perform all these steps, but you can still get an idea of what's happening by reading along. If this process doesn't work for you, it means that something with your environment is not set up correctly. Follow these steps:

1. Create a new project or scene and add a UI button to the center of the screen.

2. Set the button's Pressed Color to **Red** in the Inspector.

3. Run the scene and ensure that clicking the button changes its color. Stop the scene.

4. Attach your mobile device to your computer with a USB cable. When the computer recognizes your device, open the **Unity Remote** app on your device.

5. In Unity, select **Edit > Project Settings > Editor** and choose your device type in the Inspector under **Unity Remote > Device**. Note that if you don't have a mobile platform installed for Unity (Android or iOS), the option for it will not appear in the Editor settings.

6. Run the scene again. After a second, you should see the button appear on your mobile device. You should now be able to tap the button on your device's screen to change its color.

Accelerometers

Most modern mobile devices come with built-in accelerometers. An *accelerometer* relays information about the physical orientation of the device. It can tell whether the device is moving, tilted, or flat. It can also detect these things in all three axes. Figure 22.3 shows a mobile device's accelerometer axes and how they are oriented in *portrait orientation*.

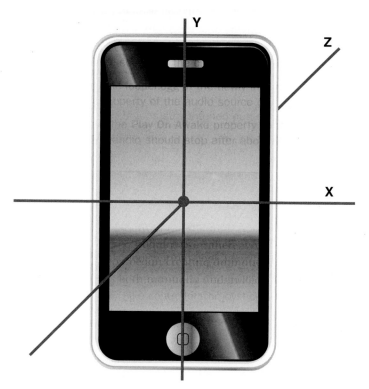

FIGURE 22.3
Accelerometer axes.

As you can see in Figure 22.3, the default axes of a device align with the 3D axes in Unity while the device is being held upright in portrait orientation directly in front of you. If you turn the device to use it in a different orientation, you need to convert the accelerometer data to the correct axis. For example, if you were using the phone pictured in Figure 22.3 in landscape orientation (on its side), you would use the X axis from the phone's accelerometer to represent the Y axis in Unity.

Designing for the Accelerometer

You need to keep in mind a few things when designing a game to use a mobile device's accelerometer. The first is that you can only ever reliably use two of the accelerometer's axes at any given time. The reason for this is that no matter the orientation of the device, one axis will always be actively engaged by gravity. Consider the orientation of the device in Figure 22.3. You can see that while the x and z axes can be manipulated by tilting the device, the y axis is currently reading negative values, as gravity is pulling it down. If you were to turn the phone so that it rested flat on a surface, face up, you would only be able to use the x and y axes. In that case, the z axis would be actively engaged.

Another thing to consider when designing for an accelerometer is that the input is not extremely accurate. Mobile devices do not read from their accelerometers at a set interval, and they often have to approximate values. As a result, the inputs read from an accelerometer can be jerky and uneven. A common practice, therefore, is to smoothly move objects with accelerometer inputs or to take an average of the inputs over time. Also, accelerometers give input values from -1 to +1, with full 180-degree rotation of the device. No one plays games while fully tilting a devices, though, so input values are generally less than their keyboard counterparts (for example, -.5 to .5).

Using the Accelerometer

Reading accelerometer input is done just like reading any other form of user input: via scripts. All you need to do is read from the Vector3 variable named `acceleration`, which is a part of the `Input` object. Therefore, you could access the x, y, and z axis data by writing the following:

```
Input.acceleration.x;
Input.acceleration.y;
Input.acceleration.z;
```

Using these values, you can manipulate your game objects accordingly.

NOTE

Axis Mismatch

When using accelerometer information in conjunction with Unity Remote, you might notice that the axes aren't lining up as described earlier in this hour. This is because Unity Remote bases the game's orientation on the aspect ratio chosen. This means that Unity Remote automatically displays in landscape orientation (holding your device sideways so that the longer edge is parallel to the ground) and translates the axes for you. Therefore, when you are using Unity Remote, the x axis runs along the long edge of your device, and the y axis runs along the short edge. It might seem strange, but chances are you were going to use your device like that anyway, so this saves you a step.

Moving a Cube with the Power of Your Mind...or Your Phone

In this exercise, you'll use a mobile device's accelerometer to move a cube around a scene. Obviously, to complete this exercise, you need a configured and attached mobile device with an accelerometer. Follow these steps:

1. Create a new project or scene. (If you create a new project, remember to modify the editor settings as described in the previous section.) Add a cube to the scene and position it at (0, 0, 0).

2. Create a new script called AccelerometerScript and attach it to the cube. Put the following code in the `Update()` method of the script:

```
float x = Input.acceleration.x * Time.deltaTime;
float z = -Input.acceleration.z * Time.deltaTime;
transform.Translate(x, 0f, z);
```

3. Ensure that your mobile device is plugged in to your computer. Hold the device in landscape orientation and run Unity Remote. Run the scene. Notice that you can move the cube by tilting your phone. Notice which axes of the phone move the cube along the x and z axes.

Multi-Touch Input

Mobile devices tend to be controlled largely through the use of their touch-capacitive screens. These screens can detect when and where a user touches them. They usually can track multiple touches at a time. The exact number of touches varies based on the device.

Touching the screen doesn't just give the device a simple touch location. In fact, there is quite a bit of information stored about each individual touch. In Unity, each screen touch is stored in a Touch variable. This means that every time you touch a screen, a Touch variable is generated. That Touch variable will exist as long as your finger remains on the screen. If you drag your finger along the screen, the Touch variable tracks that. The Touch variables are stored together in a collection called `touches`, which is part of the `Input` object. If there is currently nothing touching the screen, then this collection of touches is empty. To access this collection, you could enter the following:

```
Input.touches;
```

By using the `touches` collection, you could iterate through each `Touch` variable to process its data. Doing so would look something like this:

```
foreach(Touch touch in Input.touches)
{
    // Do something
}
```

As mentioned earlier in this hour, each touch contains more information than the simple screen data where the touch occurred. Table 22.1 lists all the properties of the `Touch` variable type.

TABLE 22.1   `Touch` **Variable Properties**

Property	Description
deltaPosition	The change in touch position since the last update. This is useful for detecting finger drags.
deltaTime	The amount of time that has passed since the last change to the touch.
fingerId	The unique index for the touch. For example, this would range from 0 to 4 on devices that allow five touches at a time.
phase	The current phase of the touch: Began, Moved, Stationary, Ended, or Canceled.
position	The 2D position of the touch on the screen.
tapCount	The number of taps the touch has performed on the screen.

These properties are useful for managing complex interactions between the user and game objects.

Tracking Touches

In this exercise, you'll track finger touches and output their data to the screen. Obviously, to complete this exercise, you need a configured and attached mobile device with multi-touch support. Follow these steps:

1. Create a new project or scene.

2. Create a new script called TouchScript and attach it to the Main Camera. Put the following code in the script:

```
void OnGUI()
{
    foreach (Touch touch in Input.touches)
    {
        string message = "";
        message += "ID: " +touch.fingerId + "\n";
        message += "Phase: " +touch.phase.ToString() + "\n";
        message += "TapCount: " +touch.tapCount + "\n";
        message += "Pos X: " +touch.position.x + "\n";
        message += "Pos Y: " +touch.position.y + "\n";

        int num = touch.fingerId;
        GUI.Label(new Rect(0 + 130 * num, 0, 120, 100), message);
    }
}
```

3. Ensure that your mobile device is plugged in to your computer. Run the scene. Touch the screen with your finger and notice the information that appears (see Figure 22.4). Move your finger and see how the data changes. Now touch with more fingers simultaneously. Move them about and take them off the screen randomly. See how it tracks each touch independently? How many touches can you get on your screen at a time?

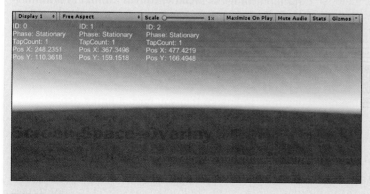

FIGURE 22.4
Touch output on the screen.

CAUTION
_____

Do Because I Say, Not Because I Do!

In the Try It Yourself "Tracking Touches," you created an `OnGUI()` method that collects information about the various touches on the screen. The part of the code where the string `message` is being built with the touch data is a *big* no-no. Performing too much processing in an `OnGUI()` method can greatly reduce the efficiency of a project, and you should try to avoid this. I used this method because it was an easy way to build the example without unneeded complexity and for demonstration purposes only. Always keep update code where it belongs: in `Update()`. In addition, you should really use the new UI because it is much faster.

_____

Summary

In this hour, you've learned about using Unity to develop games for mobile devices. You started by learning how to configure your development environment to work with Android and iOS. From there, you learned how to work with a device's accelerometer. You finished up the hour by experimenting with Unity's touch-tracking system.

Q&A

Q. Can I really build a game once and deploy it to all major platforms, mobile included?

A. Absolutely! The only thing to consider is that mobile devices generally don't have as much processing power as desktops. Therefore, mobile device users might experience some performance issues if your game has a lot of heavy processing or effects. You will need to ensure that your game is running efficiently if you plan to also deploy it on mobile platforms.

Q. What are the differences between iOS and Android devices?

A. From a Unity point of view, there isn't much difference between these two operating systems. They are both treated as mobile devices. Be aware, though, that there are some device differences (such as processing power, battery life, and phone OS) that can affect your games.

Workshop

Take some time to work through the questions here to ensure that you have a firm grasp of the material.

Quiz

1. What tool allows you to send live device input data to Unity while it is running a scene?

2. How many axes on the accelerometer can you realistically use at a time?

3. How many touches can a device have at once?

Answers

1. The Unity Remote app

2. Two axes. The third is always engaged by gravity, depending on how you are holding the device.

3. It depends entirely on the device. The last time I tested an iOS device, I was able to track 21 touches. That's enough for all your fingers and toes, plus 1 from a friend!

Exercise

In this exercise, you'll move objects about a scene based on touch input from a mobile device. Obviously, to complete this exercise, you need a configured and attached mobile device with multi-touch support. If you do not have that, you can still read along to get the basic idea.

1. Create a new project or scene. Select **Edit > Project Settings > Editor** and set the Device property to recognize your Unity Remote app.

2. Add three cubes to the scene and name them **Cube1**, **Cube2**, and **Cube3**. Position them at (-3, 1, -5), (0, 1, -5), and (3, 1, -5), respectively.

3. Create a new folder named Scripts. Create a new script called InputScript in the Scripts folder and attach it to the three cubes.

4. Add the following code to the `Update()` method of the script:

```
foreach (Touch touch in Input.touches)
{
    float xMove = touch.deltaPosition.x * 0.05f;
    float yMove = touch.deltaPosition.y * 0.05f;

    if (touch.fingerId == 0 && gameObject.name == "Cube1")
        transform.Translate(xMove, yMove, 0F);

    if (touch.fingerId == 1 && gameObject.name == "Cube2")
        transform.Translate(xMove, yMove, 0F);

    if (touch.fingerId == 2 && gameObject.name == "Cube3")
        transform.Translate(xMove, yMove, 0F);
}
```

5. Run the scene and touch the screen with up to three fingers. Notice that you can move the three cubes independently. Also notice that lifting one finger does not cause the other fingers to lose their cubes or their place.

HOUR 23
Polish and Deploy

What You'll Learn in This Hour:

▶ How to manage scenes in a game
▶ How to save data and objects between scenes
▶ The different player settings
▶ How to deploy a game

In this hour, you'll learn all about polishing a game and deploying it. You'll start by learning how to move about different scenes. Then you'll explore ways to persist data and game objects between scenes. From there, you'll take a look at the Unity player and its settings. You'll then learn how to build and deploy a game.

Managing Scenes

So far, everything you have done in Unity has been in the same scene. Although it is certainly possible to build large and complex games in this way, it is generally much easier to use multiple scenes. The idea behind a scene is that it is a self-contained collection of game objects. Therefore, when transitioning between scenes, all existing game objects are destroyed, and all new game objects are created. However, you can prevent this, as discussed in the next section.

NOTE

What Is a Scene? Revisited

You learned about the basics of scenes early on in this book. It is time, however, to revisit that concept with the knowledge you now possess. Ideally, a scene is like a level in a game. With games that get consistently harder or games that have dynamically generated levels, though, this is not necessarily true. Therefore, it can be good to think of a scene as a common list of assets. A game consisting of many levels that use the same objects can actually consist of one scene. It is only when you need to get rid of a bunch of objects and load a bunch of new objects that the idea of a new scene really becomes necessary. Basically, you should not split levels into different scenes just because you can. Create new scenes only if required by the gameplay and for asset management.

NOTE

Building?

This hour tosses around two key terms: *building* and *deploying*. Although they can often mean the same thing, they do have a slight difference. *Building* a project means telling Unity to turn your Unity project into a final, executable set of files. Therefore, building for the Windows OS will produce an .exe file with a data folder, building for Mac OS will build a .dmg file with all game data in it, and so on. *Deploying* means sending a built executable to a platform to be run. For example, when building for Android, an .apk file (the game) is built, and then it is deployed to an Android device for playing. These options are managed in Unity's build settings, which are covered shortly.

Establishing Scene Order

Transitioning between scenes is relatively easy. It just requires a little setup. The first thing you do is add the scenes of your project to the project's build settings, as follows:

1. Open the build settings by selecting **File > Build Settings**.

2. With the Build Settings dialog open, click and drag any scenes you want in your final project into the Scenes in Build window (see Figure 23.1).

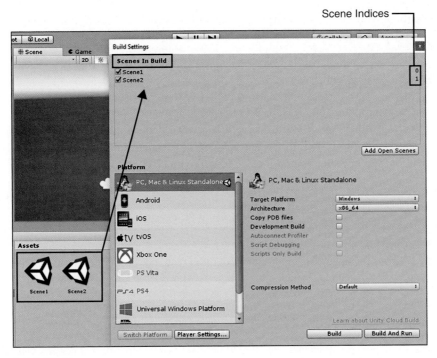

FIGURE 23.1
Adding scenes to the build settings.

3. Make note of the number that appears next to each scene in the Scenes in Build window. You will need these numbers later.

Adding Scenes to Build Settings

In this exercise, you'll add scenes to the build settings of a project. Be sure to save the project you make here because you will be using it again in the next section. Follow these steps:

1. Create a new project and add to it a new folder named **Scenes**.

2. Click **File > New Scene** to create a new scene and then select **File > Save Scene As** to save it. Save the scene in the Scenes folder as **Scene1**. Repeat this step to save another scene called **Scene2**.

3. Open the build settings (by selecting **File > Build Settings**). Drag **Scene1** into the Scenes in Build window first, and then drag **Scene2** into the same window. Ensure that Scene1 has an index of 0 and Scene2 has an index of 1. If not, reorder them by dragging them around.

Switching Scenes

Now that the scene order is established, switching between them is easy. To change scenes, use the method `LoadScene()`, which is a part of the `SceneManager` class. In order to use this class, you need to tell Unity that you want to access it. You can do that by adding the following line to the top of any script that needs it:

```
using UnityEngine.SceneManagement;
```

The `LoadScene()` method takes a single parameter that is either an integer representing the scene's index or a string representing the scene's name. Therefore, to load a scene that has an index of 1 and the name Scene2, you could write either of these two lines:

```
SceneManager.LoadScene(1);        // Load by index
SceneManager.LoadScene("Scene2"); // Load by name
```

This method call immediately destroys all existing game objects and loads the next scene. Note that this command is immediate and irreversible, so make sure that it is what you want to do before calling it. (The LevelManager prefab from the Exercise at the end of Hour 14, "User Interfaces," uses this method.)

TIP

Async Scene Loading

So far this book has focused on loading scenes immediately. That is, when you tell the `SceneManager` class to change a scene, the current scene is unloaded and then the next scene is loaded. This works well for small scenes, but if you are trying to load a very large scene, there can be a pause between levels during which the screen is black. To avoid this, one thing you could do is load a scene *asynchronously*. This "async" style of loading tries to load a scene "behind the scenes" while the main game continues on. When the new scene is loaded, the scene is switched. This method isn't instant, but it can help prevent gameplay hiccups. Generally speaking, loading scenes asynchronously can be a bit complex and is beyond the scope of this book.

Persisting Data and Objects

Now that you have learned how to switch between scenes, you have undoubtedly noticed that data doesn't transfer during a switch. In fact, so far all your scenes have been completely self-contained, with no need to save anything. In more complex games, however, saving data (often called *persisting* or *serializing*) becomes a real necessity. In this section, you'll learn how to keep objects from scene to scene and how to save data to a file to access later.

Keeping Objects

An easy way to save data in between scenes is just to keep the objects with the data alive. For example, if you have a player object that has scripts on it containing lives, inventory, score, and so on, the easiest way to ensure that this large amount of data makes it into the next scene is just to make sure that it doesn't get destroyed. There is an easy way to accomplish this, and it involves using a method called `DontDestroyOnLoad()`. The method `DontDestroyOnLoad()` takes a single parameter: the game object that you want to save. Therefore, if you want to save a game object that is stored in a variable named `Brick`, you could write the following:

```
DontDestroyOnLoad (Brick);
```

Because the method takes a game object as a parameter, another great way for objects to use it is to call it on themselves using the `this` keyword. For an object to save itself, you put the following code in the `Start()` method of a script attached to it:

```
DontDestroyOnLoad (this);
```

Now when you switch scenes, your saved objects will be there waiting.

Persisting Objects

In this exercise, you'll save a cube from one scene to the next. For this exercise you need the project created in the Try It Yourself "Adding Scenes to Build Settings." If you have not completed the project yet, do so before continuing. Be sure to save this project because you will be using it again in the next section. Follow these steps:

1. Load the project created in the Try It Yourself "Adding Scenes to Build Settings." Load **Scene2** and add a sphere to the scene. Position the sphere at (0, 2, 0).

2. Load **Scene1** and a cube to the scene and position the cube at (0, 0, 0).

3. Create a Scripts folder and in it create a new script named **DontDestroy**. Attach the script to the cube.

4. Modify the code in the DontDestroy script so that it contains the following:

```
using UnityEngine;
using UnityEngine.SceneManagement;

public class DontDestroy : MonoBehaviour
{
    void Start()
    {
        DontDestroyOnLoad(this);
    }

    // A neat trick for easily detecting mouse clicks on an object
    void OnMouseDown()
    {
        SceneManager.LoadScene(1);
    }
}
```

This code tells the cube to persist between scenes. In addition, it uses a little trick for detecting when the user clicks on the cube (OnMouseDown(); store this one away for a rainy day). When the user clicks on the cube, Scene2 is loaded.

5. Run the scene and notice that when you click the cube in the Game view, the scene transitions, and you see the sphere appear next to the cube (see Figure 23.2).

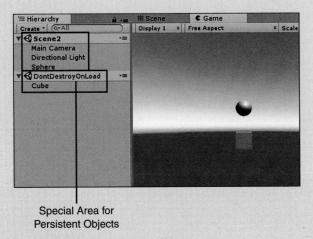

Special Area for
Persistent Objects

FIGURE 23.2
Cube persisting into Scene2.

CAUTION

Dark Scenes

You may have noticed that when you switch scenes, the new scene can be darker even though there is a light in there. This is due to not having complete lighting data for dynamically loaded scenes. Luckily, the solution is simple: Just load the scene in Unity and select **Window > Lighting > Settings**. Uncheck **Auto Generate** at the bottom and then click **Generate Lighting**. This tells Unity to stop using temporary light calculations for the scene and to commit these calculations to an asset. A folder appears next to your scene, with the same name as the scene. Thereafter, the lighting will be fine when loading into the scene.

Saving Data

Sometimes you need to save data to a file so you can access it and later. Some things you might need to save are the player's score, configuration preferences, or inventory. There are certainly many complex and feature-rich ways to save data, but a simple solution is something called *PlayerPrefs*. PlayerPrefs is an object that exists to save basic data to a file locally on your system. You can use PlayerPrefs to pull the data back out.

Saving data to PlayerPrefs is as simple as supplying some name for the data and the data itself. The methods you use to save the data depend on the type of data. For instance, to save an integer, you call the `SetInt()` method. To get the integer, you call the `GetInt()` method. Therefore, the code to save a value of 10 to PlayerPrefs as the score and get the value back out would look like this:

```
PlayerPrefs.SetInt ("score", 10);
PlayerPrefs.GetInt ("score");
```

Likewise, there are methods to save strings (SetString ()) and floats (SetFloat ()). Using these methods, you can easily persist any data you want to a file.

TRY IT YOURSELF ▼

Using PlayerPrefs

In this exercise, you'll save data to the PlayerPrefs file. For this exercise you need the project created in the Try It Yourself "Persisting Objects." If you have not completed the project yet, do so before continuing. You will use the legacy GUI for this exercise. The focus is on PlayerPrefs, not the UI. Follow these steps:

1. Open the project you created in the Try It Yourself "Persisting Objects" and ensure that **Scene1** is loaded. Add a new script named **SaveData** to the Scripts folder and add the following code to the script:

   ```
   public string playerName = "";

   void OnGUI()
   {
       playerName = GUI.TextField(new Rect(5, 120, 100, 30), playerName);

       if (GUI.Button(new Rect(5, 180, 50, 50), "Save"))
       {
           PlayerPrefs.SetString("name", playerName);
       }
   }
   ```

2. Attach the script to the Main Camera object. Save Scene1 and load **Scene2**.

3. Create a new script called **LoadData** and attach it to the Main Camera object. Add the following code to the script:

   ```
   string playerName = "";

   void Start()
   {
       playerName = PlayerPrefs.GetString("name");
   }

   void OnGUI()
   {
       GUI.Label(new Rect(5, 220, 50, 30), playerName);
   }
   ```

4. Save Scene2 and reload Scene1. Run the scene. Type your name into the text field and click the **Save** button. Now click the cube to load Scene2. (The scene switching cube was implemented in the previous Try It Yourself, "Persisting Objects.") Notice that the name you entered is written on the screen. In this Try It Yourself, the data was saved to PlayerPrefs and then reloaded from PlayerPrefs in a different scene.

CAUTION

Data Safety

Although using PlayerPrefs to save game data is very easy, it is not very secure. The data is stored in an unencrypted file on the player's hard drive. Therefore, players could easily open the file and manipulate the data inside. This could enable them to gain an unfair advantage or break the game. Be aware that PlayerPrefs, just as the name indicates, is intended for saving player preferences. It just so happens that it is useful for other things. True data security is a difficult thing to achieve and is definitely beyond the scope of this book. Just be aware that PlayerPrefs will work for what you need it for at this early stage in your development of games, but in the future you will want to look into more complex and secure means of saving player data.

Unity Player Settings

Unity provides several settings that affect how the game works after it is built. These settings are called the player settings, and they manage things like the game's icon and supported aspect ratios. There are many settings, and many of them are self-explanatory. If you select **Edit > Project Settings > Player**, the Player Settings window opens in the Inspector view. Take your time to look through these settings and read about them in the following sections so you can learn what they do.

Cross-Platform Settings

The first player settings you see are the cross-platform settings (see Figure 23.3). These are the settings applied to the built game regardless of the platform (Windows, iOS, Android, Mac, and so on) you built it for. Most of the settings in this section are self-explanatory. The product name is the name that will appear as the title of your game. The icon should be any valid texture image file. Note that the dimensions of the icon have to be square powers of 2, such as 8×8, 16×16, 32×32, 64×64, and so on. If the icon doesn't match these dimensions, the scaling may not work properly, and the icon quality might be very low. You can also specify a custom cursor and define where the cursor hotspot (the spot on the cursor that is the actual "click" location) is.

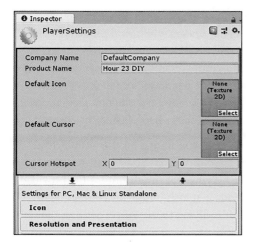

FIGURE 23.3
The cross-platform settings.

Per-Platform Settings

The per-platform settings are specific to each platform. Even though there are several repeat settings in this section, you still have to set up each one of them for every platform you want to build your game for. You can select a specific platform by choosing its icon from the selection bar (see Figure 23.4). Note that you see icons only for the platforms you currently have installed for Unity. As you can see in Figure 23.4, only the Standalone (PC, Mac, and Linux) and Android platforms are currently installed on this machine.

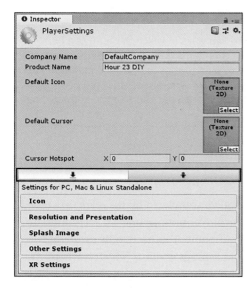

FIGURE 23.4
The platform selection bar.

Many of these settings require a more specific understanding of the platform for which you are building. You should not modify these settings until you better understand how a particular platform works. Other settings are rather straightforward and need to be modified only if you are trying to achieve a specific goal. For instance, the Resolution and Presentation settings deal with the dimensions of the game window. For desktop builds, these can be windowed or full screen, with a large array of different supported aspect ratios. By enabling or disabling the different aspect ratios, you allow or disallow different resolutions that the player can choose when playing the game.

The icon settings are auto-populated for you if you specify an icon image for the Default Icon property in the Cross-Platform Settings section. You can see that various sizes of the icon image will be generated, based on a single provided image. This is why it is important for the provided image to have the correct dimensions. You can also provide a splash image for your game in the Splash Image section. A *splash image* is an image that is added to the Player Settings dialog when a player first starts up the game.

NOTE

Too Many Settings

You probably noticed that a large number of settings in the Player Settings dialog aren't covered in this section. Most of the properties are already set to default values so that you can just quickly build a game. The other settings exist to achieve advanced functionality or polish. You shouldn't toy with most of the settings if you don't understand what they do because changes can lead to strange behaviors or prevent your game from working at all. In short, use only the more basic settings until you get more comfortable with game-building concepts and the different features you have already used.

NOTE

Too Many Players

The term *player* is used a lot in this hour because there are two ways in which the term can be applied. The first, obviously, is the player who actually plays your game. This is a person. The second way the term can be used is to describe the *Unity player*, the window that the game is played in (like a movie player or a TV). The player exists on the computer (or device). Therefore, when you hear *player*, it probably means a person, but when you hear *player settings*, it probably refers to the software that actually displays the game.

Building Your Game

Let's say that you've finished building your first game. You've completed all the work and tested everything in the editor. You have even gone through the player settings and set everything up the way you want it. Good job! It is now time to build your game. You need to be aware of two settings windows used in this process. The first is the Build Settings window, which is where you determine the final results of the build process. The second is the Game Settings window, which involves settings that human players see and configure.

Build Settings

The Build Settings window contains the terms under which the game is built. It is here that you specify the platform the game will be built under as well as the various scenes in the game. You have seen this dialog once before, but now you should take a closer look at it.

To open the Build Settings dialog, select **File > Build Settings**. In the Build Settings dialog, you can change and configure your game as you want. Figure 23.5 shows the Build Settings dialog and the various items on it.

As you can see, in the Platform section, you can specify a new platform to build for. If you choose a new platform, you need to click **Switch Platform** to make the switch. Clicking the **Player Settings** button opens the Player Settings dialog in the Inspector view. You have seen the Scenes in Build section before; this is where you determine which scenes will make it into the game and their order. You also have the various build settings for the specific platform that you chose. The PC, Mac & Linux Standalone settings are self-explanatory. The only thing to note here is the Development Build option, which allows the game to run with a debugger and performance profiler.

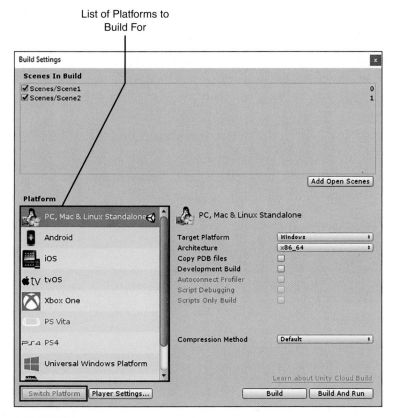

FIGURE 23.5
The Build Settings dialog.

When you are ready to build your game, you can either click **Build** to just build the game or **Build and Run** to build the game and then run it immediately. The file that Unity creates will depend on the platform chosen.

Game Settings

When a built game is run from its actual file (not from within Unity), the player is presented with a Game Settings dialog (see Figure 23.6). From this dialog, players choose options for their game experience.

The first thing you may notice is that the name of the game appears in the title bar of the window. Also, any splash image you provided in the Player Settings dialog appears at the top of this window. This first tab, Graphics, is where players specify the resolution at which they want to play the game. The list of available resolutions is determined by the aspect ratios you allowed or disallowed in the Player Settings dialog and the operating system. Players can also choose to run the game in a window or full screen and can pick their quality settings.

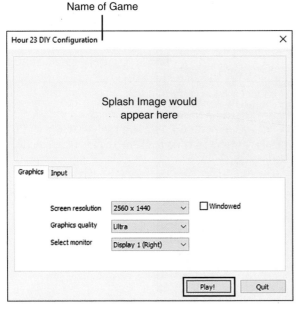

FIGURE 23.6
The Game Settings dialog.

Players can then switch over to the Input tab (see Figure 23.7), where they can remap any input axes to their desired keys and buttons.

FIGURE 23.7
The input settings.

Told You So!

You might recall that earlier in this book I said you should always try to ensure that the input you are reading from a player is based on one of the input axes and not the specific keys. This is why. If you looked for specific keys instead of axes, the player would have no choice but to use the control scheme you intended. If you think this isn't a big deal, just remember that a lot of people out there (people with disabilities, for instance) use nonstandard input devices. If you deny them the ability to remap controls, they might not be able to play your games. Using axes instead of specific keys is a negligible amount of work on your part and can make the difference between players loving or hating your game.

After players choose the settings they want, they just click **Play!** and begin enjoying your game.

Summary

In this hour, you've learned all about polishing and building games in Unity. You started by learning how to change scenes in Unity using the `SceneManager.LoadScene()` method. From there, you learned how to persist game objects and data. After that, you learned about the various player settings. Finally, you wrapped up the hour by learning to build your games.

Q&A

Q. **A lot of these settings looked important. Why doesn't this hour cover them?**

A. Truth be told, most of those settings are unnecessary for you. The fact is that they aren't important...until they are important. Most of the settings are platform specific and are beyond the scope of this book. Instead of spending many pages going over settings you might never use, it is left up to you to learn about them if you ever need them.

Workshop

Take some time to work through the questions here to ensure that you have a firm grasp of the material.

Quiz

1. How do you determine the indexes of the scenes in your game?

2. True or False: Data can be saved using the PlayerPrefs object.

3. What dimensions should an icon for your game have?

4. True or False: The input settings in the game settings allow the player to remap all inputs in your game.

Answers

1. After you add the scenes to the Scenes in Build list, each one has an index assigned to it.

2. True

3. A game icon should be a square with sides that are powers of 2: 8×8, 16×16, 32×32, and so on.

4. False. The player can only remap inputs that were established based on input axes, not specific keypresses.

Exercise

In this exercise, you'll build a game for your desktop operating system and experiment with the various features. There isn't much to this exercise, and you should spend most of your time trying out various settings and watching their impact. Because this is just an example to get you building your games, there isn't a completed project to look at in the book assets.

1. Open any project you have created previously or create a new project. (Don't worry, I'll wait.)

2. Go into the Player Settings dialog and configure your player however you want.

3. Go into the Build Settings dialog and ensure that you have added your scenes to the Scenes in Build list.

4. Ensure that the Platform is set to PC, Mac & Linux Standalone.

5. Build the game by clicking **Build**.

6. Locate the game file that you just built and run it. Experiment with the different game settings and see how they affect the gameplay.

HOUR 24
Wrap-up

What You'll Learn in This Hour:

▶ What you've accomplished so far

▶ Where to go from here

▶ What resources are available to you

In this hour, you'll wrap up your introductory journey with Unity. You'll start by looking at exactly what you've done so far. From there, you'll see where you can go to continue improving your skills. Then you'll learn about some of the resources available to help you continue learning.

Accomplishments

When you have been working on something for a significant amount of time, you may sometimes forget all that you have accomplished along the way. It is helpful to reflect on the skills you had when you began learning something and compare them to the skills you have now. There is a lot of motivation and satisfaction to be found in discovering your progress, so let's look at some numbers.

Your 19 Hours of Learning

First and foremost, you have spent 19 hours (possibly more) intensely learning the various elements of game development with Unity. Here are some of the things you have learned:

▶ How to use the Unity editor and many of its windows and dialogs.

▶ About game objects, transforms, and transformations. You learned about 2D versus 3D coordinate systems and about local versus world coordinate systems. You became a pro at using Unity's built-in geometric shapes.

▶ About models. Specifically, you learned that models consist of textures and shaders applied to materials, which in turn are applied to meshes. You learned that meshes are made up of triangles that consist of many points in 3D space.

▶ How to build terrain in Unity. You sculpted unique landscapes and gave yourself the tools needed to build any kind of world you could ever dream of. (How many people can say that?) You improved those worlds with ambient effects and environmental detail.

▶ All about cameras and lights.

▶ To program in Unity. If you had never programmed before this book, that's a big deal. Good job!

▶ About collisions, physical materials, and raycasting. In other words, you took your first steps in object interactions through physics.

▶ About prefabs and instantiation.

▶ How to build UIs using Unity's powerful user interface controls.

▶ How to control players through Unity's character controllers. On top of that, you built a custom 2D character controller to use in your own projects.

▶ How to build awesome 2D worlds with 2D Tilemap.

▶ How to make awesome particle effects using various particle systems. You also checked out each particle module in detail.

▶ How to use Unity's new Mecanim animation system. While learning that, you learned how to remap the rigging on a model to use animations that weren't made specifically for it. You also learned how to edit animations to make your own animation clips.

▶ How to sequence just about anything to create sophisticated cinematics with the Timeline.

▶ How to manipulate audio in your projects. You learned how to work with both 2D and 3D audio, in addition to how to loop and swap audio clips.

▶ How to work with games made for mobile devices. You learned how to test games with Unity Remote and using a device's accelerometer and multi-touch screen.

▶ How to polish a game by using multiple scenes and data persistence. You learned how to build and play your games.

This is quite a list, and it's not even everything you've learned in this book. As you read through this list, I hope you remembered experiencing and learning each of these items. You've learned a lot!

4 Complete Games

Over the course of this book, you created four games: *Amazing Racer*, *Chaos Ball*, *Captain Blaster*, and *Gauntlet Runner*. You designed each of these games. You worked through the concept of each one, determined the rules, and came up with the requirements. Then you built all the entities for each of the games. You specifically placed every object, player, world, ball, meteor, and more in the games. You wrote all the scripts and built all the interactivity into the games. Then, most importantly, you tested all the games. You determined their strengths and their weaknesses. You played them, and you had peers play them. You considered how they could be improved, and you even tried to improve them yourself. Take a look at some of the mechanics and game concepts you used:

▶ *Amazing Racer*: This 3D foot-racing game against the clock utilized the built-in first-person character controller as well as fully sculpted and textured terrain. The game used water hazards, triggers, and lights.

▶ *Chaos Ball*: This 3D game featured many collision and physical dynamics. You utilized physics materials to build a bouncy arena, and you implemented corner goals that turned specific objects into kinematics.

▶ *Captain Blaster*: This retro-style 2D space shooter used a scrolling background and 2D effects. It is the first game you made where the player can lose. You used third-party models and textures to give this game a high level of graphical style.

▶ *Gauntlet Runner*: This 3D running game involves collecting power-ups and avoiding obstacles. This game utilized Mecanim animations and third-party models, as well as clever manipulations of texture coordinates to achieve a 3D scrolling effect.

You have gained experience in designing games, building them, testing them, and updating them for new hardware. Not bad. Not bad at all.

More Than 50 Scenes

Over the course of this book, you created more than 50 scenes. Let that number sink in for a moment. While reading through this book, you specifically got hands-on with at least 50 different concepts. That is quite a lot of experience for you to draw upon.

By now, you probably get the point of this section. You've done a lot, and you should be proud of that. You have personally used a huge part of the Unity game engine. That knowledge will serve you well as you go forward.

Where to Go from Here

Even though you have completed this book, you are far from done with your education in making games. In fact, it is fairly accurate to say that no one is ever truly done learning in an industry that moves as quickly as this one. That said, here is some advice on what you can do to keep going.

Make Games

No, seriously, make games. This cannot be overstated. If you are someone who is trying to learn more about the Unity game engine, someone who is trying to find a game job, or someone who has a game job and is looking to improve, make games. A common misconception among people newer to the game industry (or the software industry in general) is that knowledge alone will get you a job or improve your skills. This couldn't be further from the truth. Experience is king. Make games. They don't have to be big games. Start by making several smaller games like the ones you've done in this book. In fact, trying a large game right away might lead to frustration and disappointment. No matter what you decide to do, though, make games. (Did I mention that yet?)

Work with People

There are many local and online collaborative groups looking to make games for both business and pleasure. Join them. In fact, they would be lucky to have someone with as much Unity experience as you have. Remember, you have four games under your belt already. Working with others teaches you a lot about group dynamics. Furthermore, working with others allows you to achieve higher levels of complexity in the games you can make. Try to find artists and sound engineers to make your games full of rich media goodness. You will find that working in teams is the best way to learn more about your strengths and weaknesses. It can be a great reality check as well as a confidence booster.

Write About It

Writing about your games and your game development endeavors can be great for your personal progress. Whether you start a blog or keep a personal notebook, your observations will serve you well in the present and in retrospect. Writing can also be a great way to hone your skills and collaborate with others. By putting your ideas out there, you can receive feedback and learn through the input of others.

Resources Available to You

Many resources are available to you to continue your education both on the Unity game engine and in game development in general. First and foremost is the Unity documentation, the official resource for all things Unity, which is available at http://docs.unity3d.com. It is important to know that this document takes a technical approach to Unity coverage. Don't think of it as a learning tool but rather as a manual.

Unity also provides a great assortment of online training on its Learn site, at http://unity3d.com/learn. There, you will find many videos, projects, and other resources to help you improve your skills.

If you find that you have a question that you cannot answer with the help of these two resources, try the very helpful Unity community. At the Unity Answers site, at http://answers.unity3d.com, you can ask specific questions and get direct answers from Unity pros.

Aside from the official Unity resources, several game development sites are available to you. Two of the most popular ones are http://www.gamasutra.com and http://www.gamedev.net. Both of these sites have large communities and regularly publish articles. Their subject matter is not limited to Unity, so they can provide a large and unbiased source of information.

Summary

In this hour, you've reviewed everything you have done with Unity so far. You've also looked forward. You started by examining all the things you have accomplished over the course of this book. Then you looked at some of the things you can do from here to continue improving your skills. Finally, you looked at some of the free resources available to you on the Internet.

Q&A

Q. After reading this hour's materials, I can't help but feel that you think I should make games. Is that true?

A. Yes. I believe I mentioned it a few times. I cannot stress enough how important it is to continue to hone your skills through practice and creativity.

Workshop

Take some time to work through the questions here to ensure that you have a firm grasp of the material.

Quiz

1. Can Unity be used to make both 2D and 3D games?

2. Should you be proud of the things you have accomplished so far?

3. What is the single best thing you can do to continue increasing your skills in game development?

4. Have you learned everything you need to learn about Unity?

Answers

1. Absolutely!

2. Absolutely again!

3. Keep making games and sharing them with people.

4. No. You should never stop learning!

Exercise

The theme of this final hour is retrospect and solidifying the things you have learned. The final exercise for this book continues that theme. It is common in the game industry to write something called a *post-mortem*. The idea behind a post-mortem is that you write an article about a game you have made with the intention of other people reading it. In a post-mortem, you analyze the things that worked in your process and the things that didn't. You aim to inform others of the pitfalls that you discovered so that they won't fall into the same ones.

In this exercise, write a post-mortem about one of the games you made in this book. You don't necessarily have to have anyone read it. It is the process of doing the writing that is important. Be sure to spend some time on this because you might want to read it again further down the road. You will be amazed at the things you found difficult and at the things you found enjoyable.

After writing the post-mortem, print it out (unless you wrote it by hand) and put it in this book. Later, when you come across this book again, be sure to open the post-mortem and read it.

Index

C

Sams Teach Yourself

When you only have time
for the answers™

Whatever your need and whatever your time frame, there's a Sams **Teach Yourself** book for you. With a Sams **Teach Yourself** book as your guide, you can quickly get up to speed on just about any new product or technology—in the absolute shortest period of time possible. Guaranteed.

Learning how to do new things with your computer shouldn't be tedious or time-consuming. Sams **Teach Yourself** makes learning anything quick, easy, and even a little bit fun.

C++ in 24 Hours a Day

Rogers Cadenhead & Jesse Liberty

ISBN-13: 978-0-672-33746-8

Godot Game Engine in 24 Hours

Ariel Manzur
George Marques

ISBN-13: 978-0-13-483509-9

Unreal Engine 4 Game Development in 24 Hours

Aram Cookson
Ryan DowlingSoka
Clinton Crumpler

ISBN-13: 978-0-672-33762-8

3ds Max in 24 Hours

Stewart Jones

ISBN-13: 978-0-672-33699-7

C++ in One Hour a Day

Siddhartha Rao

ISBN-13: 978-0-7897-5774-6